PSYCHOLOGY, ASTROLOGY & WESTERN MAGIC

Image and Myth in Self-Discovery

Luis Alvarado

About The Author

Luis Alvarado was born on May 6, 1959 in Bayamon, Puerto Rico, moving with his family at an early age to the United States. He had numerous psychic experiences as a child, and culturally, his parents were supportive of his metaphysical interests. All involved felt that "la obra," a Spanish phrase meaning "the work," or helping others during times of spiritual crises, would be one of the social roles the author would assume as an adult. He began to research Western occultism at the age of 12, began self-teaching astrology at 16, and read the bulk of Carl Jung's *Collected Works* at 18.

In 1981, Mr. Alvarado became an initiate of Crowley's *Ordo Templi Orientis* (O.T.O.) and in 1986 he was initiated into Crowley's A∴A∴ Both of these fraternities operate worldwide with headquarters in the United States. They are Crowley's legacy to the New Aeon, and both function as repositories of the Western occult transmission.

Concurrent with his magickal training, the author pursued his interest in understanding human change and growth; the author has 14 years of experience in the Counseling field. He received his undergaraduate degree in Psychology and in 1990 completed requirements for the Master of Arts Degree in Counseling from The Graduate Program, Vermont College. His final product for the Graduate Program, revised and re-edited, is the basis for this book.

It is the author's opinion that archetypal psychology and magick are two sides of the same coin, together providing an Understanding of the initiate's path toward attainment.

To Write to the Author

We cannot guarantee that every letter written to the author can be answered, but all will be forwarded. Both the author and the publisher appreciate hearing from readers, learning of your enjoyment and benefit from this book. Llewellyn also publishes a bi-monthly news magazine, and some readers' questions and comments to the author may be answered through this magazine's columns if permission to do so is included in the original letter. The author sometimes participates in seminars and workshops, and dates and places are announced in *The Llewellyn New Times*. To write to the author, or to ask a question, write to:

Luis Alvarado
c/o THE LLEWELLYN NEW TIMES
P.O. Box 64383-006, St. Paul MN 55164-0383, U.S.A.

Please enclose a self-addressed, stamped envelope for reply, or $1.00 to cover costs.

PSYCHOLOGY, ASTROLOGY & WESTERN MAGIC

Image and Myth in Self-Discovery

Luis Alvarado

1991
Llewellyn Publications
St. Paul, Minnesota 55164-0383, U.S.A.

FIRST EDITION

Library of Congress Cataloging-in-Publication Data
Alvarado, Luis. 1959–
  Psychology, astrology and Western magic : image and myth in self-
discovery / by Luis Alvarado. — 1st ed.
    p.   cm.
  Includes bibliographical refernces.
  ISBN 0-87542-008-0
    1. Archetype (Psychology) 2. Gods—Psychology. 3. Astrology and psychology.
4. Cabala—Psychological aspects. 5. Psychotherapy.
I. Title.
BF175.5.A72A58   1991
150. 1955—dc20   91-32831
                                                                        CIP

Llewellyn Publications
A Division of Llewellyn Worldwide, Ltd.,
St. Paul, MN 55164-0383, U.S.A.

CONTENTS

PREFACE

My own spiritual journey, the quest for soul, began early, in grammar school. I say this because ever since I can remember, *image* has held a special fascination for me. In grammar school the Brothers Grimm and the Old Testament provided outlets for my imagination; later in high school, classical Greek mythology became a passion. While still in high school the images and symbols of astrology became a full-time study; this was followed by the cerebral consumption of the works of Carl Gustav Jung. Several years later, Western magic and the Qabalah touched my soul in the same way other topics had assumed an importance in my life—through the image.

My undergraduate degree was in Psychology. My choices of work experiences after school were in mental health; specifically, I set out to understand the movements between mental illness and mental health, and how, as a professional, I could help others. Since I had already read Jung, my interpretation of mental illness was different from the standard clinical approach. I continued to develop my own ideas about mental health and mental illness, continuing to do work with the chronic mentally ill. I remained within the framework of the medical model of mental illness without fully accepting it, mostly because the medical model does not utilize an *a priori* transcedent factor in its definition of the psyche. I kept searching elsewhere for models of mental health, and my search always led me back to the image.

For many years I struggled to bring together the various disciplines of Western civilization that engage the image: Greek mythology, astrology, Jung's psychology, and Western magic. I returned to school and began my graduate work wanting to find some understanding of how these areas of experience might together become a synthetic whole that could be used in the therapeutic setting. The task I set for myself was this: to find a common denominator, if there was one, among all these currents of thought, and then, to learn the best way to apply this understanding in a counseling situation.

A beginning assumption in my graduate work was that the God-image provided a connecting thread that wove through mythology, astrology, Jung's psychology, and Western magic. In my need to understand myself and my method of counseling, I set out to explore the God-images, and how, as archetypal structures, they order our life experience.

Images allow us to know archetypal structures, archetypes being the primary forms that govern the psyche. Archetypes are preexistent patterns of emotions, behaviors, perceptions, and responses common to all of humanity. According to James Hillman, archetypes are like psychic organs that are congenitally given, basic patterns that appear in the arts, religions, dreams, and social customs of all peoples, and that manifest spontaneously in mental disorders. He states that an archetypal image must be valued as universal, trans-historical, basically profound, generative, highly intentional, and necessary. For Hillman, the archetypal image denotes intentional force and person, meaning an image is like a person whom one loves, fears, delights in, is inhibited by, etc. The image therefore presents a claim, whether moral, erotic, intellectual, or other, and demands a response. It is an affecting presence offering an affective relationship. The archetypal is always phenomenal in Hillman's view. He writes, "By means of the archetypal image, natural phenomena present faces that speak to the imagining soul rather than only conceal hidden laws and probabilities and manifest their objectification."

Most of us are familiar with the image because most of us dream. Words are usually not the primary mode in dreams. The rules of words seem to matter little and the logic of images is most important. Often we wake having more knowledge than the visual images would seem to express, alluding to the fact that although an image can be seen, an image does have to be seen to produce an effect. We awake from dreams with moods and unsought for emotions: sometimes we wake up perplexed, sometimes delighted, and sometimes afraid. We may feel that the message of the dream is important and may spend an entire day trying to decipher the dream, even if our experience of the dream image itself may have been only seconds long in duration. This is a reminder that the image as source is complex.

James Hillman, when defining his archetypal psychology, does three important things. One is to assert that a consistent theme in Jung's writings is the archetype. Two, since the archetype is knowable through the image, he gives primacy to the image, dispensing with much of Jung's theoretical definitions. And three, he realized that once we give primacy to the image, we must rediscover the metaphor of the imagining soul, for the primary data of soul as psyche is the image.

Our journey together, from beginning to end, which I present in the following pages, can be summarized as follows: God-images are archetypes. Images are the primary data of soul. We can find soul in mythology, astrology, Western magic, and Jung's psychology by way of God-images, since soul and image are never far apart. In this book God-images provide a connecting thread for mythology, astrology, Jung's concept of the archetype, and Western magic. As we follow the God-images, we will explore a psychology based on soul, and come to know a therapeutic approach based on image.

A therapeutic approach based on image means that this book presents a form of psychodynamics because the image as source is complex and phenomenal. If the image presents us with an affective relationship, then relating and right relationship is a component of a psychodynamics of soul. It is through the struggle to find the experiences of right relationship that a true psychodynamism of the soul develops.

With this in mind, let me quickly summarize my own background of learning. First, I have undergone my own Jungian analysis. Second, I have been instructed in the discipline of Western ceremonial magic. Third, work with the chronic mentally ill has taught me much about the ways of the psyche, especially how the psyche manifests pathology. All three of these areas of learning rely on the right relationship between student and teacher or helper and client. All three areas of learning have, for me, been saturated with images. My understanding of psychodynamics has come by way of the image.

Right relationship must include what I call the ego question: What is the ego's role, as the center of consciousness, in a psychology of dynamic relationships? This book serves as an attempt (only) to answer this question, for the answer is as complex and as elusive as the image.

While on the topic of the image as elusive, this book will be difficult to understand for many. There are multiple layers and levels to the images and the narrative is saturated with multi-disciplinary ideas. I have attempted to gradually introduce concepts *and* teach by example, trying to involve the reader by way of image as well as words. I have hoped that by the beginning of Chapter Five the reader will have enough of a grasp of the basic propositions to do his or her own evaluation of the case story. This book will be most difficult for those who have not had *story* as part of their life experience—those persons who are only just beginning to move beyond the tyrany of the ego structure. This book challenges us to give primacy to the image, and the image is above all, collective.

A necessary disclaimer must be included. Although I have borrowed extensively from James Hillman's works, the use of his concepts as they relate to Western magic and the occult, astrology, and the Qabalah are entirely of my own invention. I have tried, and I hope successfully, to demarcate between Hillman's concepts and my own use of them. It is my belief that Hillman's archetypal psychology is, at present, the only psychology that can be best utilized when exploring the interface between psychology and Western occult disciplines. The foundation of this opinion is, unfortunately, a whole other book currently being researched.

INTRODUCTION

This book is about understanding the story found in the God-images that shape our lives. Re-discovering the Gods is a matter of *practical* importance for anyone wishing to activate the metaphor of soul. The Gods are everywhere, at all times, and as such can offer our lives meaning though their varied and unique psychologies. Re-discovering the Gods *within* allows us to know the mythic basis of existence, the fantasies that color our perceptions of the world, and in turn, that dominate the drama which is our life. The Gods afford us with a means of transcendence beyond the ofttimes rigid ego constellation that is elegant, parsimonious, and true to the mythic basis of existence. The Gods are *pontifices*, from the root word *pontifex*, literally "bridge-maker." The Gods are the bridges within the soul between nature and nurture, body and spirit, the profane and the divine, the microcosm and the macrocosm.

God-images are archetypes and archetypes come with a story. Archetypes are preexistent patterns of emotions, behaviors, perceptions, and responses common to all of humanity. Carl Jung wrote, "The term 'archetype' occurs as early as Philo Judaeus, with reference to the *Imago Dei* (God-image) in man."[1] Men and women experience the archetypes as God-images because of the incredible power and consuming nature of these preexistent shapers of human experience.

The word "archetype" and its definition comes from Carl Jung and his psychology. It is one of his far reaching contributions to psychology, an idea whose influence has extended to other disciplines in the humanities such as anthropology, comparative mythology, the arts, history, religion, and the sciences. The archetype and archetypal psychology has inspired and sustained a wealth of research and study that continues to pour forth into the current that is the modern exploration of the human soul. Therefore, aside from our simple definition, what else do we mean by the archetype? To answer this question requires that we examine more closely Jung's psychology.

Jung differentiated between the personal unconscious and the collective unconscious. The personal unconscious contains, recorded, all of one's life experiences—every sensation, impression, emotion, fantasy, thought; in essence, one's life history in toto. It contains contents easily and not so easily available to consciousness. When we say, "I remember the time . . .," we are tapping into our personal unconscious, into easily accessible memories. The not so easily accessible memories lie, as it were, in metaphorical depths. These psychic contents are painful to consciousness and are actively removed from consciousness by the Freudian ego-defense mechanisms of suppression and repression. The personal unconscious is a buffer zone between consciousness (and its center of activity - the ego) and the collective unconscious and includes psychic contents making their way to consciousness, referred to as pre-conscious contents. The personal unconscious according to Jung is mostly subjective or individual.

The collective unconscious is impersonal, or objective. In it resides all the innate behavior patterns and ways of being of the human species. It is also, if I may use a modern metaphor, a vast library of video-tapes of the human experience. Every human being inherits, and has access to, its contents. Not only the archetypes, but the instincts also belong to the realm of the collective unconscious. The collective unconscious is general and objective rather than specific and individual.

According to Edward Whitmont, the collective unconscious is the image-producing stratum of the psyche that contains the drives and emotions as psychic energy, or libido.[2] Libido moves by way of fields:

> A field is an energy pattern or configuration that becomes perceptible to the experienced observer only through the patternings of directly observable elements susceptible to its influence.[3]

For instance, iron filings will form a pattern when exposed to a magnetic field. *Archetypes can be conceived of as fields that give form to the drives and the emotions contained within the psyche.* Archetypes, utilizing psychic energy or libido, order our life experiences in the same way a magnetic field orders iron filings.

As fields, archetypes have two attributes, a dynamic manifestation and a formal manifestation.[4] The dynamic aspect, which includes emotions and drives, implies a movement, a goal, a teleology. The formal aspect is experienced as image—in symbols, myth, art, folktale, social customs, and dreams. I use the compound noun, God-image, borrowed from Jung's references, to encompass both attributes. The word "God" alludes to the dynamic personified component expressed in the (classical) mythology of a deity. The word "image" alludes to the formal component we experience in dreams, art, and social customs. A *God-image* is a very specific kind of archetype, or preexistent pattern of emotions, perceptions, and responses.

Together, the words "God-image" relate an archetypal drama. A God-image comes with a story—with lead actors and actresses, supporting characters, stage, stage-props, scenes, flourishes—drama (sometimes comedy), theme, plot, sub-plot, climaxes, and so on. The story we call myth. As we integrate the Gods into our lives we create our own personal myth. Personal myth and collective myth merge, separate, and merge again.

For an example, let us look to the mythos of the White Goddess. Robert Graves tells us that the White Goddess, a Goddess of the Moon and of inspired poetry, had as her origin the cultures of the early Mediterranean peoples. Her worship eventually extended as far north as Ireland. If the White Goddess[5] is an archetype that structures my psychic make-up, then I must ask certain questions: Who are the actors in this drama, Who am I identifying with—when, where, how, what for? This particular Goddess story includes two young male suitors, lovers vying for her affections. These lovers represent the fertility of the new year versus the lost youth of the previous year, or the polarity of birth and death. Let us suppose that in my life experiences I identify with one lover over the other—who or what in my life fulfills the role of my adversary? Depending on whether I am a man or a woman, homosexual or heterosexual, depending on the life transition I am undergoing and who I am and what my life experiences have been, will determine my relationships to the other characters in the story. In turn, even if archetypal, the other characters will have a tendency to shift in the story to compensate for the individual preferences. The story contains an internal energy value that must be maintained.

I have said that the God-image is a very specific kind of archetype. What I mean by this is that there are many kinds of archetypal situations. James Hillman lists, for example, the archetypal situations of abandonment, sacrifice, or the descent.[6] Some archetypes are dominants, to use a word of Jung's, and dominate the psyche's constitution. These archetypes are the shadow, the anima/animus, and the Self. Some archetypes describe ordinary day to day life, as for instance, the Mother archetype, or the Wounded Healer archetype; these archetypes are usually projected onto our own mothers or our family physician, respectively. A God-image, being a complex story, may partake of all or some of the above described archetypes and archetypal situations, or none. The Greek Goddess Hera has attributes of the Mother archetype, but so does the Goddess Demeter and the Goddess Rhea. Demeter's myth, moreover, contains the archetypal situation of the descent where Hera's story does not. Another brief example is the archetype of the eternal youth. Both of the Gods Hermes and Dionysus exhibit qualities of the eternal youth, but each exhibits this quality in a different way. Dionysus' story includes the archetypal situations of abandonment, sacrifice, and the descent, mentioned above.

Every individual will interact with a God-image in any number of unique ways. As therapists, we *must* remember the story, but we allow the client to tell us the story as *they* live it. By remembering the archetypal story, we assist the client in clarifying relationships: between story characters, between client and story, between client and therapist. All these levels of relationship are to be found in the God-image, especially the right relationship between ourselves, the Gods, and life.

I depart from Jung by using, whenever possible, the plural form, "God-images," or more simply "Gods," to denote a polytheism and indicate an inclusive, gender neutral reference, as polytheism implies both Gods and Goddesses. Gender inclusion is also indicated whenever I use the words God-image and God, specifying Goddess where appropriate. And even though in my work I use whatever pantheon of God-images best contains and sustains the subtlety of the experience under consideration, I nonetheless must admit a preference for the Greek pantheon of Gods and Goddesses. This preference is elucidated by James Hillman:

Greece provides a polycentric pattern of the most richly elaborated polytheism of all cultures, and so is able to hold the chaos
of the secondary personalities and autonomous impulses of a
field, a time, or an individual. This fantastic variety offers the
psyche manifold fantasies for reflecting its many possibilities.[7]

While I am on the subject of Greece let me state that most of the
topics I reference in this work (Western magic, Hermeticism, Gnosticism, astrology, alchemy, analytical psychology, and archetypal psychology) all contain ideas originating and developed during the classical period in Greece and thereafter. This may come as a
surprise. Jim Tester in his *A History of Western Astrology* writes "It is
the 'Macarthyism' of the Classical scholar: too many Greeks in-
dulged in un-Greek activities,"[8] when he tells us that astrology was
adopted by the Greeks precisely because, in their views, it was rational. The Greeks were always interested in the systematic understanding of the universe and humanity's place in it. "The idea of the
universe as the macrocosm, and man as the microcosm, reflecting in
his nature and structure that of the whole, is a Greek one, and
largely Stoic."[9] In this work, then, we cannot but return to Greece.

This book is about a personal way of working with others in the
therapeutic relationship using God-images. I approach the God-images by way of depth psychology using astrology and the Qabalah
(also spelled Cabala, Kabala, Kabbalah), a Western system of magic
and mysticism. Both astrology and the Qabalah contain a wealth of
images—metaphors in symbolic pictures of ourselves and the universe we live in. As Western forms of initiation they belong to those
guardians of the image that existed years before the advent of modern depth psychology. I have therefore devoted a chapter to each of
these systems of the right understanding of our world.

Having briefly defined God-image, let us review what is meant
by depth psychology. Depth psychology, so named, begins with
Sigmund Freud. It presupposes a multilayered structure to the psyche, the two most important divisions being consciousness and the
unconscious. Freud was interested in the dynamic interaction between the conscious and unconscious levels of psychological life, an
interaction usually fraught with conflicts. Freud's major concern
was the understanding and the alleviation of the symptoms of these
conflicts. Freud's movement when working with the unconscious
was down and in, a reach for depth. His theory of hysteria, his development of dream analysis, and his exploration of the psy-

chopathology of day to day life were all based on the dynamics and conflicts of conscious ego life with the unconscious.

Carl Jung was a student and friend of Freud. Jung departed from Freud's psychoanalysis, and called his depth psychology analytical psychology. Jung, more than Freud, was interested in the unconscious' ability to create what he at first called splinter-psyches, and later defined as the psychological complex. The complex develops from a life trauma (Freud), and this life trauma becomes paired with a collective archetype. The conflicts between conscious life and the unconscious happen because the complex has a life of its own (autonomy) separate from the ego which is the center of conscious activity. The goal of analytical psychology is to understand how the personal trauma, paired with the archetypal drama, affects the individual.

For example, we all have a personal experience of mother; the actual experience of mother is colored by the archetype of the Mother. Consequently, we all carry within us the complex mother/Mother. The archetype of Mother is like a photographic negative, to use one of Jung's metaphors, that is "developed" or fleshed out by our actual experience of our own mothers. A priority may be given to Mother; mother may not be so bad, but if Mother for us is the Angry Mother, then we may tend to mostly remember those times when mother was angry because we have a propensity to be more sensitive to these times. Analytical psychology, as practiced, attempts to separate mother from Mother; the complex is an important focus in the work of psychotherapy. The theory of the complex in modern day psychology comes from Jung's explorations and writings.

James Hillman takes a radical departure from both Freud and Jung. He refers to his depth psychology as a psychology of soul, soul being one of the meanings of the Greek word *psyche*. He equates the soul with the Underworld of Greek myth, with "a self-sustaining and imagining substrate—an inner place or deeper person or ongoing presence...."[10] He is less interested in the traditional psychodynamics of psychopathology than in exploring *psyche*, soul. Psychologically, Hillman defines soul as a perspective that is reflective. "Between us and events, between the doer and the deed, there is a reflective moment—and soul-making means differentiating this middle ground."[11] Differentiating the middle ground where the reflective moment occurs is the focus of psychological inquiry for Hillman.

He ascribes to soul the ability to make meaning possible, *to deepen events into experiences.* Soul is communicated in love and has a religious concern because of its relationship to death; and further, he writes:

> ... by 'soul' I mean the imaginative possibility in our natures, the experiencing through reflective speculation, dream, image, and fantasy—*that mode that recognizes all realities as primarily symbolic or metaphorical* [italics mine].[12]

For Hillman soul/psyche, image/archetype, and psychology belong in the same sentence. He reduces the word psychology to its Greek components; *psyche*, soul/image and *logos*, word/mind/ reason, literally a logos of soul. He refers to his depth psychology as archetypal psychology since the archetype was the singular consistent and central theme in Jung's psychology; and because archetype, and therefore psyche, are everywhere found—in science and art, religion and mysticism, in human and non-human reaches. The activities of soul occur because soul mediates the archetype; between ego and archetype we find soul. Hillman does address psychopathology, but does not make it the beginning and end of psychological inquiry.

Freud, Hillman, and Jung suggest, respectively, the divisions of body, soul, and spirit. I will refer to these three concepts throughout this book for I wish to remain close to soul and image without losing sight of body and spirit. These three divisions, much to my surprise and delight, have structured the narrative in a way unanticipated by me. It is therefore important to look at these three men anew, from the perspective of body, soul, and spirit as these concepts pertain to their psychologies.

Freud researched the instincts, Hillman finds time for reflection, and Jung mapped the quest for the Self. If we equate spirit with intent (a goal, a teleology), and remember that Jung wrote extensively about spirit, then we can better understand his psychology. Jung's psychology is a psychology of purpose and a psychology of personality. It is a psychology of purpose because every movement within psyche has a meaning and a function. Jung was the first to view the neurosis as primarily adaptive as opposed to maladaptive; its existence within the psyche serves a function and the solution is contained within the neurosis itself.

Jung used psyche and personality interchangeably. His was also a psychology of personality. The word personality comes from the Greek *persona*, mask, implying a mask through which sounds something transcendent: the personality is the mask through which the collective unconscious becomes manifest, or sounds through. The mature personality is thus capable of containing the many voices of existence, voices that are archetypal. A theme found throughout Jung's psychology is the story of the Quest for the Grail, for the treasure hard to attain. This treasure is the *totality* of who we are, the archetype of the Self. Jung's image for the Self was that of a circle, the Self being both the center and the circumference of the circle.[13] Spirit is impersonal and objective, as is Jung's collective unconscious.

Freud's psychology is a psychology of the body and of the instincts. Mental life happens through the interaction of ego, id, and superego. The ego coordinates mental processes and has a conscious and unconscious part: the conscious ego includes perception and motor control; the unconscious ego contains the dream censor and the process of repression. The id contains repressed psychic contents and the drives, the instincts. The superego is the authority structure, the watchful, judging, and punishing agent in the individual and is the source of social and religious feelings. The superego has its origin in the *original* ego configuration, which has been superseded by family and societal needs. The superego receives its energy from the id, the source of libido. The superego, partaking of both ego and id, would seem to be the mediating construct within the psyche. But this is not so. It is the ego that becomes the mediating battle ground, the site of anxiety between instinctual needs and drives (id) and collective norms and expectations (superego).[14] Individual suffering is *personal* and subjective.

Hillman acknowledges the depths (Freud and instinct) and the heights (Jung and spirit). He calls upon us, however, to remember psyche, soul. Soul is the between place, the mediator of high (spirit) and low (body). Soul is both personal and impersonal. I believe Hillman to be correct when he suggests that we have lost soul. In the current "New Age" movement, the trinity body/mind/spirit is frequently cited. Mind and spirit are in vogue yet once and again. I picked up a catalog of workshops, one of many that exist today, and browsed through only ten pages out of eighty. The words "spirit" and "mind" occurred twelve times. Not once was there a reference to soul. The closest references seemed to be the word "emotions." "Body" rarely occurred alone, instead I read "body/mind" more often than not. Most of the workshops were goal oriented. There were workshops to increase self-esteem, job performance, mind performance, "empowerment"—whatever that means—and healing. The word "healing" occurred repeatedly, but without reference to what the pathology might be. Suffering, that special province of soul, was referred to only indirectly, and then as something to be healed, which is to say, gotten rid of.

Certainly soul and mind are inextricably linked: but we have to discipline mind in order to create soul. Soul is as real an experience as body and spirit, mediating between both, calling us to task through its gift of meaning, bringing us to the alembic where the alchemical fire of suffering turns the base metal of the instinctual life into the gold of the mature personality. We would rather refer to mind, since it is impersonal and once removed. Mind and knowledge are like the wind and the soul like a windmill; together, the metaphorical grains of our life experiences are ground into the flour that provides us with the nourishment of meaning. A wise friend of mine once said, "Knowledge contains its own imperative." How much more an imperative must self-knowledge contain! Soul is that imperative.

Having to rediscover soul in our present study, it would be helpful to look at soul's more recent history. During the years 1800 to 1830, roughly, Romanticism as a way of viewing the world gained a foothold in Germany. Romanticism was a reaction to the Enlightenment. The Enlightenment originated in France around 1730 and culminated in 1785. The Enlightenment proclaimed the values of reason and society. The Romantics held to the irrational and the individual. Romanticism encouraged a deep feeling for nature with a consequent search for the ground of nature evident in the emotional life and in the human soul. Romanticism valued the activity of "becoming," the many metamorphoses and spontaneous unfolding of the individual. It also looked to particular cultures and nations, as opposed to the idea of society in the abstract and developed a feeling for history as a means of understanding the individual. This all made for an ideal type of human being according to Henri Ellenberger:

... Romanticism produced its ideal type of Man. Its main features were an extreme sensitiveness enabling Man to "feel into" Nature and to "feel with" other men, a rich inner life, belief in the power of inspiration, intuition, and spontaneity, and the importance ascribed to emotional life.[15]

According to Hillman, the words "vale" (as valley and/or the scene of sorrow) and "soul-making" came from the Romantics, Keats in particular who wrote: "Call the world, if you please, the vale of soul-making. Then you will find out the use of the world."[16]

Depth psychology, whether it emphasizes instinct, soul, or spirit, posits the unconscious, the storehouse of images. How do we begin to gain access to the unconscious in a way available to the greatest number of persons? Dreams and dreamwork fulfill this need. Freud saw within dream images the psychopathology of the individual interpreted within the context of his psychoanalytic theory. Jung expanded the realm of the psyche to include the collective unconscious: dream images *might be wish-fulfillment* according to Freud, but they might also be symbolic of archetypal dramas never before within the purview of consciousness. Hillman gives primacy to the dream image and the dream world; Hillman suggests we honor images from *their* viewpoint, from their world, not from ego needs.

Dream images present us with uncensored raw data; unless, of course, you are from the Freudian school which assumes that all dreams are censored by the dream censor aspect of the ego. In any case, we know that clients begin to dream according to the therapeutic mode of the therapist. In Freudian psychoanalysis, the dreams become psycho-sexual. But Jungian analysis fosters dream images of personality development with the archetype of the Self as the pivot point. Hillman's focus is the myth and the image as they afford us with the materials for soul-making. Hillman's stance is one of non-interference as regards the dream image. The images speak to themselves. There is nothing beyond the image, no allusions to anything more beyond itself. In this book I side heavily with Hillman's theoretical stance. "Psyche" is interpreted to mean soul. The purpose of archetypal psychology is to understand and assist soul with its activity of soul-making.

Psyche as lived is postulated as feminine by numerous disciplines. Giving primacy to the image in counseling immediately constellates the archetypal feminine. Herta Payson in "The Transformative Image: A Feminine Approach to Therapy" writes:

> Dreams speak to us in images .... Coming from the unconscious, which is essentially a feminine place, the images of the dream yield their secrets to a feminine approach. The qualities of nurturing growth, of yielding to the unknown, and of intuitive understanding, which are essentially feminine, are far more conducive to the opening of a dream's enigma than a logical, direct approach.[17]

The archetypal feminine has as its universal image the guardian of our nighttime skies, the Moon. It is this lunar landscape which lies closest to the image, to the shapes within our dream life. Jung detailed the solar hero/heroine journey as one of individuation. I would like to suggest that there is a lunar hero/heroine whose journey is also one of individuation, but this lunar hero/heroine journeys through a landscape (dreams) that is essentially that of the forces of the Goddess Night and her children. Stated differently, the lunar hero/heroine whose journey is one of individuation actively engages in soul-making.

In addition to these three perspectives of dreamwork, reflective of the work of Freud, Jung, and Hillman, I have included my understanding of astrology and the Qabalah, with God-images providing the ordering field. As I have said, astrology and the modern Qabalah both contain a wealth of images. In my own work I utilize these images as a means of enhancing the soul's ability to imagine, to fantasize. This idea will develop gradually over the course of the book. It is here only necessary to explain the value of imagining for soul. Hillman writes:

> Fantasy in our view is the attempt of the psyche itself to re-mythologize consciousness; we try to further this activity by encouraging familiarity with myth and folktale. Soul-making goes hand in hand with deliteralizing consciousness and restoring its connection to mythic and metaphorical thought patterns. Rather than interpret stories into concepts and rational explanations, we prefer to see conceptual explanations as secondary elaborations upon basic stories which are containers and givers of vitality.[18]

I have kept the story as paramount throughout this work. I have attempted to speak less *about* story than to let the story and its images speak about themselves. There are, consequently, many voices in this work. I have quoted extensively some of those voices, both actual and imaginal. This has allowed me to remain close to story.

If there has been a struggle for me in preparing this book, it has been whether or not to include the Qabalah and Western magic. At first I thought it possible to leave the Qabalah out of the text—I would simply give my conclusions, divorced from the process by which I arrived at these conclusions—a process that for me includes knowledge and training in the use of the Qabalah. I realized that this was not practical. It would be like presenting a finished garment expecting someone else to wear it, one size fitting all. I cannot write about a process by giving only conclusions. The Qabalah and Western magic is how I order the God-images in my own fantasies and it is such an *important* process for me, that I have devoted the whole of Chapter One to its definition and history.

I will be using the God-images along every step of the way. Chapter One gives the history of the Qabalah and Western magic as they pertain to God-images. Also in Chapter One are James Hillman's four factors in a psychology of soul, and some of my ideas as to the commonalities of Western magic and a psychology of soul. Jean Shinoda Bolen's use of God patterns in the therapeutic setting is also included. The purpose of Chapter One is to describe a topography of the place where we begin our journey, using the Qabalah and a psychology of soul to paint broad strokes on a canvas from which, by the end of this book, we can stand back and away from, to see where we have been.

Chapter One is a chapter about beginnings, and beginnings usually contain a certain fragility; it has been the most difficult chapter to write. Since each chapter in this book works off the previous chapter, Chapter One has the decided disadvantage. Each subsection in Chapter One can stand on its own, and should be so read. The threads of each subsection will come together as the book proceeds. Patience is indicated, as there are many levels to this book and I have tried to momentarily suspend our habitual ego way of approaching things. This is a magician's trick carefully executed: how do we keep the ego happily distracted while the image is given primacy? The Qabalah is a technique used by Qabalists to accomplish this magician's trick and so is central to the beginnings of this book.

Chapter Two contains a brief history of astrology and its connection to God-images. Chapter Three looks to the fate that comes with our experience of the image, and outlines Carl Jung's analytical psychology as the evolution of the theory of the archetype. The first three chapters form a unity. In Chapter One we begin with the opposites as exemplified by the interrelation of word and image. In Chapter Two we begin from without and move inwards to soul using astrology, and how, beginning with the images of astrology, we can find ways of fantasizing from externals thereby engaging in soul-making. In order to do this we must at least agree with the Stoics that the microcosm (man/woman) reflects in its nature that of the whole (the universe as symbolized by the heavens). In Chapter Three we begin within, from soul's images, and move outwards from the primacy of psyche and image and how the encounter with image affects our lives.

Chapter Four presents us with soul-ideas, derived from the first three chapters, of what a therapy utilizing the transformative image as primary data might look like. With these soul-ideas in mind, we will move to Chapter Five which is a case story of how God-images manifest within a particular life.

I should note the use of gender inclusive language throughout, and the capitalization of certain words to emphasize archetypal and cosmic forces and principles, an inheritance from the Qabalah and the Western Magic Tradition. The need for capitalization is threefold: to draw attention to the soul's native ability of personifying experience; to populate our narrative with the many Others whose voices will be heard throughout; and to remind us that the merely human is limiting.

There are three other topics that I need to quickly address. One is the use, in this work, of the words "masculine" and "feminine." When I use these as modifiers, I do so from an archetypal stance, and do not necessarily refer to the gender of the person experiencing the archetypal structure. A man can experience a feminine archetypal structure as easily as a woman can, and, men and women being who they are, the experience is usually different for each. Two, there is the question of the transliteration of the Hebrew Qabalah into English, which presents a problem. The Hebrew alphabet does not have a one-to-one correspondence with the English alphabet, e.g., from Hebrew the word QBLH (Hebrew letters Qoph, Beth, Lamed, and He) can be transliterated as Cabala, Kabballah, or Qabalah, among others. I have used the transliterations of Western magic to differentiate this use of the Qabalah from other disciplines' use of the Qabalah. And three, all case materials are given with the stipulation of confidentiality; names have been changed or data withheld.

The present work is ambitious in its scope. I wish to share a very personal way of working, my own personal myth. I wish to invoke the Gods and their images as guides and teachers that can help us become more than merely human. I wish to give primacy to soul by remembering that though the Gods are guides and teachers, as archetypes they are more than simply psychology. It is we, by way of psyche, that do the psychologizing: the Gods exist everywhere and at all times. I wish to help restore soul to its rightful place as mediator between body and spirit; this is the between realm. And lastly, I wish to remind us that we have been unfaithful to the Greek ideal of learning where microcosm and macrocosm love one another by discarding and discrediting much of what they helped create rationally. We can no longer ignore the Western traditions of *gnosis*, the intuitive apprehension of spiritual truths.

In summary: a certain number of archetypes of the collective unconscious clearly contain a story, a movement towards a goal, which is the fulfillment of the story (archetype) within the context of the individual's life. The interaction of individual myth and collective myth is observable to the therapist, whose task it is to know these stories in their universal form and thereby assist the client in the clarification of these universal myths as they "play" themselves out in the individual life. The task of the therapist may or may not be assisted by knowledge of Carl Jung's psychological constructs, although, in my opinion, they make the task easier. To date, therapists have resorted to classical mythology in order to learn about mythic themes embodied by the Gods. I propose that the Qabalah of Western magic and Western astrology can each contribute to the therapist's knowledge base, both practical and theoretical, because both of these disciplines are saturated with God-images. In using the image and moving towards the universal concept contained within the image, a therapist becomes free to move beyond one particular pantheon of deities thereby deepening for the client the meaning of the image, for the image is above all else collective. This deepening of the image into a multifaceted experience is one of the tasks of the therapist, whose overall goal is the assistance in the healing that the client is seeking, for therapy is from the Greek word meaning "to serve," to deeply care about.

CHAPTER ONE

To Begin With: God-Images, the Qabalah, Magic, and Depth Psychology

... if we consider the Gods as expressing themselves each in a specific mode of being, each with symbolic attributes, landscapes, animals and plants, activities and moralities and psychopathologies, then part of the specific mode of being of each God is a style of reflection. *A God is a manner of existence, an attitude toward existence, and a set of ideas.* Each God would project its divine *logos*, opening the soul's eye so that it regards the world in a particularly formed way. A God forms our subjective vision so that we see the world according to its ideas.
— James Hillman, *Re-Visioning Psychology*

The Gods call. The Gods arrive. The Gods demand. The Gods inspire. The Gods leave. The Gods come and go in images, in images charged with feelings, with ideas, with percepts. Many are the voices clamoring within me, God-images wanting access to my hands, to the written word. As I begin to write about images, I am lost in words that insufficiently convey the images. The approach to the image is circular, while communication by means of the written word is a linear process. We have only to remember our dreams to appreciate the difference between the word and the image, for in our dreams words are few.

Herta Payson suggests an approach to a beginning exploration of the image when she writes:

> Exploring an image means circling around it, looking at it from all sides, as one examines a piece of sculpture, until the whole emerges, multifaceted, in several dimensions.[1]

1

This is not so with the word, for the word, whether we speak it or write it, must be uttered according to prescribed rules. The image as an affecting presence offering an affective relationship allows us to converse with it, curse it, bless it, or surrender to it. The image can grow and change until the dreamworld is as real as our world of words. It may appear that there are no rules in the dreamworld; more precisely, the rules are different and not as constricting as the rules of words.

The word and the image, like any pair of opposites that can come to mind, are the perennial inhabitants of the psyche. And herein lies a problem: how to do justice to both, the word and the image—and by extension young and old, black and white, up and down, and so on—without getting lost in dichotomy, in the world of the opposites? True it is: a work that claims to be based on Carl Jung's psychology cannot dispense with the tension of opposites. But the opposites can rend a human being asunder, like being tied to two teams of horses moving in contrary directions. This is so, for once we begin to interpret everything, as for example, in terms of male and female, we are condemned to seek gender in everything and we forget that maleness and femaleness can also be relative qualities.

We are beginning our chapter with a dilemma as old as humanity itself—the tension of opposites. We could separate the opposites, develop each one accordingly, and then attempt to unify them. Or we can choose the more difficult path, to bind and separate the opposites simultaneously, never chosing the absolute poles of any one pair, but the relative shades of grey in between. Our beginning dilemma, getting lost in the dichotomy of word and image resolves itself if we remember that the word and the image complement each other. To complement is to make complete, to make whole, to bring to perfection.[2] Experientially, the word and the image are complements found within the God-image; together they make God-images complete, whole, perfect. We must approach the word and the image differently and experience them differently; but the word must cede before the image and the image cede before the word in a mutual rhythm of ebb and flow.

Restated, we can by-pass the either/or modality of the primal pair of opposites—which the Chinese call Yin and Yang, Female and Male—by getting to know their children, the God-images of our experience. I propose from the beginning a pantheon of Gods and

Goddesses. Trapped in the either/or mode of the primal pair, we can forget that the word as idea and the image as symbol exist simultaneously in the gifts of the Gods, as Hillman assures us in our introductory quote. Let the primal pair dance their eternal dance. Let their children fill the pages of this work, for by degrees, as one understands the child, one comes to know the parents.

And how prolific are the Gods! It is not enough to know their personalities, their animals and stones, their plants and ideas. They sing, they laugh, they join in love, they mate with mortals. They weave their spells with unseen webs of meaning that dazzle the human imagination as we sit, rapt, not sure of whether we fight or flee, or dance with them out of sheer bewilderment. In this book we will come to know the Gods, both their image and their word, and also remain connected to their incessant mating, their all too complex mythologies of relationships.

We will utilize the Qabalah, astrology, and depth psychology to accomplish the goal of knowing the Gods. In this first chapter we will explore the God-images as they are found in the modern Qabalah of Western magic, move to James Hillman's four activities native to soul and how these activities of soul appear in Western magic, introduce Jean Shinoda Bolen's use of the Gods as patterns of behavior, and end, using the Qabalah to structure the remaining narrative of the book. I will be using the Qabalah on two different levels: to maintain the unity of word and image; and as the structure of the movements and chapters of this work.

The Qabalah and Magic

It is difficult to *write* about images. The word and the image are complementary, and both are needed if we are to utilize the image in any manner, especially therapy. We are reminded by Hillman that the word "psychology" comes from the Greek words for soul (psyche) and word (logos). To interpret life and living from a *psychological* perspective, therefore, requires that the primary datum of soul, the image, be understood as bringing with it an experience of logos, or ideas that are usually expressed in words.

But how can the word and the image be maintained together, even though logically we move to one and then the other? One method is the Qabalah of Western magic. The Qabalah is workable because it assists the initiate to order universal constructs contained within the image as archetype, and vice-versa. The Qabalah can assist in maintaining the complementarity of word and image. What is the Qabalah and what is its history?

The Qabalah has its origin in Judaism.[3] It is a mystical tradition based upon the religious beliefs of the Jewish faith. Mysticism differs from religion, in that the goal of the mystic is to experience the Divine directly, without the intercession of an appointed religious body. The Qabalah's history is synonymous with Judaism's, until the Middle Ages of our modern era, when it was reinterpreted and used in the fabric of a much younger Christian mysticism. It is this Christian contribution to the Qabalistic literature that is most germane to the study of God-images.

The early history of the Qabalah begins with the five Books of Moses in the Old Testament known as the Pentateuch. For the Hebrews, the Pentateuch is the written Torah, Hebrew for Law. The written Torah is believed to contain a quantum of divine energy, being as it were, a receptacle for the divine spirit. The reverse process, coming to know God by way of the Torah is thus implicit; as the Jewish religion and its literature evolved, so too did the mystical interpretations of the Torah.

The earliest recognized Qabalistic literature developed between 538 B.C. and 70 A.D. It was known as Merkabah mysticism, after the Throne Chariot of God, or Merkabah, a vision in Ezekiel 1: 26-8. Merkabah mystics believed that by a shamanistic and therefore magical, ecstatic ascent or descent, they could reach the Throne Chariot of God. The ascent to God's throne was a journey the mystic had to undertake. There were seven heavenly halls, or hekhaloths, and each entrance to a hall was guarded. To ensure safe passage, the initiate would memorize magical names and seals pertinent to each hall, the journey to God's Throne being thus expedited. Merkabah mysticism also made use of a magic: the controlling of Nature's forces to achieve a stated goal.

Merkabah mysticism was the longest phase of Jewish mysticism lasting roughly from 100 B.C. to 1000 A.D. The surviving fragments of Merkabah mysticism were written down and edited sometime between the fifth and the sixth centuries A.D., and became the scaffolding upon which practical Qabalism developed. The magic of Merkabah mysticism became the magic of practical Qabalism.

There are two historical divisions in Qabalah the speculative Qabalah and the practical Qabalah. Charles Poncé, whose history of the Qabalah I have used almost exclusively, writes:

> The speculative branch concerns itself solely with the operations of the spiritual dimension of the universe, in an attempt to discover how it meshes with this world. Speculative Kabbalism aims also at revealing how man may find a place in both dimensions at one & the same time. The practical Kabbalah is primarily concerned with winning the energies of the spiritual world for the purposes of magical control .... Practical Kabbalism greatly influenced the magic of Western Europe during the Mediaeval period .... [4]

Practical Qabalism was brought to Germany by way of Italy in 917 A.D., by the Kalonymus family. This is the history given by Eleazor of Worms (1165-1238) who had been instructed by his teacher, a member of the Kalonymus family, to spread the word and literature of practical Qabalism. Meanwhile, speculative Qabalism flourished in Spain. The appearance of the *Sepher Zohar, The Book of Splendor*, in Spain between 1280-1290 helped to unite both divisions, and with the exile of the Jews from Spain, the *Zohar* was carried to the various countries the Jews were forced to settle in. In this manner, the Jewish mystical tradition spread throughout Europe.

We possess no definitive dates, but the Qabalah, most importantly the practical Qabalah, eventually reached the attention of Christian thinkers and scholars who were rediscovering classical art, literature, and learning during the Renaissance.[5] The rediscovered classical learning included Hermeticism, Gnosticism, and Theurgy (Western magic). Western magic would in time not only absorb the teachings of the practical Qabalah, but the teachings of Hermeticism and Gnosticism as well; this new Western magic would eventually be brought into the 20th century by a succession of scholar-magicians and secret societies versed in the Qabalah. Before continuing with our history, let us digress somewhat and briefly examine Hermeticism, Gnosticism, Theurgy.

Hermeticism, also known as Hermetism, was originally comprised of works written in Alexandria between the first and third centuries A.D. These works were not many, and were collectively known as the *Hermetica* because the author was believed to be Hermes Trismegistos, "Thrice Greatest Hermes." From its beginnings Hermeticism was a secret mystical tradition.

Hermeticism is an important historical contributor of several key ideas found in modern esotericism and occultism. One contribution is the importance of an eclectic mentality that seeks a unity between the human and the universe; any and all ideas can help us to learn about this unity. A second contribution from Hermeticism is the appreciation of the symbolic *value* of the universe which consequently allows us to move away from the negativity of Western dualism, which is that matter (i.e., the world and those things of this world, as for instance, our bodies) is evil, only the deity being wholly good. And third, Hermeticism reinforces the myth of the Fall, or man/woman's process of reintegration; Hermeticism is in essence the journey of the *initiated* soul that finds its way back to the source as deity.

Gnosticism comes from the Greek word for knowledge, *gnosis*. It is a current of antiquity that ran parallel with early mainstream Christianity, and in many cases Gnostic sects were direct offshoots of traditional Christianity; of course, these sects were considered to be heretical. In 1966, scholars defined Gnosticism as a religion in its own right with the following beliefs: 1) the unknown God did not create the world, 2) the world is an error, the result of the Fall because of a split in the deity, and 3) spiritual man and woman are alien to the natural world but related to the deity; he/she becomes conscious of his/her deepest self when he or she hears the divine words of revelation which implys that unconsciousness is the cause of evil. Gnostics believed that the deity could be experienced directly by initiation in the secret tradition of gnosis.

The third current of antiquity rediscovered by Renaissance scholars was that of Theurgy, or magic performed with the aid of beneficient spirits. For pre-Christian pagan magicians, or Theurgists, the Gods and Goddesses were both personalities in their own right and personifications of cosmic principles. Theurgists believed that man-made objects could be imbued with a life and intelligence of their own through the use of symbols, or tokens, based upon the Hermetic law of correspondence: "As above, so below."[6] The tokens were the stones, plants, perfumes and other associated symbols of the deity invoked, placed within the image of the deity. A properly performed rite would culminate with the presence of the deity, especially in the form of mystical illumination; hence such works as the *Corpus Hermeticum*, one of several works of the *Hermetica* said to be inspired by the God Hermes. According to Francis King, Theurgy "was popular with the late pagan philosophers, who saw it as a barrier against the rising flood of Christianity—something *above* philosophy in that it gave direct access to the gods."[7]

These three philosophies (Hermeticism, Gnosticism, and Theurgy) together contributed to the development of four core beliefs. First, the material universe reflects Divine intent. Second, divinity is defined as including a pantheon of Gods and Goddesses. Third, direct access to the Gods is possible by way of correct procedure and ceremonial that includes the active, magical use of God-images. And fourth, secret initiation is the means of transmission of the ways one can personally attain to the divine knowledge, or *gnosis* (we can remember here the mysteries of Eleusis and the rites of alchemy, also). Practical Qabalism employed these four concepts in a broad sense if we but remove the pagan polytheistic element. Western magic and Jewish magic could only eventually meet. From historical fragments, we can even conjecture the whole of magic's inception to have been beneath the nighttime skies of Babylonia, a romantic speculation that both magic traditions had a common origin within the womb of the sands of the desert.

Summarizing, Western magic has as its antecedents the Hermetic and Gnostic literature of the Roman Empire, especially the still extant *Corpus Hermeticum*, and the surviving fragments of Theurgy's most sacred book, The *Chaldean Oracles* said to have been written by Zoroaster. Renaissance scholars made use of Hermeticism, Gnosticism, and Theurgy in their need to understand humanity's place in the universe. Marsilio Ficino, favored scholar during the Renaissance of the Florentine banker family Medici, translated the *Corpus Hermeticum* in 1463, even when the entire works of Plato were also awaiting translation. Since the Qabalah had been spread throughout Europe by exiled Spanish Jews, Christian scholar-magicians familiar with the literature proceeded to reconcile the *Corpus* with the Old and New Testaments using the Qabalah. King writes:

> The scholar-magicians were influenced by all three of these tendencies, Hermeticism, the Kabalah and Christian mysticism; they understood the nature of the pagan gods in the sense of the *Corpus Hermeticum*; they interpreted the Old Testament by the Kabalah, and the New (*lumen Christi*) by the speculations of the mystics. They saw the magic, the occult philosophy, that they built on these foundations as true Christianity, a Christianity which was the religion of eternity .... [8]

The history of the Qabalah and its absorption into the Western Magic Tradition is complex. What we need to remember is that Jewish mysticism and its brand of magic was introduced into Europe by the Jews. The practical Qabalah in particular, with its secret names of the one God and an angelic hierarchy, was adopted by an evolving Christian magic and mysticism. One can understand how the fire and passion of the Jewish practical Qabalists to experience the divine captured the imagination of Christian scholar-magicians who were creating a mysticism of their own. Christian scholar-magicians were versed in Christian mysticism, astrology, alchemy, and the philosophies of Hermeticism, Gnosticism, and Theurgy. By adopting the Qabalah, they performed a curious and unique marriage of Judeo-Christian monotheism and Greek polytheism, two currents that have greatly influenced Western history. Theirs was a synthesis of these two currents by way of a magic fueled by a mysticism based on the traditional Qabalah reinterpreted. This became the *new* Western magic.

Christian scholar-magicians kept their new-found tradition alive by way of secret societies and fraternities, an inheritance from the schools of Gnosticism. The belief in a secret brotherhood whose purpose it is to preserve the knowledge leading to divine illumination engendered the various groups such as the Templars (founded about 1118 A.D. at Jerusalem by the Christian Crusaders), the Rosicrucians (allegedly founded by Christian Rosenkreutz sometime in the 15th century, there have been splinter groups since then), and the Masonic Lodges. A.E. Waite in The *Holy Kabbalah* writes that all these fraternities have attempted to preserve the ancient mysteries of initiations of Egypt, Greece, and Rome—if not in actuality, then at least in spirit:

> During the Christian period the knowledge which would otherwise have perished was preserved *ex hypothesi* among successive occult fraternities, some known to history, such as the Templars and Rosicrucians, the rest working in complete silence. Corporately or otherwise, they were all affiliated with each other, and Symbolical Freemasonry forms the last link in the western chain of transmission.[9]

For our purposes, we can move ahead in time from the magic of the Middle Ages to England and to *The Hermetic Order of the Golden Dawn*. The Order was founded in London in 1888 by three men (Dr.

William Wynn Westcott, Samuel Liddell McGregor Mathers, and Dr. W. R. Woodman) who were well versed in Symbolical Freemasonry (a Christian mysticism), astrology, alchemy, magic, Tarot, and the Qabalah.[10] The Golden Dawn in turn continued the transmission of a Christian occult philosophy animated by the Western Magic Tradition. Western magic had by this time expropriated the Qabalah from the Hebrews. Western magic, by history and definition, actively engages the image. The Qabalah, by history and definition, actively engages the word. Together they became the magic of the Golden Dawn. The Golden Dawn standardized the interchangeability of the words "Qabalah" (with a 'Q') and "magic" (of Western origin). Israel Regardie tells us about the Order teachings when he writes:

> In the opening passages of the very first initiatory ritual of the Order is found the remarkable phrase "By names and images are all powers awakened and reawakened."
> This simple phrase sets the stage, as it were, for all subsequent Order teaching. In effect it reveals the essential fact involved in all practical magical work.[11]

The Tree of Life

What is this Qabalah with a 'Q,' also known as the Western magic tradition, that brings us back to the complementarity and unity of word and image? To answer this question it is essential for us to examine the foundation of both traditional Jewish mysticism and the more recent Christian magical mysticism, the image of the Tree of Life which is comprised of the Ain Soph and the Sephiroth. According to Poncé:

> No matter how much one Kabbalist may differ from another in his theoretical speculations he will agree that without the concepts of the *En-Sof* & the *Sefiroth* there is no Kabbalism.[12]

The Tree of Life is the beginning and the end of Qabalistic study and the literature cannot be fully understood without the image of the Tree. The Tree of Life (illus. 1) consists of the ten emanations of God, the Sephiroth (singular Sephirah), numbered from one to ten. These are represented as circles interconnected by twenty-two paths. The twenty-two letters of the Hebrew alphabet are attributed to these twenty-two paths, which are numbered 11-32 (illus. 2).

AIN SOPH

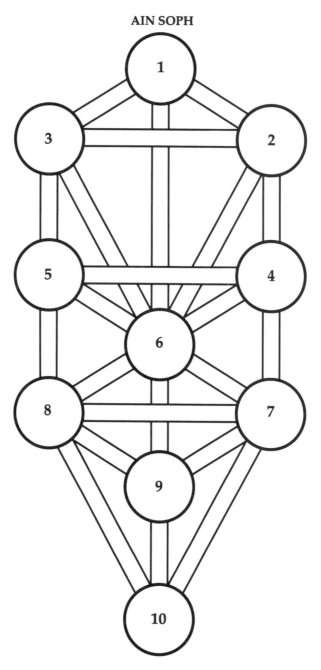

Illustration 1
Otz Chiim—The Tree of Life

The ten Sephiroth and the twenty-two letters of the Hebrew alphabet give us thirty-two paths in total. Note that the Sephiroth, or spheres, are also known as paths when a reference is made to the complete Tree; whenever Qabalists reference the twenty-two paths, they mean the paths that connect the ten spheres.

The Sephiroth have their origin in the Ain Soph, the Limitless, the true God. According to Poncé:

> The En-Sof is something beyond human comprehension, but He is at the same time the fluid in which the entire universe of the Sefiroth, the emanations of His totally uncommitted affluence, reside.[13]

The Ain Soph, meaning "without end," Limitless, is the wellspring of this universe, yet cannot be understood in terms of this universe. The Ain Soph generates the Sephiroth (numbers, spheres, emanations), this generation forming the basis of the created universe; ultimately, we are the final recipients of the outpouring of the Ain Soph. The Ain Soph is in effect, unknowable, which we should not confuse with unknown, but knowable.

Poncé tells us that there are many metaphors concerning the relationship between the Ain Soph and the Sephiroth. They are inseparable, the Sephiroth being the internal psychic organs of the body of God, much as the nerves of our bodies are representative of us. The Sephiroth can be thought of as stages or operations of God, like the glands in our bodies that operate without our consideration or awareness. Later Hasidic theory relegated the operations of the Sephiroth to the plane of the human mind, "a theory of the operations of the human mind at the deepest level where it merges with the soul."[14] Poncé offers one final metaphor:

> *En-Sof*, I would further suggest, is the meaning in creation, the limitless meaning which our scientists seek to discover in their attempts to unveil the origin of the universe. *En-Sof* is what they seek.[15]

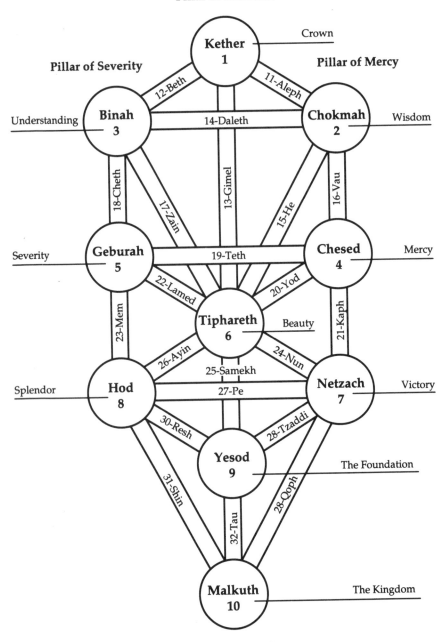

Illustration 2
The Tree of Life—The Spheres and the Paths

The Hebrew name and the English translation of each of the Sephiroth is as follows:

Kether — The Crown	Tiphareth — Beauty/Harmony
Chokmah — Wisdom	Netzach — Victory
Binah — Understanding	Hod — Splendor
Chesed — Mercy	Yesod — The Foundation
Geburah — Severity	Malkuth — The Kingdom

The ancients were familiar with seven planets: Sun, Moon, Mercury, Venus, Mars, Jupiter and Saturn. Sun and Moon were considered planets, and continue to be so considered in astrology and alchemy. The planets are attributed to each sphere, and the modern planets, Uranus, Neptune, and Pluto have been added by modern Qabalists (illus. 3).

The twenty-two paths numbered 11-32 have a Hebrew letter assigned to each. *The Sepher Yetzirah* or *Book of Formation*, written between the third and sixth century A.D., establishes the Hebrew alphabet as a divine instrument of creation, God's utterance becoming the foundation of the created universe.[16] The Hebrew letters are broken down into three mother letters, seven double letters, and twelve simple letters. The three mothers, Aleph, Mem, and Shin represent the three elements of Air, Water, and Fire. The seven doubles contain the opposites that make up the cosmos and also represent the seven planets of the ancients. They are Beth, Gimel, Daleth, Kaph, Pe, Resh, and Tau containing the opposites of life and death, peace and strife, wisdom and folly, wealth and poverty, grace and sin, fruitfulness and sterility, and dominion and slavery, respectively; and the planets Mercury, Moon, Venus, Jupiter, Mars, Sun, and Saturn. In addition, the twelve astrological signs are attributed to the twelve simples. Tzaddi to Aries,[17] Vau to Taurus, Zain to Gemini, Cheth to Cancer, Teth to Leo, Yod to Virgo, Lamed to Libra, Nun to Scorpio, Samekh to Sagittarius, Ayin to Capricorn, He to Aquarius, and Qoph to Pisces.

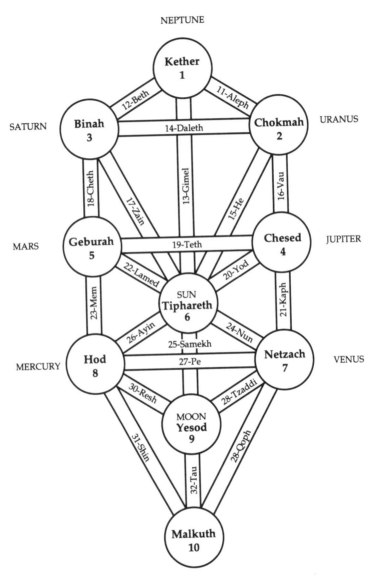

Illustration 3
The Tree of Life—The Planets

Pluto is attributed to an imaginary sphere. Daath, that is found half-way between Chokmah and Binah, and is the child of their union.

The ancients used the planets, the constellations and the elements in their understanding of the universe. The Qabalah gives meaning to the astrological signs and the elements especially, by placing them within a larger universal context. The Hebrew letters, their English translation, their path number on the Tree and their correspondence to sign, element, and planet are included in table 1.[18] One can note that the planets have a sphere and a path each.

A way to differentiate the spheres from the paths is this: The Sephiroth are *objective* forces, akin to Jung's definition of the collective unconscious and the archetypes which exist therein as potential, unknown, but capable of ordering experience once activated. Hillman would remind us that the archetypes exist everywhere and at all times apart from the human subject. The paths that connect the spheres are the *subjective* experience of the path treader since a path must lead somewhere, hopefully to another sphere. A path is energized by the two spheres it connects. The path is akin to the activated archetype that is knowable because it orders our experience. A path may be likened to Jung's definition of a psychological complex. The complex has an archetypal core which is given substance by a person's actual life experience. In the spheres "We Be."[19] Treading the paths "We Become."

TABLE 1

THE HEBREW LETTERS AND THEIR PATHS ON THE TREE

Letter	*English Meaning*	*Path Number*	*Correspondence*
Aleph	Ox	11	Air
Beth	House	12	Mercury
Gimel	Camel	13	Moon
Daleth	Door	14	Venus
He	Window	15	Aquarius
Vau	Nail	16	Taurus
Zain	Sword	17	Gemini
Cheth	Fence	18	Cancer
Teth	Serpent	19	Leo
Yod	Hand (Grasping)	20	Virgo
Kaph	Hand	21	Jupiter
Lamed	Ox-goad	22	Libra
Mem	Water	23	Water

Letter	English Meaning	Path Number	Correspondence
Nun	Fish	24	Scorpio
Samekh	Tent-peg; prop	25	Sagittarius
Ayin	Eye	26	Capricorn
Pe	Mouth (as the organ of speech)	27	Mars
Tzaddi	Fish-hook	28	Aries
Qoph	Back of head	29	Pisces
Resh	Head, face	30	Sun
Shin	Tooth (serpent's)	31	Fire
Tau	Cross; mark	32	Saturn

The philosophy of the Qabalah includes the four planes of existence, the four worlds. Atziluth is the Archetypal World, the World of Emanations; Briah is the World of Creation; Yetzirah is the World of Formation; and Assiah is the World of Action, the World of Matter (illus. 4). These planes correspond *roughly* to the four realms of human experience: the Godhead, spirit/soul, mind/emotions, and body, respectively. Atziluth as the archetypal world of emanation is the Godhead (Kether); Briah as the world of formation is spirit (Chokmah) and soul (Binah); Yetzirah as the world of creation is mind (Chesed, Geburah, Tiphareth) and emotion (Netzach, Hod, and Yesod); and lastly, Assiah as the world of matter and action is the body (Malkuth). The lesson from the Qabalah is that the planes of existence are separate but interrelated. If the God-images are to remain alive for us they must touch our lives on all planes.

The early Christian scholar-magicians found in the Qabalah an efficacious device to control the mind. In Oriental philosophy the mind is likened to the intractable ox which is stubborn and difficult to mold. The Jewish Qabalists had for centuries utilized their philosophy based on the Ain Soph and the Tree as a focus for the mind, allowing for the contemplation of the Ineffable, the created universe, and humanity—the union of thought and symbol leading them to ever greater levels of illumination which they translated into meaning.

The practical Qabalists had developed a magical system early on. The rediscovery of magic in Europe during the Renaissance, derived from the classical period, found in practical Qabalism a wonderful yoke for the mind. Dion Fortune in 1935 wrote:

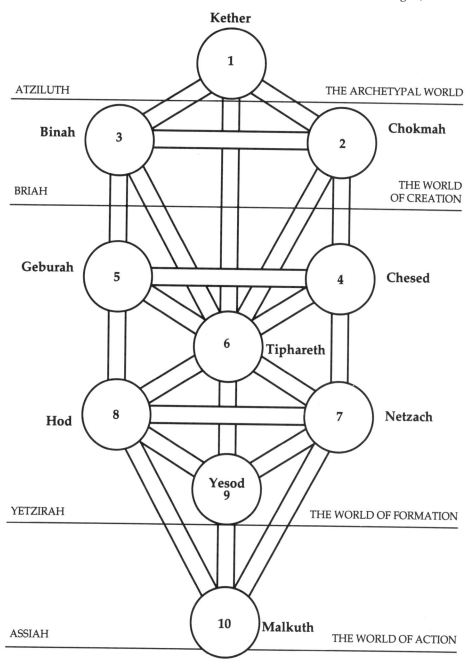

Illustration 4
The Four Worlds on the Tree

Upon the Tree of Life with its Ten Holy Sephiroth the modern occultist bases both a metaphysic and a magic. He uses a philosophical conception of the Tree to interpret what it represents to his conscious mind, and he uses a magical and ceremonial application of its symbolism to link it up with his subconscious mind. The initiate, consequently, makes the best of both worlds, ancient and modern; for the modern world is all surface consciousness, and has forgotten and repressed the subconsciousness, to its own great hurt; and the ancient world was mainly subconsciousness, consciousness having been but recently evolved. When the two are linked up and brought into a polarised function they yield superconsciousness, which is the goal of the initiate.[20]

The thirty-two paths of the complete Tree have been likened to a filing system of thirty-two drawers, and not unlike the current filing systems used in computer software. Computer filing systems are developed along sequential lines beginning with a root directory that branches out into sub-directories, and the sub-directories in turn branch out into other sub-directories. "Files" are stored this way.

Fortune further wrote:

The curious symbol-system known to us as the Tree of Life is an attempt to reduce to diagrammatic form every force and factor in the manifested universe and the soul of man; to correlate them one to another and reveal them spread out as on a map so that the relative positions of each unit can be seen and the relations between them traced. In brief, the Tree of Life is a compendium of science, psychology, philosophy, and theology.[21]

The skeleton of the modern magical filing-system aspect of the Tree of Life was developed by *The Hermetic Order of the Golden Dawn*. The Order incorporated the 78 card deck known as Tarot cards as the best and easiest way of "labeling" a "file" known as a path. The earliest actual copies of Tarot cards were prepared in 1392, but there is reason to believe that the cards themselves date much earlier in medieval times. There are 22 major arcana, or Trumps, in the deck corresponding to the 22 Hebrew letters and to the paths on the Tree (table 2).

TABLE 2
THE TWENTY-TWO TAROT TRUMPS WITH ASTROLOGICAL ATTRIBUTIONS, HEBREW LETTER, AND PATH NUMBER ON THE TREE

Trumps based on Paul Foster Case's *The Tarot: A Key to the Wisdom of the Ages*

Trump No.	Title	Hebrew Letter	Astrological	Path No.
0	The Fool	Aleph	Uranus, Air	11
1	The Magician	Beth	Mercury	12
2	The High Priestess	Gimel	Moon	13
3	The Empress	Daleth	Venus	14
4	The Emperor	He	Aries	15*
5	The Hierophant	Vau	Taurus	16
6	The Lovers	Zain	Gemini	17
7	The Chariot	Cheth	Cancer	18
8	Strength	Teth	Leo	19
9	The Hermit	Yod	Virgo	20
10	Wheel of Fortune	Kaph	Jupiter	21
11	Justice	Lamed	Libra	22
12	The Hanged Man	Mem	Water	23
13	Death	Nun	Scorpio	24
14	Temperance	Samekh	Sagittarius	25
15	The Devil	Ayin	Capricorn	26
16	The Tower	Pe	Mars	27
17	The Star	Tzaddi	Aquarius	28*
18	The Moon	Qoph	Pisces	29
19	The Sun	Resh	Sun	30
20	Judgement	Shin	Fire, Spirit	31
21	The World	Tau	Saturn, Earth	32

*Aleister Crowley changed the attributions of The Emperor from Trump 4 to Trump 17, from He to Tzaddi. Therefore, He is still Trump 4, path 15 but is now Aquarius, The Star—Tzaddi, The Emperor, Aries is now Trump 17, path 28. Crowley felt this was in keeping with the symbolism of the New Age of Aquarius.

Richard Roberts feels that the 22 major arcana are an alchemical revelation of the descent and ascent of Hermes/Mercury/Thoth. In any case, it can be argued that the 22 major arcana are representative of numerical archetypes depicted through imagery.[22] Included, in illustrations 5A—5D, are reproductions of the 22 major arcana as designed by Arthur Edward Waite and drawn by Pamela Coleman Smith known as the Waite deck. Although the Waite deck is here reproduced, I have used Paul Foster Case's written analysis of the Major Arcana from his book *The Tarot, A Key to the Wisdom of the Ages*.

More than any other occult inheritance, the Tarot presents with pure image. It is a tool that I recommend highly to anyone who has never worked with images. To use them is sheer simplicity. One simply picks a Trump and looks at it. The goal is to make the Trump as real as possible in the imagination; one then steps into the imaginal landscape. Almost all of the persons I know who have utilized the Tarot for meditative purposes report an activation of archetypal forces, both within psyche and around them in actual life events. The Tarot is a powerful imaginal tool that requires no prior knowledge, only perseverence and an openness to its influence. Combining the Tarot with the Tree of Life was a most ingenious marriage, as the Tree itself is a potent symbolic glyph. Together they give the conscious mind and the ego a focus; this allows the collective archetypal image to be activated within the psyche without interference from the conscious mind.

The Hermetic Order of the Golden Dawn emphasized the importance of God-images for the purposes of practical magic. Initiates of the Golden Dawn spent considerable time and energy in researching the classical God-images and ordering them using the Tree. The Golden Dawn's writings often speak of the importance of knowing and using "God-forms," visual representations of the God under consideration. A God-form is a fantasy image, to be worn as one would a garment. To assist in the invocation of a particular force identified with a particular deity, they developed the file system to order the symbols particular to any one path.

Aleister Crowley, an initiate of the Golden Dawn, compiled these attributions of the thirty-two paths of the Tree into a work titled *777*, begun in 1907 and first published in 1909. Table 3 gives some of the specific attributions given to the second path, the sphere of Chokmah, as an example. The magician employs every symbol

Illustration 5A
The Waite—Rider Deck
Major Arcana

Illustration 5B
The Waite—Rider Deck
Major Arcana

Illustration 5C
The Waite—Rider Deck
Major Arcana

Illustration 5D
The Waite—Rider Deck
Major Arcana

within the Temple of Art to invoke a particular deity contained within a particular path. The Temple and the Ceremonial must focus the *mind* upon the path one is working. To this end colors, shapes, sounds, smells, and accoutrements must all correlate with the archetype under consideration and the God-image being invoked. The mind thus focused is preoccupied and the collective unconscious is given a free outlet.

In Chokmah, for instance, the essence of the deity, the general energy or archetype, is contained in the number of the sphere and Qabalistic lore: Chokmah is the archetypal Phallus. As objective experience it is dynamic force. Chokmah is formless cosmic energy, the impulse to dynamic creation. Its title in Hebrew is Wisdom.

We can also apply the Eastern Tantra philosophy of the chakra system (illus. 6), and assign to Chokmah the Ajna chakra, the third eye, seen in Michaelangelo's famous statue of Moses as two wisps of hair resembling horns, essentially priapic in meaning. Chakra is Sanskrit for wheel. The seven major chakras represent energy centers in the subtle body that appear to correspond to major nerve plexuses and glands within the physical body. For example, the Manipura chakra corresponds to the solar plexus of the body and is given control over the element of fire, and the body function of digestion.

The chakras come to us from the Eastern traditions of Tantra, which is Sanskrit for warp or loom; hence a doctrine, a work, a handbook. The Tantras are the traditions of Indian religion outside of Brahmanism and classical Hinduism. The Tantras are revelations that appear apart from the Vedas and the Upanishads, the holy books of Indian religion, and contain different rites and practices. The Tantras are esoteric, procuring benefits that the holy books cannot give. The Tantras are the mystical initiatic aspect of the Indian religion. A Tantra is a practiced path to supernatural powers that leads to liberation. These include specific practices and techniques of ritual, bodily, and mental practices associated with the various doctrines, therefore the various Tantras. The core belief of the Tantras is that *kama*, desire, in all its aspects, can serve towards one's liberation from the world.

Returning to Chokmah: from the *general*, objective number archetype and Qabalistic attributions of Chokmah—"dynamic creative force" is too abstract—we can move to the specific God-images that are subjectively experienced. Although a masculine sphere,

TABLE 3
ATTRIBUTIONS ASSIGNED TO THE SPHERE OF CHOKMAH
FROM ALEISTER CROWLEY'S 777

Hebrew: ChKMH (Chokmah)	
Cheth, Kaph, Mem, He	*Wisdom*
Mystic Number:	*3*
Root of the Element of:	*Fire*
The *Sepher Yetzirah* refers to Chokmah as:	*The Illuminating Intelligence*
Queen Scale of Color	*Grey*
Selection of Egyptian Gods	*Amoun, Thoth, Nuith, Isis (As Wisdom)*
The Perfected Man	*Disk Of Ra/Face*
Hindu Deities	*Shiva, Vishnu, Lingam*
The Forty Buddhist Meditations	*Joy*
Scandinavian Gods	*Odin*
Greek Gods	*Athena, Uranus*
Roman Gods	*Janus*
Christian Gods	*God The Father*
Animal, Real & Imaginary	*Man*
Plants, Real & Imaginary	*Amaranth*
Precious Stones	*Star Ruby, Turquoise*
Magical Weapons	*Lingam, The Inner Robe Of Glory*
Perfumes	*Musk*
Vegetable Drugs	*Hashish*
Mineral Drugs	*Phosphorus*
Magical Powers (Western Mysticism)	*Vision Of God Face To Face*
Lineal Figures	*Line, Cross*
Eastern Tantra	*Ajna Chakra*

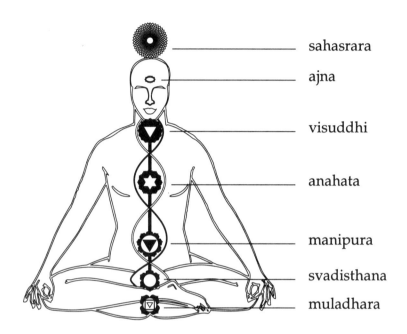

sahasrara

ajna

visuddhi

anahata

manipura

svadisthana

muladhara

Illustration 6
The Chakras and the Body

The seven chakras or power zones in the subtle body. The two power streams known as "Ida" and "Pingala" wind round the central axis or "Sushumna." The leaf design on the head represents the highest chakra, the "thousand-petaled lotus."

CHAKRA	SPHERE(S)
Muladhara	Malkuth/Yesod
Svadisthana	Yesod/Hod
Manipura	Netzach
Anahata	Tiphareth, Geburah, Chesed
Visuddhi	Binah
Ajna	Chokmah
Sahasrara	Kether

The Chakras on the Tree. Based on Aleister Crowley's 777

Sophia as Wisdom and Athena as Daughter of Her Father, reside in Chokmah. Uranus, God of the Sky and the realm of the fixed stars, the Germanic God Odin, and the Christian God the Father are all images of Chokmah. The motive force of the Qabalah is above all practical. It is to be used so that subject and object merge; the Qabalah facilitates the union of ego and archetype. The Qabalah as practical magic is a fluid medium and as individual as the person using it. Fortune says of the Qabalah:

> A technique that is being actually practiced is a growing thing, for the experience of each worker enriches it and becomes part of the common heritage.[23]

The Qabalah and God-images

Summarizing, we can say that the Qabalah offers the mind a bridge between word and image, or as Dion Fortune wrote in 1935, a bridge between conscious and the unconscious, whose primary datum is the image. One can begin with idea and locate the appropriate image as symbol on the Tree, or one can begin with symbol and explore the ideas associated with it. More, the Tree offers a way of understanding complex relationships by way of a mental ordering system, which one can then use in exploring an image, an exploration that can only be multifaceted. It will perhaps be helpful if I give examples of the use of the Tree, both in a general and in a particular application.

Let us take the Moon as an example of the general application. In my experience and research I have come to believe that the Moon represents the image itself; a strong Moon by placement in a birth chart seems to indicate that a person has easier access to the perceptible image, to the imagination. The imagination is paired with the Moon in most astrology texts. On the Tree, the Moon corresponds to the sphere of Yesod.

Yesod is known in Hebrew as the Foundation, for the influences of the preceding eight Sephiroth spill into the reservoir of the astral waters of Yesod. Western magic teaches that the astral plane is the plane where the emotions are most active in animating and creating the images found within the imagination. This is Yesod.

Yesod is the sphere of perceptible images, a fluid ever-changing world that underlies the world of form, binds the world of form, gives shape to the world of form. Here the Moon is the creator of organic organisms, the builder of the structures of life and consciousness by way of the generative factor of feeling. We feel first, which is to say respond, and secondarily have emotions around our response. Feeling is a total organismic event, exemplified by the fight or flight response. Dane Rudhyar states:

> The main function of the Moon is to deal with the element of solar *heat* and use it in conjunction with the element of *moisture* ....
> The feelings are psychological expressions of biological instincts, which in truth are waves and eddies in the tidal flow of the lunar forces acting upon the "moisture" in man's body and psyche.[24]

The spiritual experience assigned to Yesod is the Vision of the Machinery of the Universe. In this sphere the Moon contains the images that shape organic structures, the organic "machines" that operate within the universe.

The Moon can also be found on the Tree in Qoph, the 29th path, the Tarot trump known as The Moon, the sign of Pisces. Qoph means "the back of the head." It is at the back of the head, where the cranium and spine meet, that the medulla oblongata of the brain can be found, the site where the unconscious body processes like breathing and circulation are maintained; also at the back of the head can be found the reticular formation, the seat of unbridled emotion. The Qoph-zone is the zone within the body that induces dreams, according to occult philosophy. The *Sepher Yetzirah* calls Qoph "The Corporeal Intelligence," and very appropriately assigns sleep to Qoph. According to Hillman, the images of our dreams fulfill the desires of instinct.[25] Here the Moon is Enchantress, Hecate at the cross-roads, weaving her night spells of unintelligible images under the dark of the Moon. She is awake when the body and consciousness are asleep, delighting in images that perpetuate the organic processes of cell movements, the beating of our hearts, the rhythm of our lungs. In Qoph the Moon is image as representative of instinctual processes, and instinct is of the body.

Higher on the Tree the Moon resides in the sphere of Binah. Here She is Sakti, feminine archetypal power. Arthur Avalon in The *Serpent Power* defines Sakti:

> All that is manifest is Power (Sakti) as Mind, Life and Matter. Power implies a Power-Holder (Saktiman). There is no Power-Holder without Power, or Power without Power-Holder. The Power-Holder is Siva. Power is Sakti, the Great Mother of the Universe.[26]

Binah in Hebrew is referred to as Marah, the Great Sea, the Waters in the chapter of Genesis of the Old Testament over which the Spirit of God moved. According to Crowley in 777, almost any feminine figure shows some aspect of Binah. The Moon in Binah is the Giver of Form, not organically as in Yesod, but in potentia, image as the vehicle of Power.

The Higher Moon is also the 13th path, Gimel, the Tarot trump known as The High Priestess. Here She is the Goddess Diana of the Bow, Chaste, Nature as The Veil that conceals the primal unity, Kether. She is the Soul as the Mediator between Mind and Spirit. The Moon in astrology is said to be exalted in Taurus. A planet exalted in a sign manifests its positive side most purely. In Taurus, a fixed Earth sign, the changeable and ever-changing Moon becomes focused. Taurus, the Tarot trump known as the Hierophant, is Vau, the 16th path. Here the Moon is Europa, abducted by Zeus who had transformed himself into a white bull; as the Virgin mated with the solar-phallic bull She is the Fecundity of Nature, an allusion to the creative aspect of the archetype as image which can find an infinite number of variations to express a root idea. The Moon astrologically rules Cancer, the 18th path, Cheth. Cheth is the Tarot trump known as The Chariot. Here the Moon is the Universal Womb, the Chalice of Ecstasy where feminine archetypal Power is stored, the image as the Nurturer of All.

How complex is the Moon upon the Tree! She is found in many places. She is many Goddesses, all lunar in nature and each Goddess offers us a different image. There is a higher Moon which mediates our spiritual quest and a lower Moon that maintains the organic children of her fertility. The one image, the Moon, becomes many images, many Moons, many Goddesses from which the face of Luna peers down on us. More, She *is* the image. In one image She is accessible, the Universal Mother of the sign Cancer. But She changes, and as Diana She will send her hounds to devour anyone who would pollute her Sanctuary. It is to the merit of the magical Qabalah that the archetypal feminine as Luna can be found in so many places, for the Moon in our experience is just so many Goddesses. The validity of the use of the Tree to order God-images resides in its practicality, a practicality that can be validated by application of any other discipline based upon Nature. The Tree is Nature, the World Soul of the Romantics.

Let us explore a specific application of the Tree to order God-images. I will also make brief reference to a birth chart; this anticipates Chapter Two on astrology and God-images. The following is a dream from a young professional woman, Susan, who has never worked with myths or images or astrology.

> I find myself walking down a corridor. A little girl is leaving with her mother. A cute girl about five or so. Fair-skinned, brown hair, full lips and mouth. She starts running ahead of mom. Mom turns through side door away from child. I go after child, tell her mom has gone a different way. She gets in my car, we drive a little ways. I'm talking to her and tell her she has to go back to mom. We have a conversation. I cannot remember most of it. It seems innocuous—except at the end. She says, "I'll take your headache away."
> "How did you know I had a headache?"
> "I know," and she touches my forehead.
> And I say, "Take it away!"
> She smiles, gets out of car.

When I heard this dream, two mythic themes came to mind. The first, that the little girl in the dream has extraordinary powers: a psychic form of knowledge and the ability to heal by empathy. Healing by empathy seems to be a receptive mode, the healing of women's mysteries, and reminds me of Luna. The second striking image is the touching of the forehead. When I asked Susan, she stated that in the dream the little girl touched her at the center of the forehead between the eyes. This is the Ajna chakra in Eastern Tantric philosophy, "the third eye," the place of control of mental faculties. The Ajna corresponds to the sphere of Chokmah and the God Uranus on the Tree (review table 3). This dream left me with two God-images, Luna and Uranus.

I then reflected on Susan's natal chart. Susan has natal Moon in Pisces, the leading planet in a locomotive-type planetary arrangement. Referring to table 2 we see that Pisces is the Tarot Trump *known* as The Moon, the Hebrew letter Qoph, and the 29th path on the Tree. Referring to illustration *5D*, we see the Tarot image called The Moon and referring to table 1 we find the Hebrew meaning of

Qoph, which translates as the "back of the head." Referencing the Tree, Susan's Moon in Pisces is a strong emphasis, for the planetary Moon is in the sign of the Tarot Trump known as The Moon. The Tree shows a rulership not usually found in traditional astrology between Pisces and the Moon.

Traditional astrology tells us that a Moon in Pisces indicates psychic and intuitive abilities. Qabalists have also come to this conclusion. For astrology the logic is straight-forward: the Moon is the planet of the imagination and of psychic abilities, as is the sign Pisces; together they produce a double emphasis on psychism and intuitive abilities. The beauty of the Tree is that we can find an equivalent logic that is more profound because we look to the ground of Nature. If we suppose the Tree to represent the World Soul, then we can look to the Tree for an explanation of why the Moon as planetary energy and the path of Qoph are paired.

The planetary ruler of Pisces is Neptune. Neptune is attributed to the sphere of Kether. Kether is the first manifestation of the Unknowable God and contains the universe in potential. The path from the sphere of Kether to the sphere of Tiphareth is Gimel, the Tarot Trump known as The High Priestess. The High Priestess is ruled by the planet of the Moon. The High Priestess is the mediator between the Godhead, Kether, and the enlightened individual, Tiphareth. The individual in Tiphareth can know Kether only indirectly, by way of the infinite images that manifest the universe; these infinite images are referred to as the Veils of the Goddess Isis, another description of the High Priestess.

Lower on the Tree, the relationship between Moon and Neptune, the path of Gimel, The High Priestess, is mirrored by the path of Qoph, Pisces, the Trump known as The Moon. Qoph joins the sphere of Malkuth to the sphere of Netzach. Malkuth is the body. As stated, the images of Qoph serve the manifestation of instinct, or the body. We know that the first appearance on the Tree of the Moon is Gimel, and Gimel represents the archetypal image. We know the path of Qoph as Pisces flows from Malkuth, the body. The Tarot Trump known as The Moon (Qoph) unites body and image. Looking at The Moon Trump we find a story summarized as follows: the lower Moon has to do with instinctual processes, therefore the image finds a home on the lower Tree by uniting body and mind, the path of Qoph, the sign of Pisces. A natal Moon in Pisces in a birth chart emphasizes the archetypal association on the Tree between the path of Qoph, Pisces, and the Moon, an association that is "backed up" by referring to the Tree's inherent imaginal logic.

Susan's sun sign is Taurus, the Moon's exaltation; we can follow the same procedure outlined above for Pisces and find the Tarot Trump, the Hebrew letter and the path on the Tree for Taurus. These are The Hierophant, the letter Vau, and the 16th path on the Tree, respectively. Susan's natal Moon is in the angular seventh house, lending the Moon added emphasis by house placement. The Moon in Susan's natal chart is emphasized by her Sun sign of Taurus, her Moon sign of Pisces, and the placement of the Moon in an angular house. Looking to our second God-image from Susan's dream, Uranus, we find that Uranus is the release planet in a T-square configuration in Susan's chart, giving Him emphasis in releasing creative energies for Susan. This is all to say that in Susan's natal chart Luna and Uranus are strong by placement.

Uranus being assigned to the sphere of Chokmah, we look at the other attributions of the sphere. Athena is here. In the Greek myth, Athena was born as an adult in full armor from her father Zeus' head. Zeus had been suffering from a raging *headache,* and the God Hephaestus split Zeus's head open with a double ax, giving Athena exit. We now have a Goddess image, based on Susan's dream image of a headache. We began with the forehead, moved to the Ajna chakra, thence to Chokmah. Chokmah leads us to Uranus and Athena. Now we have Luna, Uranus, and Athena. How do we begin to examine the dream practically and continue the circular work of exploring the image?

The first question we can ask, is there an archetypal association between the Moon and Uranus? The answer is yes. "The Lotus named Ajna [which corresponds to the sphere of Chokmah and therefore to Uranus] is like the moon, beautifully white," writes Purananda, a guru from Bengal, in the *Shat-chakra-nirupana,* written in 1577.[27] We can envision the crescent of the Moon, points upward between the brows of the Gods: the Ajna chakra, essentially phallic/ spiritual. The phallus in myth and Nature must have a matrix wherein its creative focused energy can take on form. The Moon as Virgin and the Creative Impulse have always been paired, either as two separate forces, Europa and the Bull; or as one image containing both forces, like Athena, the Virgin Warrior. In Susan's dream, the Virgin Child touches the Ajna, the Creative Impulse. Susan's dream shows an activation of the psychic Moon and the logos quality of

Uranus; the Virgin and the Creative Impulse.

The Goddess Athena is the perfect God-image, for she combines the quality of logos with the quality of maternal nurturance. Athena nurtured numerous heroes, guiding them to fulfill their destinies. Athena being a Virgin Goddess, what she mothered were children of the mind. Susan's dream seems to indicate this pairing of child with mind; at the time we were working together, her progressed Moon was applying to exact aspect with natal Uranus. We spent time exploring the Goddess Athena, for Susan's individual predisposition to the Moon archetype came through a strong logos quality; indeed, the Virgin Child of her dream represented a different mode of the Moon archetype, one of receptivity, a quality Susan stated she was aware of having, but one that she had never fully explored. For Susan, our image exploration, from a single dream, seemed to say that Athena was strong natally (emphasis on Moon and Uranus in her chart), and that a non-predominant archetypal quality (the child) of nurturing receptivity (natal Moon in Pisces) within Susan, was needing attention.

The Magic of Soul-making:
Magic and Archetypal Psychology

> If we wish identity with a greater power, let us seek a union with ourself - our total self raised to its highest potential of wisdom, knowledge, and experience. If we wish to unite with the universe, let us court the whole of nature, all experience, all truth, the wonder and the terror, the splendor and the pity and the pain of the awesome cosmos itself.
> —John Whiteside Parsons,
> *Freedom is a Two-Edged Sword*

Magic, religion, mysticism, and mythology have coexisted for millennia. They enrich each other, and in that richness they offer meaning to our lives. Western magic has a long history even if we postulate its beginnings in a pre-Christian Rome. It has remained alive and has been transmitted secretly by way of various occult lodges and fraternities. The power of the early Church along with the advent of modern science have conspired to define what is rational and therefore acceptable as a topic of study, and what is not. Magic is not considered rational. Along with most forms of Western gnosis, it has been discarded to the woodshed as something to be feared and depotentiated.

This century has seen few proponents of magic. By contrast, mythology, mysticism, and religion have fared much better, gaining a backdoor access denied magic through depth psychology. Carl Jung in his landmark work *Symbols of Transformation* paired myth and the archetype, and assigned to myth a psychology. Jung used mythological motifs to understand how archetypes shape our lives. He realized that the myth was a key that could unlock the gates of the collective unconscious as mythological motifs have an incredible consistency throughout differing cultures worldwide. For instance, many cultures have variations on the myth of the flood which destroyed the world. Jung came to realize that the archetype and the mythological motif are one and the same.

Jung emphasized the power and the value of myth as depth psychology. He felt that the whole realm of human experience was the province of psychology. Jung therefore addressed the topics of God and religion and spent a good part of his later life researching the subject of alchemy as representing a process of psychological development.

Magic has yet to receive the same psychological attention or legitimization. I believe that Western magic has much to contribute to our understanding of the world as its history is co-extensive with Western culture. A subject matter consisting of at least two thousand years of history and contributions to Western civilization must have something to say to us, especially psychologically.

There are some who attempt to understand magic "as if" it were a psychology, following Jung's lead, and it is from this perspective that magic is explored in these pages. In this book magic is postulated as a Western guardian of the image before the development of modern depth psychology—along with myth, religion, and mysticism. Of all the Western inheritances, magic has consistently been true to the image; this is its greatest value to image exploration. It is time to explore its psychological dimensions.

The word magic comes from the root word meaning to be, to have power, and can be traced to Old Persian, *magus*, a member of a priestly class, and possibly meaning "mighty one." Two modern dictionary definitions of magic are: 1) The art that purports to control or forecast natural events, effects, or forces by invoking the supernatural and 2) The practice of using charms, spells, or rituals to attempt to produce supernatural effects or to control events in nature.[28] Combining both of these definitions, we can define magic as the controlling of natural events by means of charms, spells, and rituals that invoke the powers of the supernatural.

This combined definition of magic is illustrated by Sir James George Frazier who wrote *The Golden Bough* in 1922, a truly classic work in the field of anthropology. Frazier's book traces the ritualistic practices of many groups of peoples throughout the world, practices which have as their goal the controlling of nature's forces. Primitive men and women rely on ritual to ensure survival of the group, ceremonial being the propitiatory rites to the Gods that guarantee a successful hunt or that sanctifies a developmental milestone like the transition from childhood to adult status.

Psychologically, Frazier's text demonstrates Jung's concept of "canalization of libido," the redirecting and sublimating of instinct as energy potential into the functions of consciousness through the use of symbol, ritual, and magic.[29] Our definition of magic so far is a standard one, and I do not believe it coincidence that Frazier reflects this predjudice. The modern perception of magic as reflected in Frazer's book and as found in the dictionary is a valid one as far as it goes, yet this definition dismisses magic as a misperception of the primitive man/woman who sees ghosts everywhere.

Aleister Crowley defined his magick, with a 'k,' as the science and art of causing change to occur in conformity with will. Crowley's subsequent postulate is that any change may be effected by the application of the proper kind and degree of force in the proper manner through the proper medium to the proper object. Crowley then developed twenty-eight theorems, the first one being that any *intentional* act is a magical act. Crowley emphasized the scientific method as essential to the modern day magician and his definition of magic extended magic's domain to encompass all areas of life, including those areas of existence unknowable through the usual five senses.

Crowley's extensive and enlightened works on the art of magic cannot be given justice in one brief paragraph, but what I have given thus far is helpful in moving the art of magic away from the constricted view of the Western scholar and back to the initiate's own perceptions. One such initiate was John Whiteside Parsons. He was a student of Crowley's who lived in California. Parsons was a principal scientist in the rocket research group attached to the California Institute of Technology that eventually came to be known as the Jet Propulsion Laboratory in Pasadena. Parsons died in 1952 in a laboratory explosion, but not before leaving us several essays giving his ideas about magick (with a 'k').

Parsons wrote regarding the background of magick:

> The experimental animistic basis of magick is a general field theory which regards the individual as a network (field) of forces interacting in and directly related to a similar cosmic network (field) which includes the total universe. (From certain viewpoints these two fields are regarded as identical). It is therefore a postulate of magick that every man and every woman is a star. In magical terminology certain aggregate categories or clusters of forces in a field are termed gods, angels, elementals, or demons. Such terminology may be reasonably applied to a partiality of consciousness (point of view or state of mind), a city, a culture, an era, a star cluster or nebula, providing that proper definition follows.

> From this field view naturally follows the law of similarity (homeopathy or sympathy) from which are derived images, talismanic and mantra magick, and the law of bipolarity, which has its physical counterpart in the second law of Newtonian mechanics.[30]

Parsons further defined the purpose and object of magick:

> It may be stated that magick is the method of training individuals towards total consciousness by stimulation of various centers of the mind and by the cultivation of field thinking.[31]

And:

> It is therefore the function of magick to lead each individual to the realization and expression of his total self on all the planes of being and experience.[32]

I have quoted Parsons extensively because his understanding of magic brings us back to a general field theory, a field being defined as an aggregate cluster of forces experienced as gods, demons, angels, and elementals. I must qualify again that I cannot do justice to the whole of modern magic in a few paragraphs. This is the limit, for I am only concerned here with a psychological appreciation of modern day magic, and Parson's field theory fits nicely with Jung's and Hillman's understanding of the archetypal image.

Edward Whitmont in the Introduction of this book was quoted as writing that the archetype is a field that orders our life experience. Archetypes are the primary forms that govern the psyche, and, according to Hillman, archetypes are the primary data of soul. It is through the soul's mediating function that the voices of existence speak to us, and the archetype is the means by which soul deepens events into subjective experience. Magic is many things, but with Parson's definition magic is the process by which the individual soul comes to know the elemental and angelic forces of Nature, the Gods of existence, the fields that make up the cosmos. We are reminded of the Golden Dawn's injuction, "By names and images are all powers awakened and reawakened," logos and image, a logos of psyche.

The main interface, the basic commonality, between magic and archetypal psychology is the image. True magic must include active work with the archetypal image. The right understanding and use of the archetypal image is an important ability to be acquired in order to do practical magic as developed by Western occult schools. Western magic teaches that the image cannot be fully appreciated with linguistic thought alone. The power of the image lies in its ability to transcend linear thinking and then to bring us back to thought, in the manner of a boomerang set aloft by its owner. With the image we are momentarily air-borne, and with the image we return to home-base, wiser for this experience.

Hillman's *Re-Visioning Psychology* affords practical magic a modern psychological starting point. In my own experience with magic, Hillman's four concepts defining a psychology of soul not only describes work with the image, but the psychological components of magic as well, since, as I have stated, practical magic utilizes the image. Hillman's four activities native to soul are: personifying, pathologizing, psychologizing, and dehumanizing.

Personifying is "the spontaneous experiencing, envisioning, and speaking of the configurations of existence as psychic presences."[33] We all know about personifying. The West calls it anthropomorphism and dismisses it with a snicker and some such statement about primitive thinking. Anthropomorphism is the giving of human attributes and motivations to inanimate objects or natural phenomena. Mythology is often seen as an earlier culture's attempt to explain Nature to itself through anthropomorphism. For example, the Greeks experienced the Dawn as a Goddess they called Eos. Since Homer she is described as "rosy-fingered." When, as a student of the classics, we read about Eos as being the rosy-fingered Dawn, we were told to consider this an example of anthropomorphism, and most other students, following the instructor's lead, left well enough alone.

But what are we to make of it when, researching the myth, we find that Eos had an amorous nature? "Aphrodite, the Goddess of Love, caused Eos to long for young mortals perpetually because she had caught her mate Ares in Eos's bed."[34] Eos had a dilemma: she was an immortal Titan Goddess perpetually in love with mortal youths. Anthropomorphism as the explanation for why the Greeks spent so much energy describing Dawn seems to be a dismissal of their actual experience. As we will see when we examine the concept of dehumanizing, the purely human in attributes is limiting and attributing human motivations to the Gods (anthropomorphism) does little in the way of explaining the nuances and richness of the mythological motifs. We are forced to look deeper for an explanation that does justice to the actual experience of the meeting with Eos. This experience is *personifying*.

To personify is to engage in imagining things. Soul-making depends upon the psyche's ability to personify. Hillman writes:

> By refusing to go along with the usual arguments against personifying, we expect to find a new way or refine an old way: (a) of revivifying our relations with the world around us, (b) of meeting our individual fragmentation, in our many rooms and many voices, and (c) of furthering the imagination to show all its bright forms. Our desire is *to save the phenomena of the imaginal psyche.*[35]

There are numerous ramifications when we honor the psyche's ability to personify. From the outside, it seems that psyche takes our life experiences and personifies them. From within, it appears that the archetype, as we have already said, clothes itself in representational forms which we call image. Instinct and archetype take on form. It is the ego who anthropomorphizes, who assumes that the rest of the universe is derivative, based upon its existence. We do not give the archetype a personality; *the archetype allows us to experience a personality*. Eos, then, is a personality. We can imagine, if we but try, that she spreads her arms wide, across the early morning horizon, the air cool and sweet; we can appreciate the hunger in her arms, for she is of an amorous nature, as she yearns for the Sun and as she heralds the Day. When we can do this, we enter into a different form of consciousness that is not ego based, but that is image based. We find soul in the simplest of life's experiences.

Magic, with its history of image animation partakes of both movements, inner to outer and outer to inner, when it utilizes psyche's ability to personify. All forms of magic teach the primacy and importance of the image, directly or indirectly, and of the process of personifying. The elementals of Earth are Gnomes. A true vision of Aphrodite, the Goddess of Love, should not have any Ares symbols—Ares being an opposite nature—or the vision is tainted. In magic we learn that the archetype will clothe itself in the appropriate symbolic image, and, the attention of the magician will add power to the image by animating it. The human and the archetypal are equally necessary. It is a tenet of practical magic that a properly performed rite should invoke the deity who will then offer Divine illumination. Aleister Crowley wrote:

> There must always be some slight pang of pain in a true Astral Vision; it hurts the Self to have to admit the existence of a not-Self; and it taxes the brain to register a new thought ....
> There is a deeper effect of right reaction to a strange Self: the impact invariably tends to break up some complex in the Seer.[36]

This description should warn against the assumption that personifying is "idle" imagination. Anyone who has had the experience of the numinosity[37] of the archetype will understand immediately what Crowley means.

Our second activity of soul is *pathologizing*. Pathologizing is

> ... the psyche's autonomous ability to create illness, morbidity, disorder, abnormality, and suffering in any aspect of its behavior and to experience and imagine life through this deformed and afflicted perspective.[38]

Hillman suggests that the medical profession and psychology exist because the psyche maintains the archetypal fantasy of falling apart. The care of souls is the care of suffering, of attending the wounds of soul:

> Psychopathology as an archetypal fantasy means that the soul produces crazed patterns and sicknesses, perversions and decay, within dreams and behavior, and in art and thought, in war and politics, and in religion, because pathologizing is a psychic activity per se. Psychic sickness remains as an archetypal category of existence independent of its contents.[39]

Healing is equally a fantasy of soul that balances the archetypal experience of falling apart. Perhaps, as Hillman suggests, becoming an individual means that we touch the places where we suffer, where we are wounded. There are many who avoid this experience. Nor does Western society allow us our pathologies. Compulsions, depressions, anxieties, and perversions are to be found instead on the many television talk shows. We have become a nation of voyeuristic pathology junkies, outraged but fascinated by others' sickness. Pathologizing as an activity of soul continues even when we choose to ignore it. Our pathologies return to us under the guise of the media's concern to "inform" us.

Magic has much to say about pathology. It can be found in the diaries, journals, and lives of many occultists throughout the ages (this is also true of many of our foremost Western thinkers and scholars, psychologists included). This is seen in Colin Wilson's *The Occult*,[40] a history of magic through the ages. This work is a Who's Who of compulsions, inflation and grandiose thinking, fragmentary personalities, liars and swindlers, charismatic personalities, true geniuses, power crazed individuals, political intrigues, illness and depression, sexual perversions, and genuine abilities. But this is to be expected. If a quality of an archetypal situation includes its pathology, and if magicians actively seek the "psychic presences" of existence, the archetypes, then it would appear that they would be susceptible to the pathologies of their craft. On a different note, these same magicians were also on the cutting edge of healing as shamans, medicine men and women, spiritual counselors and astrologers, alchemists, and, yes-physicians.

Pathologizing leads us to the next activity of soul, the attempt to find a meaning within its suffering. This activity is psychologizing, or seeing through. Psychologizing *"goes on whenever reflection takes place in terms other than those presented.* It suspects an interior, not evident intention . . . . It goes on whenever we move to a deeper level."[41] Psychologizing has to do with ideas; not just any ideas, but ideas that allow soul to reflect back upon itself. "By psychological ideas I mean those that engender the soul's reflection upon its nature, structure, and purpose."[42] Hillman reminds us that the primary activity of soul is reflection, or seeing through. Ideally, soul's reflections of itself through its ideas engenders appropriate activity; in Western culture however, we are active precisely because we wish to avoid knowing what soul wants, what soul needs, and what soul is doing.

Hillman details the process of psychologizing.[43] First, there is the "psychological moment" when we reflect, wonder, or puzzle, when soul intervenes, moving us from the apparent to the less apparent, from the scientific or philosophical explanation to something deeper—soul is only satisfied by its own process of seeing through:

> Moving from the outside in, it is a process of *interiorizing*; moving from the surface of visibilities to the less visible, it is a process of deepening; moving from the data of impersonal events to their personification, it is a process of subjectivizing.[44]

Second, psychologizing justifies itself in terms of depth; we justify the activity by appealing to an ultimate hidden value which Hillman refers to as the hidden God who appears only in concealment. Third, the present moment is given a narrative, a tale elaborated by fantasy, a process of mythologizing. And fourth, ideas are the tools with which the whole operation of psychologizing proceeds.

> The most important is that seeing through requires all four so—called steps, and all four may simultaneously proceed. We tell ourselves a justifying story as we penetrate inward by means of ideas. Or an idea may start us off psychologizing, or a fantasy about an event may prompt the moment of reflection and the search for something deeper.[45]

This elaboration of psychologizing is an elaboration of how the soul reflects.

It can be safely said that magic's basic psychological process is psychologizing. From the universal and archetypal situations represented by the Qabalistic Tree of Life, each aspirant is taught and encouraged to reflect, to search for the hidden God, to develop his or her own story through the discovery of those archetypal situations that dominate the individual life. Magical training encourages one to ask, "What is my God trying to tell me in this event, in this person, in this dream, in this revelation?"

Our last activity native to soul is the activity of dehumanizing, which has a specific meaning in Hillman's use. Hillman writes:

> But the statement that soul enters into everything human cannot be reversed. Human does not enter into all of soul, nor is everything psychological human. Man exists in the midst of psyche; it is not the other way around. Therefore, soul is not confined by man, and there is much of psyche that extends beyond the nature of man. The soul has inhuman reaches.[46]

The word "dehumanizing" has a negative and pejorative connotation in common usage. In simple English, to dehumanize someone is to take away their humanity, and this leads to the abuse of the person or persons. Hillman means something different, i.e., that the purely human is limiting. A possible synonym for dehumanizing might be de-anthropomorphizing, although I suggest this with reservation. Psyche is supraordinate to our conception and definition of "human." Meeting the images within soul is dehumanizing, i.e., images move us away from our presumed literalness as a human being, towards the collective ground that animates all of existence, the ground which is the world soul of the Romantics. This is echoed by the Golden Dawn which attempted, through its various rites of initiation, to invoke the Divine nature within, to move beyond the limitation of the human personality.

God-images are archetypal structures within the soul, and bring with them all four soul activities. Jean Shinoda Bolen gives us the attitude I believe necessary to a magic of soul-making. In *Goddesses in Everywoman*, Bolen takes a departure from traditional Jungian theory. In essence, Bolen presents the argument that Goddesses as archetypal patterns of feminine behavior do not necessarily need an explanation other than the primacy of the God-image. "When a woman has Athena and Artemis as goddess patterns, 'feminine' attributes such as dependency, receptivity, and nurturing may not be facets of her personality ...."[47] Bolen describes the God-image, when experienced, as having a primacy and an imperative as attributes. God-images need no explanations beyond themselves.

The archetypal God-image contains its own explanation and its own justification, its own wholeness that includes a way of falling apart, a way of pathologizing. The God-image draws us inward, sparks our imagination and releases into the soul those fantasies relevant to the particular God-consciousness.

God-images arise as spontaneous events within the human psyche. When we actively pursue the God-image, we can call it many things—Hillman's psychology of soul, or magic. In either case, Bolen reminds us of the inherent integrity of the God-image. This applies whether we view image from depth psychology or from true practical magic.

I present what I call a magic of soul-making as a beginning personal resolution between depth psychology and the psychology of magic. When I am with a client, it is my fantasy that we are engaged in a depth psychology of soul-making, and magic (and the Qabalah) becomes a way of thinking, an adjunct to the amplification[48] of individual work with the archetype. Engaging the image initiates a movement that is the same in a psychology of soul-making as in a psychology of magic. Their difference is the intent, the goal for which the image is actively engaged. Having a goal is an injustice against the image, Hillman might say; practical magic seeks to control and direct the forces of the archetype. This is the major difference between a psychology of soul and practical magic. God-images simply are. It is the soul who interprets. This ability of the image to afford the human imagination with limitless possibilities is its magic.

The God-images Within as Patterns of Behavior

This is a chapter on Beginnings, the place from where we start our journey. We have so far looked at the Tree, dialogued with word and experienced image, understood the definitions of archetypal psychology which first and foremost must be a psychology of soul, and given primacy to the image. We need to add one more strand to our fabric: Jean Shinoda Bolen's two works—*Goddesses in Everywoman* and *Gods in Everyman*. Contained in these works are God-images of the Greek pantheon as patterns of behavior or ways of being. Bolen writes in the Preface to *Gods in Everyman*:

Every archetype is associated with particular "god-given" or "goddess-given" gifts and potential problems. Appreciating that this is so makes either arrogance or self-blame less likely. And because whatever we do that arises out of our archetypal depths has meaning for us, a man who knows which god or gods are active in him may be able to make choices knowing which options or directions are likely to be personally more satisfying.

Reading about the gods sometimes turns out to be a means of "re-membering" cut-off (dismembered) parts of ourselves. This process may also be aided by dreams, memories, and myths that tap into our unconscious.[49]

I have found that Bolen's easy style of writing and well researched material makes the God-images readily accessible. In addition, Hillman has said that the ability to imagine is easier for those persons who have had story as part of their life experience.[50] The man or woman who remembers the Brothers Grimm or Star Wars from their childhood is more likely to appreciate and utilize the fantasy material that archetypes constellate. In my therapeutic work with clients, I have found that if they read Bolen's descriptions of God-patterns, it allows them to begin to imagine, affording them with the first steps towards engaging in a psychology of soul. Besides encouraging fantasy material, Bolen's integration of Jungian concepts as a dynamic of the God-image itself reduces the temptation to intellectualize, an activity that takes us away from soul and interferes with our activities *within* soul.

Bolen also describes the God-patterns as they may appear at different developmental stages in our lives and how these ways of being might interact with our society, within our families, and close relationships. Each chapter is a wonderful way to begin to fantasize, to appreciate the archetype, to open discussion with someone not used to story. Bolen's descriptions of the God-images give us much working material for the imagining activity of soul. Client and therapist can together explore the archetypal, imagining the fantastic, giving soul the freedom to do what it does best—reflect by way of images. Each moment becomes a story with many voices. Together client and therapist can ask the questions 'what' and 'who' moves within soul, the whys ignored, for we only know why after the fact, for it is said that hindsight is 20/20.

The Tree as Structure for this Work

There is one more use of the Tree—it provides the structure for this book. This is in keeping with the need of soul to have ideas and images by which to reflect upon itself. This book represents my soul's need to reflect upon itself in a special way. But rather than using only words, soul requires that we use image (see illus. 7).

Kether, Chokmah, and Binah are known as the Supernal Triad, in that they come into being before the phenomenal universe. From the ground of Kether appears Chokmah, the masculine principle. Chokmah is in essence a projection of Kether, the fantasy of movement, development, and growth. The Self creates and perceives a not-Self. The dyad now requires a third principle—that of relationship. This is Binah, the feminine principle. The Self requires the fantasy of relating to the not-Self. In occult lore, three is the necessary number for manifestation; this is the triangle or trinity.

For our purposes, Chapter One reflects Kether. In this chapter we give, define, and enjoy the mutuality of word and image, the excitement of soul in the union of complements. Chapter Two reflects Chokmah—logos and spirit, and we will examine astrology from the bird's eye view of the soul, taking cosmic order (logos and spirit) and internalizing it into the fantasies of soul. Chapter Three reflects Binah, the true house of soul and archetypal psychology. Here we will descend to the Underworld with the guidance of soul.

Between the noumenal world of the Supernal Triad and manifest existence lies the Abyss. The Abyss is Chaos, Dispersion, Dissociation and is related to Binah, for Binah is the giver of form, of personality, and must therefore contain its opposite. Below the Abyss is the sphere of Tiphareth, the Sun. Tiphareth is also the Son, as Binah is the Mother, Chokmah the Father, and Malkuth the Daughter. These are not to be taken literally, for Father, Mother, Son, and Daughter are best thought of as qualities, four in number, described by the elements of Fire, Water ,Air, and Earth, respectively. It would also appear that Hillman's four activities of soul could be attributed to these four spheres, giving us an example of how the Tree orders our ideas. Hillman's *personifying* would relate to Chokmah, *dehu-*

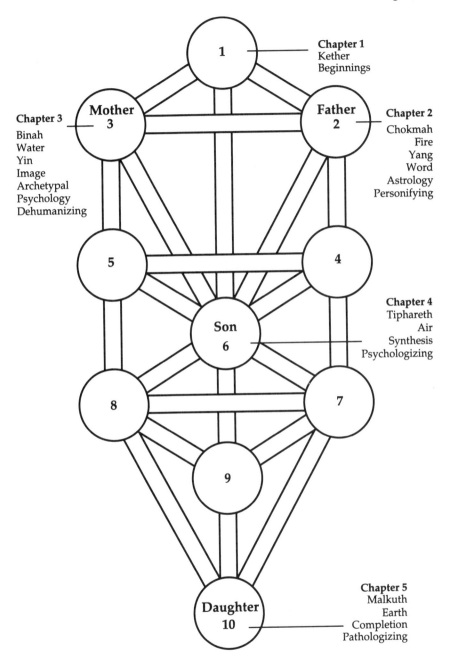

Illustration 7
The Tree as Structure for This Work

manizing to Binah, *psychologizing* to Tiphareth, and *pathologizing* to Malkuth. We will develop each idea accordingly, by chapter.

Chapter Four will reflect Tiphareth as we psychologize about therapy and what it can mean. We will use the images afforded us by the Tree in this psychologizing of the sphere of Tiphareth. Chapter Five, Malkuth, will be a case story, including God-images, dreams, memories, astrology, and artwork. This case story will show us by example how soul touches a life through images.

Kether and Beginnings

As Dion Fortune has pointed out, the Qabalah is a compendium of science, theology, philosophy, and psychology. I have made the case that the Qabalah affords us with a way to begin to understand God-images that is inclusive and non-oppositional. I purposely emphasized the apparent oppositional quality of word and image in the beginning of this chapter so that we could better understand their differences. It is better to think of polarity as complementary pairs, Chokmah the necessary complement of Binah, as logos (ideas) is the complement of the image.

Let us end this chapter with the concept of Beginnings and with the Greek God-images Poseidon and Hermes, in Roman mythology the Gods Neptune and Mercury, repectively. The Tree of Life is generated by the Ain Soph, the first manifestation being Kether, The Crown. For Hebrew Qabalists, Kether was the Sephiroth of "the first swirlings," quite an accomplishment considering science and astronomy as we know it did not exist, and the "Big Bang" theory of how the universe formed had not been expounded. Kether is the God Neptune, the ocean, the collective unconscious or the ground of existence of the Romantics. It is the first swirlings of soul. One fantasy found in Western culture is that from the water all life comes. Kether is the ocean as abundance, as the source of all life. It is our highest aspiration and vision of God.

Within Kether lies the universe in potential; the opposites have not yet separated out. The God name of Kether is Eheieh, "I AM." We can equate Kether with God in contradistinction to Man/Woman and the sphere of Malkuth. Kether is the goal of magician and mystic alike. Kether, The Crown, is above every head. It is the Sahasrara chakra of Eastern Tantra.

Neptune is the God of the Sea, of the *between* places. Since human experience happens on many planes or dimensions—body, emotions, thought, and beyond—Neptune as Ocean flows between these dimensions, offering us an understanding of the subtle threads that bind existence if we can let go of the mind and intuit with the soul. Neptune, being a water deity, had the ability to shape-change, meeting each plane, each experience with the appropriate form. Thorough knowledge of the Qabalah allows us to meet each plane, each dimension with the appropriate form, which is to say, with the appropriate image. The eagle is more appropriate to air and to Jupiter, less so to earth and to Venus. So, as Neptune, we too will shape-change in order to meet in the *between* spaces. Neptune is the ability of soul itself to shape-change, presenting us ever anew with the infinite facets of itself. Neptune is the ability of soul to swim through the waters of the unconscious, exploring the rich life to be found there.

If Neptune is intuition, then Mercury is the flash of insight. Mercury, the Messenger of the Gods, carried the staff called the caduceus. This staff had two serpents intertwined around it, very much like the Eastern Tantra drawing of the three major nadis, or nerve channels, of the Ida, Pingala, and Sushumna (see illus. 6). We can carry this image further by remembering that the Tree of Life has three columns. On the left, headed by Binah is the feminine column of form, The Pillar of Severity. On the right, headed by Chokmah, is the masculine column of force, The Pillar of Mercy. And in the center, headed by Kether is the column of equilibrium, The Pillar of Mildness (illus. 2).

We can use the image of Mercury's twin serpents, intertwined, weaving left and right from Severity to Mercy, around the central Pillar of Mildness with Kether at the top. Hillman writes about Mercury (Hermes) and the between spaces:

> To focus on the opposites is to miss the opportunities, the Hermes whose presence is precisely in the *between*. Perhaps this has been the Hermes function all along: to double our awareness by returning a portion of it to the serpent who can move only by wriggling left and right at the same moment. Let us imagine Hermetic awareness less as a transcendent function that holds the opposites together, or overcomes them, and more as a consciousness that requires and even creates a betweenness in which to operate.[51]

At first glance, Mercury and Neptune are an unlikely pairing. But Mercury is the fast, sleek, darting silver fish in the waters of the unconscious, and these waters are ruled by Neptune. Together, Mercury and Neptune represent the *union* of insight and intuition, the union of word and image which is the realm of the *between* places. This is what we mean by Kether: ending where we began, now, in the present. An aspect of soul is its wholeness[52] as represented by Kether. Movement is an illusion. Here, now, with soul, is all there is.

CHAPTER TWO

The Cosmic Influence:
Astrology and Archetypal
Structures

This leads to the ultimate conclusion that *we* do not actually personify at all. Mythical consciousness is a mode of being in the
world that brings with it imaginal persons. They are given with
the imagination and are its data. Where imagination reigns, personifying happens. We experience it nightly, spontaneously, in
dreams. Just as we do not create our dreams, but they *happen* to
us, so we do not invent the persons of myth and religion; they,
too, happen to us. The persons present themselves as existing
prior to any effort of ours to personify. *To mythic consciousness,
the persons of the imagination are real.*
— James Hillman, *Re-Visioning Psychology*

We reviewed in Chapter One how the Tree of Life has evolved
from its Hebraic monotheistic origins into a system that accommo-
dates the God-images of our experience, whether we believe in one
God or many. Practitioners of the modern schools of initiation, Fortune for instance, hold the Gods to be the "creations of the created,"[1]
which is to say that out of the universal mind-stuff created by the
one unknowable true God, human worshippers have created the
other Gods in their own image. God creates the universe with humankind, and humankind in turn creates the Gods. With this reasoning the Gods are reduced to images representative of nature's
impersonal forces or cosmic laws and nothing more.

This same logic was applied in the early studies of mythology.
Myths, went the argument, are the primitive and therefore juvenile

perceptions of our ancestors, early explanations of natural phenomena. For this our ancestors may be excused, one does not blame the child for its inexperience and naivete. However, anyone who has taken the time to read myths soon discovers the stark beauty and power of their narrative, the oftentimes religious tone, and the reverence for the world which they depict. This quality of the myth led Jung, Kerenyi, and others to explore myths as something more than quaint attempts at science. With their scholarship, our understanding of the existence of myths became broader, including the psychological and religious realms. We began to see myths as spontaneous creations of the psyche, projective activities containing power and elegance.

Myths come from within us. Myths are soul's way of explaining ourselves to ourselves and our universe to ourselves. Myths reflect the soul's native ability to personify, to experience the world through its imaginings and its persons. As we begin to examine astrology, we will keep in mind that astrology from its very beginning was, among many things, a means of personifying. Western astrology has come to us via the Greek inheritance. The Greek tradition regarded personifying as a necessary mode of understanding the world and of being in it.[2]

This chapter on astrology has as its main goal the reclaiming of soul's ability to personify, and in personifying, rediscovering the Gods. Nowhere else do we find the Gods more visible than in the night skies of our ancestors, the vault of heaven: that supposed cosmic bowl turned upside-down with holes through which the Divine light glittered, creating myriad pinpoints of light, that, taking on form, as persons cried out to psyche.

The Supernal Triad and the Archetype: A Metaphor

In Chapter One we set up some parameters through definitions. Kether the Crown, our first sphere on the Tree, contains the other nine sephira and twenty-two paths in potentia but as yet have we to reach our manifest world, the sphere of Malkuth. The journey is long. The first movement is the separation of the World Parents, the breakdown of Kether's unity into the Yang and Yin of creation. Erich Neumann summarizes what occurs when the World Parents are separated:

> Through the separation of the World Parents heaven and earth
> are distinguished from one another, polarity is created, and the
> light [of consciousness] set free.[3]

On the glyph of the Tree, the Yang principle corresponds to the
sphere of Chokmah, and Yin to the sphere of Binah (see illustration
7). In Chapter One we remained on the Middle Pillar headed by
Kether, the Pillar of Equilibrium, because we wanted to understand
the creative tension that accompanies any attempt to remain at the
midpoint of the opposites. We learned that our experience of soul
can help us remain balanced, that soul by definition resides in the
middle ground between word and image. But as Neumann points
out, the journey cannot happen if we remain in the undifferentiated
potential of the World Parents—Kether on the Tree. We must engage the fantasy of movement, growth, and development—the
child (archetype) of the World Parents. We will therefore explore
the opposites and their corresponding pillars.

Chokmah is pure dynamic force. It is the sphere of the fixed
stars or zodiac according to Qabalistic doctrine. Chokmah heads the
Pillar of Mercy, the masculine pillar. The principle of Chokmah is
defined by the Chinese as Yang and its power elaborated under the
trigram[4] of the Creative (also known as the trigram of Heaven) in
the *I Ching*, or *Book of Changes*. Of the trigram of the Creative it is
said:

> Its energy is represented as unrestricted by any fixed conditions
> in space and is therefore conceived of as motion. Time is re-
> garded as the basis of this motion. Thus ... [the Creative] in-
> cludes also the power of time and the power of persisting in
> time, that is, duration.[5]

The Creative is further defined in the *I Ching*, and we are reminded of the Western concept of Logos, the Divine Will, which can
be attributed to the sphere of Chokmah:

> The beginning of all things lies still in the beyond in the form of
> ideas that have yet to become real. But the Creative furthermore
> has power to lend form to these archetypes of ideas.[6]

Let us imagine that the "power to lend form to the archetypes
of ideas" is what personifying is about. A further suggestion is that
the dynamic energy aspect of the field theory of the archetype is cor-

relative here; the field, through its dynamic quality (Chokmah) in-duces forms (Binah), i.e., the binding *energy* that gives and main-tains the form of the iron filings of our introductory analogy[7] is what we mean by Chokmah. The concepts of Heaven, Logos, Yang, the Father, the Phallus, the Creative, the Masculine, Time, and cognate ideas will help us to archetypally understand Chokmah and in turn astrology, for the art of astrology is under the guardianship of Chok-mah.

The sphere of Binah is the first sphere of form on the Tree, as Chokmah is the first sphere of force. Binah is the Great Mother and Qabalists call Her Marah, the Sea. Binah heads the Pillar of Severity, the feminine pillar. Binah is the Womb as Chokmah is the Phallus. The Chinese know the principle represented by Binah as Yin. The trigram of the Receptive (also known as the trigram of Earth) in the *I Ching* is an elaboration on the powers of Yin and describes the attrib-utes of Yin:

> It is the perfect complement of the Creative—the complement, not the opposite, for the Receptive does not combat the Creative but completes it. It represents nature in contrast to spirit, earth in contrast to heaven, space as against time, the female-maternal as against the male-paternal.[8]

Binah correlates to the formal aspect of the archetype; it is the *form* taken by the iron filings in our analogy or *the form seen of the force informing*. The concepts Earth, Eros, Yin, the Mother, the Womb, the Receptive, the Feminine, Space, and cognate ideas will help us to understand Binah, and in turn archetypal psychology, since the image is under the guardianship of Binah. We will speak of Binah and its relationship to the image in Chapter Three.

In Kether we have the archetypes in a *psychoid* state, to use Jung's own word. Psychoid refers to processes that occur some-where between body and psyche since, being psychoid, it is not of the psyche. Jung writes: "it is meant to distinguish a category of events from merely vitalistic phenomena on the one hand and from specifically psychic processes on the other."[9] Psychoid also means irrepresentable as describing the archetype. It was Jung's conten-tion that the archetype per se is not directly knowable or represent-able, only its effects are available to us. And what are its effects? The dynamic and the formal aspects of the image.

The archetype in Kether is unknowable. The dynamic aspect of the archetype is analogous to the sphere of Chokmah, the energy behind the form. The formal aspect of the archetype is analogous to the sphere of Binah; it is the Mother that gives form, that clothes force. Binah is the engine as Chokmah is the steam, while the potential for the totality of this interaction lies in Kether.[10]

Two being the number of Chokmah, we will find several occasions in this chapter where the archetype of the dyad is illustrative. For instance, the dyad expresses itself in the dichotomy of outer and inner—*what* is out there versus *how* we experience it. Our reality as mediated by soul must contain an inner and an outer condition, like the two sides of a coin. Another occasion where we can make use of the dyad concept is in contemplating Hillman's description of the archetypes:

> They have a double existence which Jung presented in several ways: (1) they are full of internal oppositions, positive *and* negative poles; (2) they are unknowable *and* known through images; (3) they are instinct *and* spirit; (4) they are congenital, yet not inherited; (5) they are purely formal structures *and* contents; (6) they are psychic *and* extrapsychic (psychoid).[11]

The number two is reflective of the double existence of the archetype and in turn of the God-image.

Personifying as an activity of soul with its mythic consciousness and its relationship to astrology is what we will develop later in this chapter. We will take a brief look at a history of Western astrology first: where it began, how it developed, and where it is today. For the moment we can make use of the dyad by remembering that our ancestors experienced the Gods directly, person to person, one-on-one which is two.

Chokmah and Uranus:
The Tree of Life, the Birth Chart, and the Gods

The history of Western astrology has many parallels with the history of Western magic. Both disciplines guarded the God-images of polytheistic Greece. Both disciplines had periods in history where they were eclipsed, and where they were resurrected. Astrology and magic both, and sometimes together, were transmitted via occult or hidden traditions, their secrets kept from the profane. Being disciplines of the imagination, there have always been men and women who maintained the knowledge of these traditions, passing the torch of knowledge to the next generation.

I have included the history of Western astrology in summary form because the ideas it contains pertaining to God-images as archetypal structures help us give form to images beyond what myth has to tell us. Astrology, like magic and alchemy, is a practiced art, and each practitioner contributes to the common pool of knowledge. Astrology's major strength is that it allows us, through the birth chart, to see what archetypal God-patterns are dominant in a life, or in any moment of time. If the Tree of Life represents the body of the archetypal man and woman, and is representative of the objective relationships among the presences of existence, then the birth chart is reflective of how these universal and objective presences will color the psychic life of the individual. Gregory Szanto writes:

> Astrologers have, in the Horoscope [birth chart], a model of the individual psyche but when we look at these planetary energies in the Horoscope we tend to see them in isolation for there is no natural connection between them. By looking at the energies on the Tree we can see them as parts of the whole in their natural state, for not only do they flow from each other but they are each connected with each other by the twenty–two paths of the Tarot major arcana.[12]

The Romantics saw the individual soul as also being part of the world soul. Szanto is referring to the relationship of the individual soul to the world soul. Psychologically this means that the individual psyche is rooted in the collective, archetypal ground of being. The Tree as the symbolic representation of the topography of the collective unconscious tells of the universal condition of existence. The birth chart, sharing the same universal elemental energies as the Tree, forms a symbolic picture of how the universal constellates within the individual psyche. The examples towards the end of this chapter will help clarify this.

The Babylonians, the Egyptians, the Greeks, and later the Romans contributed to astrology's development of both inner experience and outer world observation through the activity of imagining, or personifying. The history and evolution of astrology reflects the gradual separation of the World Parents as astrology and astronomy finally parted ways in the eighteenth century, and as the God-images of astrology were gradually dismissed and the personification of science ascended the throne; as reason gained strength, and the imaginal world became limited to the child, the primitive, and the insane.

The early Qabalists attributed to Chokmah, in the material world of Assiah, the circle of the fixed stars. Our very early ancestors worshipped the heavens and the stars with the center being the Pole Star. As humanity changed, stellar cults gave way and lunar cults became dominant; they in turn were superseded by solar religions. The Cults of the Mother were superseded by those of the Father. Kenneth Grant summarizes:

> It [Father cult] reigned upon the earth and was figured in the heavens by the sun having superseded both the stars and the moon, as a true teller of time.[13]

The sphere of the fixed stars was humanity's first time reference. The fixed stars were given names and are known to us as the constellations. The constellations that form the background against which the planets appear to move do not remain stationary, their movement is slow, a complete cycle lasting approximately 26,000 years. The constellations were relatively stable structures and could therefore be counted upon for the telling of time. The question of time is one consistent thread in astrology to this day; time as the essence of the evolution of all of Nature's creatures. Astrology continued to exist through its low historical periods precisely because of our need to tell time. In keeping with the sphere of Chokmah we begin with time and with *what is out there*—in particular the fixed stars and in general anything that we experience as external to us, especially the personifyings of psyche.

The fixed stars are strewn across the vault of heaven. For the Greeks, unlike earlier cultures, heaven was masculine, and was known as the God Uranus. He was the first born of the Goddess Ge, or Earth, Ge having been born from Chaos. Uranus and Ge mated and produced several generations of progeny—the monsters and the giants and lastly the generation of the Titans. Uranus banished each of his children into the bowels of the Earth for he hated them. Ge, understandably upset, persuaded the youngest born, Cronus (the Roman Saturn), to hide in ambush for his father when next he came to lie with Ge. Cronus castrated Uranus and cast the genitals into the sea; from the genitals sprang Aphrodite, Goddess of Love.

The Titans were released and assumed the new rulership.

Cronus married his sister Rhea and they in turn parented the first Olympians: Hestia, Demeter, Hera, Hades, Poseidon and Zeus. Cronus, learning from Ge and Uranus that a child of his was destined to usurp his power and authority, swallowed all of his offspring, except for Zeus, who was cleverly hidden by Rhea. The other Olympians were released when Cronus was given an emetic and they waged a war against the Titans, with Zeus as leader. The Olympians won, and the Titans, except for the few who sided with Zeus, were banished into the depths of the Earth, to Tartarus:

> And so a circle of major deities (fourteen in number) is evolved: Zeus, Hera, Poseidon, Hades, Hestia, Hephaestus, Ares, Apollo, Artemis, Demeter, Aphrodite, Athena, Hermes, and Dionysus. This list was reduced to a canon of twelve Olympians by omitting Hades (whose specific realm is under the earth) and replacing Hestia with Dionysus, a great deity who comes relatively late to Greece.[14]

The modern names for the planets come from the Roman counterparts of the Greek Gods and Goddesses. Following the order of the above paragraph we have the Roman names, respectively: Jupiter, Juno, Neptune, Pluto, Vesta, Vulcan, Mars, Apollo, Diana, Ceres, Venus, Minerva, Mercury, and Bacchus (see table 4). The Greek/Roman variations present us with difficulty. We use the Roman names for the planets but we use the Greek myths as they are more complex, more subtle, and more contributive to the psychology of the Western inheritance.

The story of Uranus is the story of the separation of Heaven and Earth. A castrated Uranus is no longer able to mate with Ge—above and below are permanently divorced, each complementing the other. Richard Roess, writing for the Astrological Society of Connecticut, says about Uranus:

> He inseminated from the outside and then, not wanting any connection with his offspring (creation), buried them in the bowels of the Earth. I suppose this says that Uranus creativity while from without Earth, is for Earth. So, the energy and messages related to Uranus have nothing to do with earthly existence but with something from outside its realm.[15]

TABLE 4
*SOME GREEK GODS AND THEIR ROMAN
COUNTERPARTS*

GE, GAEA	TERRA, TELLUS
URANUS	URANUS
CRONUS	SATURN
RHEA, RHEIA	OPS
ZEUS	JUPITER
HERA	JUNO
APHRODITE	VENUS
ATHENE, ATHENA	MINERVA
APOLLO	APOLLO
DEMETER	CERES
DIONYSUS	BACCHUS
ERINYES	FURIES
EROS	AMOR, CUPID
FATES, MOERAE	FATA, PARCAE
HADES, PLUTO	DIS
HECATE	HECATE
HEPHAESTUS	VULCAN
HERMES	MERCURY
HESTIA	VESTA
KORE, PERSEPHONE	PROSERPINA
ARES	MARS
POSEIDON	NEPTUNE
ARTEMIS	DIANA

Uranus represents what we experience as external to us, but also what we attempt to unite with, because Aphrodite, Love, is born from the foam of his genitals mating with the Sea.

Cross-generationally, we have the right hand Pillar of Mercy on the Tree: Uranus in the sphere of Chokmah (Wisdom), Jupiter in the sphere of Chesed (Mercy), and Venus in the sphere of Netzach (Victory). The Pillar of Mercy becomes the pillar of relationship. Uranus seeks to mate with Ge; Jupiter and Venus parent countless Gods, Demi-gods, and Heroes. Personified consciousness seeks union and conversation with others like itself whether actual others or imaginal others. The separation of Heaven and Earth is painful to psyche who, through creative imagination, brings the Gods together again within us. This need is not infantile regression; one of psyche's gifts to us is the will to love.

A Brief History of Western Astrology

The art of astrology as we know it was mostly the invention of the Greeks, according to Jim Tester in his *A History of Western Astrology*.[16] We know that the Greeks were not star, Sun, or Moon worshippers so that the roots of astrology had to come from elsewhere. This elsewhere was Babylonia:

> From the second millennium B.C. there was developed in Mesopotamia a vast bulk of omen-literature, which was collected and organized in the work known as the Enuma Anu Enlil, about 1000 B.C. The astronomy of these omens was purely descriptive, and all concern the nation as a whole, or the king and royal princes. None is concerned with the fate of individual men.[17]

And the Greeks themselves believed their astronomy to have been derived from Babylonian sources.

The fate of individual men and women was a prime concern for the Greeks and a later contribution to astrology. At this point in astrology's history, notice that Tester uses the term astronomy. He feels that astrology as we know it could not have developed unless the basic principles of astronomy were first known. Astrology could not have developed unless:

> ....an accurate, or fairly accurate, mathematical system was devised which enabled men to plot such 'configurations'—that is, the relative positions of earth and planets against the back-

ground of the fixed stars. This gives us an earliest date for the beginning of astrology proper, so to speak.... that date is about the end of the fifth or the beginning of the fourth century B.C.[18]

It is Tester's contention that astronomy was developed first and astrology second. Any references to astrology before the fifth century B.C. he labels "proto-astrology."

The Babylonians were pre-occupied with the creation of a lunar calendar, and Kidinnu, a Chaldean astronomer around 380 B.C., calculated the length of the lunar month to be . 43 seconds greater than what modern science believes it to be.[19] This is a remarkable achievement when we remember that the Babylonians had only crude instruments at their disposal. The Babylonians used the constellations as the backdrop against which to calculate their lunar calendar and to predict meteorological phenomena, i.e., weather patterns; and auspicious versus inauspicious days. To modern day astrology they contributed the naming of the stars, the identification of the constellations, and the naming of the specific star groups (zodiac) along the ecliptic, the ecliptic being the apparent path of the Sun, Moon, and planets through the sky.

In 280 B.C., a Chaldean priest from Babylon, Berosus, wrote the *Babyloniaca*, an account of the history and traditions of his people, including their astrology. This work was in Greek and so reached a wide audience.[20] He is known to have settled on the Greek island of Cos where Hippocrates had started his medical school and it is here that astrology and medicine became fast friends, a relationship that existed well into the seventeenth century. The Greeks adopted the Babylonian astrology and Western European astrology was quickly developed by the Greeks, culminating in the two works of the Greek Ptolemy in the middle of the second century A.D., the *Almagest* and the *Tetrabiblos*.

Ptolemy was a Greek living in Egyptian Alexandria, the city having been established by Alexander the Great when he was twenty-four, in the year 332 B.C. The importance of Alexandria is that of a city in whose womb Babylonian, Egyptian, and Greek thought brought forth the child known as astrology, this child having other siblings as well. Tester reminds us of the glory that was Alexandria:

It was, at its height, a large city of about half a million inhabitants, of all sorts. For it was not only a port, but a manufacturing centre, of glass and metal (from which alchemy takes its origins), of paper, of scents and incense, and of weaving, especially of carpets. It had a reputation for culture and also for extravagance and luxury, similar to that of fifteenth century Florence, or nineteenth century Paris.[21]

It was in Alexandria that astrology attained its coherence, where Hermeticism found a voice, where alchemy gained a foothold, and where various occult and mystery schools developed under the Greek influence.

Ptolemy was a systematizer and organizer. He presents the whole of the Greek *astronomia*. In the *Almagest* he details what we today would call astronomy—the movements of the Sun, Moon, planets, and stars in relation to the earth and their configurations. In the *Tetrabiblos*, he gives an account of how these configurations produce changes in the world, what we call today astrology. For the Greeks there was no difference between astronomy and astrology, the one logically co-existed with the other.

The unity of astrology/astronomy is understandable when we realize that Stoicism contributed much to the Greek world view and to astrology. Zeno founded his brand of philosophy, Stoicism, around 308 B.C. According to Tester, the Greeks were already turning towards more personal and mystical religions when astrology found its way to the island of Cos in the third century B.C.[22] Widespread popular astrology did not exist until the second century A.D. On the way to popular support, astrology was reconciled with the philosophies of Pythagoras, Aristotle, Plato, and the Stoics. All these philosophies had in common the passion to understand the relationship between humanity and the cosmos. In Greek, *cosmos* means order. Good order was, for the Greeks, beautiful and so the verb derived from *cosmos* meant to make beautiful, adorn, hence the word cosmetic.[23] The Greeks found that the art of astrology when combined with these philosophies created "good order." The Greeks were above all else rational and logical. Astrology provided for the harmonious interplay between inner and outer, heaven and earth, metaphysics and directly observable reality. The mechanics of planetary motion and the philosophy explaining corresponding changes on earth could be detailed separately *and* share one word to describe them both. There was only one *astronomia* composed of two parts. The Greeks understood well the archetype of the dyad.

Tester considers the Stoics to be the greatest logicians and physicists of their times, contributing the most to the development of astrology. They did not admit a distinction between matter and spirit, spiritizing matter and materializing spirit. The Stoics considered astrology a learned and scientific study:

> ... and its acceptance as a learned and scientific study was the common, if not the normal, attitude to it down to the eighteenth century, and it is impossible to understand men like Kepler and Newton unless astrology is seen for what the Greeks made it, a rational attempt to map the state of the heavens and to interpret that map in the context of that "cosmic sympathy" which makes man an integral part of the universe.[24]

One ramification of the cosmic sympathy for the Stoics was the idea of divination, the ability to anticipate the future. If there existed a cosmic sympathy between the human and the divine, between the heavens and what transpired on earth, then it would logically follow that the movements of the planets, correctly perceived, would coincide with earthly phenomena. The potential for gaining wise counsel from the Gods clearly existed within astrology's parameters.

All the arguments for and against the validity of astrology first made their appearances among the Greeks. They knew, for instance, about the precession of the equinoxes.[25] If we look to the sky every Spring along the ecliptic at the point where the Sun crosses the equator, the vernal equinox, and note what star group lies behind the Sun, we would realize that the constellation that forms the backdrop to the Sun as it rises at the vernal equinox changes, a complete cycle taking 26,000 years. When the Greek astrology began, the sign Aries and the constellation Aries coincided at the vernal equinox. Currently the Sun at the vernal equinox appears towards the end of the constellation of Pisces, and is moving into the constellation of Aquarius, hence the astrological ages.

The Greeks developed the individual horoscope, known as genethlialogy. They chose the path of the ecliptic as the background to the planets' movements. They developed the idea of aspect or angular relationship between any two planets in relation to earth. They expounded upon the dignities or rulerships of the signs; standardized the zodiac to twelve signs of equal degrees consistent with the ancient elements of fire, air, water and earth; adopted the Egyptian system of the division of night and day into twelve equal hours each; created the astrological houses; and, important to our study, incorporated their mythology as part of astrology's language. By the time of Ptolemy, astrology as we know it was in place and did not change much until the end of the nineteenth century A.D.

Greek astrology flourished for about one thousand years, between the fifth century B.C. and the fifth century A.D., finding a home in Italy after the Roman conquest, where it was alternately accepted and rejected by the various Roman emperors, most of whom retained astrologers. Astrology saw its first eclipse towards the end of the Roman period, but at the beginning of the Roman conquest and through the first century A.D. it was to be found within the courts of the upper classes.

The emperor Diocletian divided the Roman empire into two halves at the end of the third century A.D. with administrative centers in Constantinople and Milan. The Latin West, composed as it was of Italy, Gaul, Britain, Spain, and North Africa, crumbled under the barbarian invasions by the mid-fifth century A.D. The eastern part of the Roman empire continued virtually uninterrupted for it was wealthier, stronger, and contained a greater number of persons. The West maintained what unity it could by way of Latin and the Church.

After the fall of the Roman empire, education in the West was confined to the monasteries until the eleventh century A.D. According to Tester:

> ... the old curriculum with its pagan authors and textbooks was preserved in church schools, in theory always and for centuries in practice also only as a preparation for the study of Scriptures and the understanding of the Faith.[26]

Pagan authors were retained in Christian curriculums because of their mastery of *rhetoric* (words). The livelihood of free men for centuries, whether Greek, Roman, or Christian, was based on rhetoric (words): in law, courts, politics, polemics, in arguments for and against everything.

By the beginning of the fifth century, there were few good books in Latin on astrology. A copy of Ptolemy in Latin certainly did not exist. But education included the "artes liberales," among which astronomy was included as a matter of course. No one in the Latin Middle Ages made any real distinction between astrology and astronomy as we know it, so that astrology/astronomy, under the aegis of the liberal arts, was part of every educated person's curriculum.

The Latin Middle Ages had a rudimentary form of astrology/astronomy. During the Christian development, the words *astrologia* and *astronomia*, different words beginning to reflect the modern separation of astrology and astronomy, were used interchangeably. These two words reflected the distinction being made by the Christian thinkers between "signs" and "causes" (see below). Clearly, the astrology question became a point of contention for the early Christians. All important Church figures, as for example, St. Augustine, addressed the topic of astrology. The Church Fathers never questioned the validity of astrology, its validity was implicitly accepted. The Christian dilemma with astrology was a many headed nail: does a person have free will, or can planetary influences determine a person's life—especially so-called evil influences; is humanity primarily subject to God's influence, or the planets' influence; does astrology point to signs (that is, is astrology symbolic of the cosmic sympathy) or to causes (do the planets *cause* a thing to happen)? Even Augustine ends his arguments by saying that where astrology accurately predicts a future event it does so due to the intervention of evil spirits or demons. Tester stresses the one single position that the Church consistently held:

> What had to be preserved through all this was the freedom of man's will, his responsibility to God. His physical make-up might be subject to the influences of the heavens, but never his personal being, his will.[27]

The Renaissance began, as we saw in our last chapter, with the re-discovery of classical works. The Turks captured Constantinople in 1453 and the Greek scholars took their learning and fled to Italy, and the Latin West became aware of the Ancient Greek world firsthand. The beginning of the influx of classical ideas to the Latin West had begun much earlier than 1453, coming by way of the Islamic world, for Arabic scholars had taken the Greek ideas and texts and preserved them, adding their own contributions. These were then translated into Latin by the Arabic scholars, the Arabic influence seeping into the Latin West through the country of Spain. Among these classical works was the Greek *astronomia*, which was in the West's possession by the thirteenth century; and by the end of the fourteenth century, astrologers were the norm in both lay and ecclesiastical courts. The Middle Ages began with the rejection of astrology as necessary to the world view and ended with its almost universal acceptance. Astrology was in its own renaissance before the Renaissance, thanks to the Arab world.

Astrology was crucial to medicine and its practice since the Greek island of Cos, and many universities during the Middle Ages had a Professor of Astrologia whose duty it was to publish yearly almanacs detailing planetary motion. No practitioner of medicine would dare perform an operation without consulting the heavens, and to this end there developed a four year course in astrological medicine in the universities. Astrology/astronomy was kept vivified by the ever present need for accurate time-keeping and because medicine and astrology were completely enmeshed until the late 1600s.

Medicine, astrology's strongest ally, eventually became astrology's strongest foe. Empirical science, *scientia* (knowledge), began to develop in the late medieval schools of medicine. More and more, physicians came to rely upon observation of body processes. A cadaver could be dissected and the causes of diseases, even of death, could be detected. Losing the support of medicine, the importance of astrology began wane. Add to this the development of astronomy as a science, and even less attention was paid to the art.

Astronomy had begun to develop separately from astrology for many years. We need only remember the contributions of such men as Copernicus (1473–1543), Galileo (1564-1642), Brahe (1546-1601), Kepler (1571-1630) and Newton (1642-1727). All these men either practiced astrology or knew more than the average person about the subject, but their interests lay with *scientia*, science. By the eighteenth century, astrology was dead in educated circles due to neglect and the advent of The Age of Reason, when reason became deified in its own right.

Where reason, science, and Christianity colluded was in the dismissal of the imaginal psyche—psyche's personages were no longer "real," and astrology as a form of personifying also lost its appeal. Tester's *History* stops at the end of the seventeenth century with this lack of interest in, and excitement about, astrology: "So astrology died, like an animal or plant left stranded by evolution. It was not killed."[28]

The gradual separation of "science" from the imaginal realm of the human psyche is a story repeated again and again. Uranus hides his children, for he thought them to be ugly. And so astrology was hidden in favor of astronomy, magic in favor of the scientific method, alchemy in favor of chemistry, and Hermeticism in favor of our modern rational philosophies. There appears to be a certain shame and guilt that science attempts to hide, becoming ever more rigid in what it considers appropriate study. Not that science in itself is bad, it is not. But the imaginal realm is never far from our ordinary consciousness: Uranus's children may not be visible, but they are just "under the surface." Ge will not allow her children to be imprisoned for too long, lest we forget that Uranus's children waged war against their father. *Scientia*, knowledge, originates in the imaginal realm, which we seem to have forgotten, as we also forget that many of science's revolutionary discoveries happened because men and women continued to be inspired by the imagination, and responded to their images.

Astrology and the Modern World:
Body, Soul, Spirit

Astrology, divorced from any creative attention, withered, but was kept partially alive in the occult circles of Freemasonry and Rosicrucianism[29] of the eighteenth century onwards. According to Sandra Shulman, in the late 1800s there occurred a revival of interest in Eastern doctrines and philosophy, spurred by Madame Helena Blavatsky, founder of the Theosophical Society in England:

> Through its lively propaganda and display of arcane wisdom Theosophy became socially acceptable .... it gave astrology an introduction into the polite drawing rooms and allowed all sorts of highly respected and educated people to re-examine the subject.[30]

The Hermetic Order of the Golden Dawn of our first chapter was chartered towards the end of the nineteenth century and coincided in time with Theosophy and the activation of other secret and not so secret societies.

This occult revival requires us to seek deeper, into the spirit of the time itself, a spirit best described by the idea of relativity. Robert Anton Wilson writes:

> The major intellectual discovery of our age is Relativity; which is why the general public, with intuitive accuracy, always classifies Einstein as *the* archetype of modern genius .... the same principle [Relativity] was—synchronistically and inevitably—being discovered/created in a dozen other fields.[31]

Wilson goes on to identify anthropology's cultural relativism, the discovery that the Western Christian perception of the universe is not the only valid one. Wilson reminds us of Freud and Jung who were discovering psychological relativism, the discovery that a person's psychological make-up filters their perceptions of life and the world. According to Wilson, relativism is found in the Western novel, in Joyce's *Ulysses* where we experience Dublin as it impacts on Stephen's brain; and in Picasso's use of space in his art. The revival of Eastern philosophies, magic, the occult, Hermeticism, alchemy, and astrology at the turn of the last century was necessary for the intellectual discovery of relativism to emerge in the Western world.

What do we mean by relativity? Most people assume that Einstein held that all things are relative. According to Nigel Calder in his *Einstein's Universe*, Einstein considered calling his theory just the opposite: the invariance theory. Einstein's quest was to find the common ground, the essential features behind the appearances in this our universe:

> Not only is everyone's point of view equally valid, but all should agree on the essential features behind appearances.[32]

To understand relativity we can make use of the archetype of the dyad. For example, my vantage point when viewing an object is different from yours—you see one feature, I see another. We can both agree that what we are looking at is a table, but my *perceived* table is different than yours, even though it is the same table. It was Einstein's reasoning that there should exist some natural invariable laws by which my relative observation and your relative observation could be reconciled, i.e, the essential features behind appearances, if we know them, should be able to both predict and describe each relative viewpoint. There are relative viewpoints and invariant natural laws that describe these viewpoints. This is not that much different than the Stoic's perception of the universe.

Astrology, finding itself resuscitated by the occult revival of the late nineteenth century, quickly and effectively moved towards becoming reputable, respectable, and scientific! Astrology began to tackle the problem of the newly discovered planets Uranus, Neptune, and Pluto. New schools of astrology emerged, fueled by the rediscovery that astrology could contain, and continues to contain, as many different viewpoints as there are astrologers. Astrology, no longer dependant on any other discipline for its validity, caught the imagination of some very different and unique thinkers. In this century astrologers have ceased being on the defensive and have begun to accept each other's researches and ideas. We are finding knowledge that is new and different from what the Greeks first developed millennia ago. We have learned that astrology's strength, grace, and beauty resides in its fluidity, in its special sense of relativity.

I utilize three divisions in the current status of astrology: the astrology of the body, or scientific astrology as exemplified by Michel Gauquelin; the astrology of soul as exemplified by Liz Greene; and the astrology of the spirit, as exemplified by Dane Rudhyar. My purpose is to contribute one way of examining the various theories of astrology that are current, based on the trinity of body, soul, spirit. Let us begin by reviewing the work of the scientific astrologers, in particular the work of Michel Gauquelin.

The determinism of the body (matter) as reflected by astrology, is exemplified by the many discoveries in this century of the cosmic influence upon the earth and its inhabitants. John Nelson, working for RCA in 1951, showed that radio disturbances during transmission coincided with certain planetary positions; in particular, magnetic storms were greatest when two or more planets as viewed from the earth were at right angles to one another, or 180 degrees apart—the traditional stress aspects in astrology of the square and the opposition. Dr. Frank Brown conducted experiments on biological organisms and their internal rhythms and concluded that rhythmical cycles were triggered by the movements of the Sun and Moon, not so-called biological clocks. Rats in total darkness, for instance, were found to be twice as active when the Moon was above the horizon as below it. Other studies have shown that the Moon's cycle has a positive correlation with increased agitation in persons with mental illness and with the increased likelihood that excessive bleeding will occur after surgery.[33]

On a more cosmic scale, we now know that space is not a void, that energy particles fill up space. The Sun emits energy in the form of protons and electrons. This is known as the solar wind. Radio waves have been recorded from all the other planets and are believed to emanate from their magnetic fields. The planets also leave a magnetic tail behind them, created by the planets' magnetic fields interacting with the solar wind. Our solar system now seems to be involved in an intricate play of activity as each planet and the Sun and Moon interact gravitationally and energistically. With these discoveries in mind, Michel Gauquelin undertook to statistically examine the age old theories of astrology.[34]

In his introduction to *Cosmic Influences on Human Behavior*, Gauquelin tells us that his fascination with astrology began in childhood. He became proficient in astrology's methods and theories, and in adulthood decided to test them with the help of statistical analysis. His research methods have been shown to be above reproach. Gauquelin did not find any strong statistical support for the traditional astrological divisions of signs (zodiac), aspects, or houses.[35] He did discover that certain planets appeared in the sky, having either just risen above the horizon or having just culminated at the zenith, with greater frequency at the time of birth than could be explained by chance, for individuals who selected certain types of careers:

> Of the 3647 famous doctors and scientists, 724, instead of 626 (the calculated theoretical number), were born after the rise or the culmination of Mars ... The probability is only 1 in 500,000 that chance could be the cause of such an excessive number of births in these sectors. In the same group of scientists, 704 instead of 598 were born after the rise or culmination of Saturn. The probability of chance being the cause is 1 in 300,000.[36]

Much of Gauquelin's book is devoted to searching for plausible explanations for his findings, and he comes to the conclusion that the individuals born under certain planetary configurations have a predilection to *choose to be born* under those planetary aspects.

I equate Gauquelin's work with the determinism of the body because of his traditional scientific approach, i.e., staying with verifiable and observable facts. Further, his explanations for the positive statistical results include many qualifiers based on genetic, socioeconomic, psychological, and physical determinants. Like any good scientist, he looks to every area of possible explanation. His work begins and ends with the "matter" at hand, the material plane.

The astrology of the spirit, as I refer to it, has its modern roots in the works of Dane Rudhyar. Dane Rudhyar is concerned with human suffering, but his ideas are Logos oriented. Rudhyar defines astrology as:

> ... the result of man's attempt to understand the apparent confusion and chaos of his life-experiences by referring them to the ordered patterns of cyclic activity which he discovers in the sky.[37]

Rudhyar's philosophy of astrology begins and ends with the sky, from his first major work in 1936, *The Astrology of Personality*, to more recent titles like *From Humanistic to Transpersonal Astrology* (1975), and *The Sun is also a Star* (1975). Where Liz Greene, as we will examine next, would help us journey through the Underworld to find soul, Rudhyar consistently tells us to look up, to reach beyond, to find Divinity:

> Astrology is born of the poignant need in every man for order .... He learns to identify his consciousness and will with the "celestial" patterns and rhythms. He becomes one with the principle of universal order, which many call "God." And living an ordered life he becomes an integrated person: a man of wisdom.[38]

In Hebrew, Chokmah means Wisdom, and given everything said so far about the sphere of Chokmah, Rudhyar's words—celestial, order, consciousness, will, and God—should sound familiar. Wisdom and will in particular are both attributed to the sphere of Chokmah, the sphere of spirit.

The astrology of the body is found whenever statistical methods and scientific requirements are met; whenever cause and effect are the sought after results. The astrology of spirit is found whenever we aspire to God and to Logos, whenever the need is for transcendence, whenever we search for intelligent activity. Both of these views are standard to Western society and remind us of the sign/cause argument in early astrology; cause alluding to body, sign alluding to spirit. For the Western mind there exists a body/spirit fusion with no space in between, although we like to pretend that they are separate, one above and one below. To view them as truly separate requires something or *someone* in between which we know as soul.

An astrology of soul has been slowly forming over the past several decades. Just as there can be a psychology of the soul (Hillman), a magic of the soul (our first chapter), so we can posit an astrology of the soul. What I call the astrology of soul is to be found nestled between the lines, so to speak, of Liz Greene's book, *The Astrology of Fate*, specifically, and generally in all her writings. Liz Greene is a Jungian analyst and an astrologer who has for many years combined one with the other. She uses the archetype, myth, and dreamwork in her practice. She responds to the body/spirit duality by invoking fate, which she equates with soul:

> It is not surprising that the modern astrologer, who must sup with fate each time he considers a horoscope, is made uncomfortable and attempts to formulate some other way of putting it, speaking instead, with elegant ambiguity, of potentials and seed plans and blueprints. Or he may seek refuge in the old Neoplatonic argument that while there *may* be a fate represented by the planets and signs, the spirit of man is free and can make its choices regardless.[39]

Greene finds the interpretations of astrology as a trend or set of possibilities (spirit) or as applying only to the corporeal nature (body) wanting. Greene questions the separation of the spiritual from the physical as two distinct and irreconcilable opposites.

What first appears as Greene's pragmatism is the struggle of soul caught between a modern day contradiction: the implied determinisms of the body and of spirit on the one hand, and the simultaneous denial of fate on the other. This dilemma is illustrated by Gauquelin in his early work. He did research which implied that a certain planet rising at the time of birth correlated with a certain career and then spent the rest of an entire book qualifying the findings, because fate as a word and as a concept is abhorrent to the Western scientific mind.[40]

Soul has need of the feminine, imaginal realm, which Greene introduces in her work. Greene speaks about fate, Providence, natural law, karma or the unconscious. . .

> . . . that retaliates when its boundaries are transgressed or when it receives no respect or effort at relationship, and which seems to possess a kind of 'absolute knowledge' not only of what the individual needs, but what he is going to need for his unfolding in life . . . . It appears to be both psychic and physical, personal

and collective, 'higher' and 'lower', and can wear the mask of Mephistopheles as readily as it can present itself as God.[41]

She challenges us to acknowledge the "it" she prefers to call fate. Caught between Necessity, the fate of the body, and Providence, the fate of the spirit, soul struggles. And soul is precisely that middle ground between psychic and physical, personal and collective, higher and lower, God and Devil.

We are here interested in pursuing an astrology of soul. An astrology of soul would use the birth chart as a way of searching for fate (soul) by looking for the God-images that shape our lives.

Astrology and the Gods Within

The Greeks combined their full understanding of their world with the art of astrology. Their understanding of the universe made extensive use of their mythology, a mythology that is very intricate for its incredible detail of relationships and genealogy. What the Greeks did with astrology is what Richard Roess states about Uranus—both astrology and Uranus reside outside the earthly realm, yet the Greeks made astrology an art that was very much for the Earth. The movements of the Earth, planets, and fixed stars remain the same from Earth's perspective whether we mean astrology or astronomy. The main point of divergence is the belief that the planetary configurations have some direct correlation with events in human lives—at whatever level this correlation occurs. In whatever terms we imagine the cosmic influence to be, I agree with Liz Greene: we can call the cosmic influence whatever we like, but when we contemplate a birth chart we find ourselves walking a middle ground, a middle ground not easily dismissed.

The process of image work usually relies upon the dreams of clients, their art works, or active imagination.[42] The use of astrology can assist in the process of engaging the image. Sometimes it is difficult for a person to engage the image as they may be reluctant, for many reasons, to befriend the image. Sometimes a person is incapable of engaging the image since, not having had story in their development, they find it difficult to imagine, and finding it difficult to imagine, cannot appreciate the personifyings of psyche. With an astrology chart before us, we can begin to explore the themes or

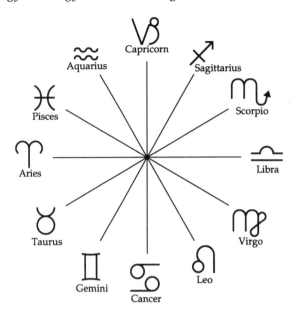

Illustration 8
The Tropical Zodiac—The Signs and their Symbols

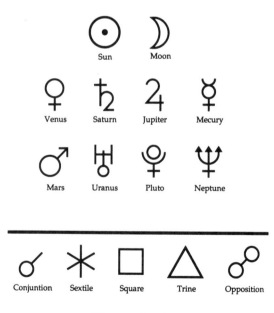

Illustration 9
The Planets and Aspects—Their Symbols

archetypal situations contained in the symbolism of the chart, search our memory for the myths, the God-images, and then, if we need to further explore the concepts within the myth, use the Tree to find different stories and correspondences. Using this technique, relying on the cues from the client, a therapist may be able to engage the individual images of the client by relating to the client the myths seen in the birth chart. I will describe the techniques of various authors, in a progression that begins with the planets and ends with the individual's experience of the God-image.

An astrology chart contains more initial data than is immediately utilizable. As noted, there are ten planets, twelve signs and twelve houses and any number of aspects between planets. Theories abound as to what to look for and how to interpret a chart. Stephen Arroyo suggests that when examining a birth chart, we search for astrological themes:

> For example, if one's chart not only has Mars in Scorpio (an interchange between astrological letters 1 and 8, thus coloring or *toning* the expression of the Mars energy with a Pluto quality) but also includes a close Mars-Pluto aspect (another interchange of letters 1 and 8), there is a double emphasis on the same combination of energies; and hence, the expression of Mars energy will be powerfully characterized by Plutonian qualities. If Mars is also in the 8th house or if Pluto is in the 1st, this theme will be even more dominant.[43]

What Arroyo is making use of is astrology's own language. If we pair the signs with the houses we have what is termed the natural zodiac. The sign Aries rules the first house of initiation as the sign Scorpio rules the eighth house of shared sexuality. The first house, the cardinal sign Aries, and the ruling planet of Aries, Mars, all share the attributes of initiative, assertion/aggression, and other dynamic qualities. The first house, the sign Aries, and the planet Mars all share the same astrological letter of 1. The same is true for the rest of the signs and houses. A sign, a house, and a planet share the same number archetype.

We can take Arroyo's use of theme as quoted above and flesh out the traditional astrological Mars/Pluto aspect qualities with myth. Mars, the God of War, was disliked by the Greeks, for he was considered a blood-thirsty coward who instigated chaos on the battlefield. The Greeks were more likely to invoke Athena in matters of war, for she was considered the best strategist in the field of battle. The Romans, being warriors, looked more favorably upon Mars. Pluto is the God of the Underworld. In Greek myth, there is no interaction between Pluto and Mars, yet they do have some things in common. Pluto's Mars-like qualities are exemplified by his rape of Persephone, his most violent act. The rape was spurred by the Mars quality of passionate lust. Mars has Pluto qualities in his love of blood–shed in the battlefield; their secret relationship appears in astrology where both planets co-rule the sign of Scorpio. Mars-Pluto images, then, would contain a combination of violence (Mars) mixed with very primitive (undeveloped) needs (Pluto), at its worst; and an intuitive understanding and appreciation of strong instinctual drives at its best.

Let us use astrology's language on an actual chart, chart 1. Diane is 35 years old, has extensive knowledge of and practices astrology; she is very much involved in the Western occult tradition through an established mystery school. The first thing we note are the four planets in Scorpio distributed within the ninth house: the Sun, Venus, Saturn, and Mercury. The ruler of Scorpio is Pluto. Pluto is in the seventh house in the sign of Leo. The Sun rules Leo. The Sun and Pluto are in mutual reception, which is to say, they are in each other's home sign, they "receive" each other as guests in the other's domicile. *Furthermore, they are in square aspect to each other.* So not only do they reside in each other's homes, a time-share if you will, they are in stressful aspect to each other. It is as if they need to trust each other and respect each other's domiciles.

This is not easy. The Sun and Leo archetype has been equated with the solar hero/heroine and the Quest for the Holy Grail. Pluto and Scorpio are given to night forces and have been equated with the legend of Faust; the descent and eventual redemption of the soul through the fires of the instincts.[44] The Sun and Leo seek the light, creativity, and the treasure in the cave guarded by the dragon. Pluto and Scorpio *are* the cave and the dragon, respectively; they seek the dark and are content to keep the treasure hidden.

There is one more astrological sequence we can utilize. It is said that a planet in a sign other than its own is disposed by the ruler of that sign. For example, in our chart of Diane, Mars is in Aquarius in the first house. The ruler of Aquarius is Uranus. Uranus is in Cancer. Cancer is ruled by the Moon. The Moon is in Leo. Leo is ruled by the Sun. The Sun is in Scorpio and Scorpio's ruler, Pluto, is in Leo. We are back where we started. All the other planets by disposition lead us back to the Sun/Pluto mutual reception. So we have three different ways that the astrological language of 5 (Sun and Leo) and 8 (Pluto and Scorpio) interact: mutual reception between the Sun and Pluto, a square aspect between Sun and Pluto, and emphasis by planetary disposition. We could add Neptune in the eighth house for another emphasis on the number eight of our language. The greatest difficulty that this chart attests to is the incessant feedback loop between the astrological numbers 5 and 8 which manifests itself in Diane's life.

Having an intimation of what the images might look like, we can proceed with what would appear to be the next step—invoking the image. Astrologer Jesse White-Frese, in a lecture for the Astrological Society of Connecticut, spoke about initial image work with astrological configurations.[45] Let us use Diane's dilemma. Jesse White-Frese would ask: What would a Sun/Pluto square relationship look like? What would it smell like? What color would it be? What shape? Where in my body would I experience this quality? Do I like it? What happens when I touch this quality? What words come to mind to describe it? Is there an image? The replies to these questions would initiate the gradual invocation of an image based on the mythology of the astrological factors reflective of archetypal situations and the client's unique perceptions and associations. Using Jesse White–Frese's technique, we invoke an image to work with, to relate to. This is not so artificial as it first might sound, since we rely on the person's unique image structure and associations. Dreams tend to produce these images spontaneously.

When I worked with Diane, we both became frustrated with the astrological language. I looked everywhere in the chart for a way that the Sun/Pluto conflict might be creatively approached. Add to this the planet Mars in the first house as the only planet East (to the left of the chart) and we have an added player. Mars and the first house share the dynamism of the number 1. Whereas the Western half of the chart contains nine of the planets, Mars singly carries the burden of the assertion of self, which is the Eastern quality of hemisphere emphasis. Mars is in square aspect, or stress aspect, to Diane's Sun and in an opposition with wide orb of influence to

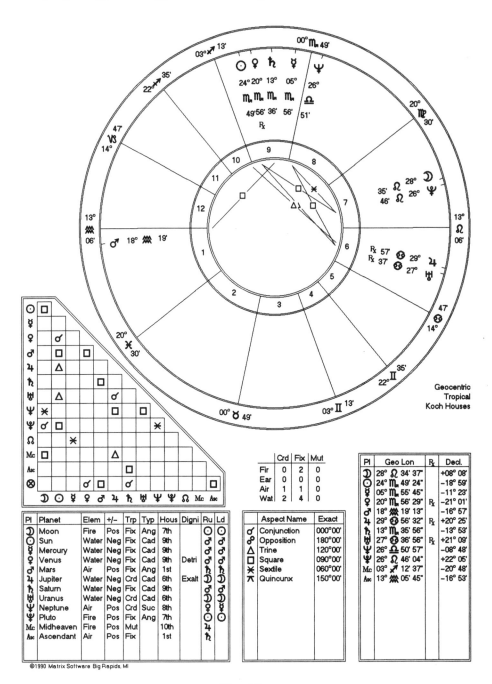

Chart 1
Diane

the Pluto/Moon conjunction. This is known as a T-square configuration. I use the image of a barbell with uneven weights on either side to which we suspend by twine another weight from the middle of the bar, and then try to lift gracefully. There is an enormous amount of frustrated energies competing against each other. Mars with a Sun/Pluto configuration adds urgency to an already difficult impasse.

Diane's learning through astrology and her experiences from her mystery school training has allowed her to understand some of the difficulties in her chart. She sees the Sun/Pluto dilemma as the need to let go of the personal ego (Sun) so that she can find the "spiritualized sun" (Pluto's ability to transform). She thinks of this as finding the light within the darkness: the Midnight Sun of the Egyptians, the Sun-God Kephra, portrayed as a Scarab holding the sun. Diane views the the Pluto/Mars aspect as the need to transform the sexual/creative energies within her.

Looking to myth, what we settled on were two key concepts: the heroine's journey (Sun) and the archetype of the descent (Pluto). Can the heroine's journey happen in the darkness? Can the Quest for the Grail, the quest for the totality of oneself, happen in the dark; in other words, is there a night equivalent? In the myth of Persephone there is a night equivalent (the descent of the Sun into the Underworld). Persephone is the Queen of the Underworld and wife of Pluto.

Jean Shinoda Bolen describes the Persephone Goddess–pattern as usually introverted. The Persephone personality is prone to depression, manipulation, and withdrawal into unreality; she has the ability to be receptive, appreciate imagination and dreams, and can have psychic abilities.[46] Bolen writes:

> Once a Persephone woman descends into her own depths, explores the deep realm of the archetypal world, and does not fear returning to reexamine the experience, she can mediate between ordinary and nonordinary reality .... And a Persephone woman who has been to the underworld and back can also be a therapist-guide who can connect others with their own depths, guiding them to find symbolic meaning and understanding of what they find there.[47]

Diane has a long history of depression (also borne out by Moon semi-square Saturn) and when we talked in depth, she stated that physical death (Pluto) as an option has always been with her. What has stopped her are her spiritual beliefs, especially a belief in reincarnation. Pluto and Scorpio both point to depression as a mode of being in the world. Diane has indeed lived a Persephone's life. The Mars' need to exert an influence extravertedly is thwarted by a Goddess-pattern that pulls downwards, away from the world. Diane has no planets in the Earth element so that her intuitive connection to this plane is non-existent, something to be created and believed in through sheer force of willing to live. Her understanding of living with death as companion is deep and poignant and she related nuances of this understanding that touched me deeply.

Finding the Persephone pattern is relatively easy, but other images are also represented in her chart. Diane has her natal Sun trining the Uranus/Jupiter conjunction. This is a planetary configuration of three God-images that are related to the realm of the Sky. Another set of images: Leo is a Fire sign, and Pluto is in Leo. Scorpio, ruled by Pluto, where the Sun is found, is a Water sign. Fire and Water produce steam, or Air. Qabalistically, Father (Fire) and Mother (Water) give birth to the Son (Air). Diane's rising sign is Aquarius, fixed Air. Air, like Water, is an element that flows easily. Maybe the Air/Sky God-images can be invoked to facilitate a flow of conflictual energies. Thus we convene what Howard Sasportas refers to as the inner congress to order.

The next and more involved step in invoking God-patterns is supplied by Howard Sasportas, who has training in Psychosynthesis. Sasportas writes about subpersonalities:

> To put it simply, we all have different parts or different bits. One part of us may want one thing; another part of us wants something else. Each of our different parts—what we call subpersonalities or subselves–may have its own way of walking, its own way of talking, its own type of body posture, its own drive, will and particular wants. Subpersonalities are "psychological satellites" which co-exist within the personality.[48]

He goes on to say that the planets and signs in the birth chart represent those different bits or parts of us.

The psychology of subpersonalities is probably the strongest impetus in the development of a dynamic psychiatry—from tribal folk healing to mesmerism and hypnotism to Freud and Jung. One has only to read Ellenberger's *The Discovery of the Unconscious* from

Table 5
SUBPERSONALITY TYPES AND THEIR ASTROLOGICAL ATTRIBUTIONS

Type	Basic Drives	Signs	Planets	Houses	Elements	Distortions
Love Type	Strong need to belong, relate and be included. Sensitive and receptive to the environment.	Builds up around placements in ♋, ♎, ♓.	Builds up around a prominent ☽, ♀ or ♆.	Strong 4th, 7th or 12th.	Emphasis in water signs.	Too concerned with what others think. Lack of discrimination. Difficulty establishing boundaries.
Will Type	Expresses a drive for power and self-expression "you adjust to me."	Builds up around placements in ♈, ♌, ♏, ♑, ♒ (also ♉ and ♐).	Builds up around a prominent ☉, ♂, ♅, (also ♃, ♄, ♇).	Strong 1st, 5th or 10th.	Emphasis in fire signs.	Power-tripping; selfishness; over-conpetitive; over-controlling; boundaries too tight.
Change Type	Driven by a need for progress, transformation and change.	Builds up around placements in ♈, ♐, ♊, or ♒.	Builds up around a prominent ☿, ♄, ♅, or ♂.	Strong 3rd, 9th or 11th.	Emphasis mainly in fire and air.	Changing for the sake of change; an inordinate fear of boundaries and limits.
Maintenance Type	Strong need to consolidate and contain; desire to ground, anchor, preserve and maintain.	Builds up around placements in ♑ and ♉ (also ♋ and ♍).	Builds up around a strong ♄.	Strong 2nd, 4th, 6th or 10th.	Emphasis in earth signs.	Stubbornness and inertia; too much conventionality; maintaining the *status quo* because of fear of the unknown.
Mystic Type	Seeks escape from the mundane, transcendence and spiritual expansion; right-brain types.	Builds up around placements in ♐ and ♓ (also ♒).	Builds up around a strong ♃ or ♆ (also ♅).	Strong 9th, 11th or 12th.	Emphasis mainly in fire and water.	You have to "drop out" or "destroy the ego" to be spiritual; too much dreaming and living in realm of possibilities and not enough grounding.
Pragmatist Type	Exhibits an urge to make boundaries and draw distinctions; ability to deal practically with the environment; left-brain types.	Builds up around placements in ♉, ♍ and ♑ (sometimes ♊).	Builds up around a prominent ♄; or a strong ♀ in earth.	Strong 2nd, 3rd, 6th or 10th.	Emphasis mainly in earth signs.	Too down to earth, not enough vision; lacks an over-view of life. "If I can't see it, then it doesn't exist."

This table is from Liz Greene and Howard Sasportas: *The Development of the Personality* (York Beach, ME: Samuel Weiser, Inc., 1987), pp. 208-209. Used by permission.

start to finish to appreciate this consistent theme. Jung originally called the subpersonalities within the unconscious splinter-psyches, and postulated the unconscious as a multiple consciousness. The multiple consciousness quality of the unconscious he later called the archetypes. Jung makes reference to the fiery sparks, the *scintillae* of the alchemists:

> It strikes me as significant, particularly in regard to our hypothesis of a multiple consciousness and its phenomena, that the characteristic alchemical vision of sparks scintillating in the blackness of the arcane substance should, for Paracelsus, change into the spectacle of the "interior firmament" and its stars. He beholds the darksome psyche as a star-strewn night sky, whose planets and fixed constellations represent the archetypes in all their luminosity and numinosity.[49]

Sasportas brings the concept of what Jung called splinter-psyches together with the birth chart, detailing various subpersonality structures, for example the Love Type. The Love Type has a strong need to relate. This subpersonality is sensitive to the environment and constellates around the signs Cancer, Libra, and Pisces; the planets Moon, Venus, and Neptune; the 4th, 7th, and 12th houses; and an emphasis in water signs (see table 5).[50] Sasportas then uses the technique of encouraging the subpersonality to become an internal personality image that can be related to, allowing for the subpersonality to become a psychological reality, i.e., he encourages psyche to share with us its personifyings.

The experience of an archetypal situation as a subpersonality can only happen if the subpersonality constellates around the mythical, as Jung showed in his definition of the complex. It is my understanding that the concepts of subpersonality, splinter-psyches, and the complex all have an autonomous reality within the psyche because all three constellate around an archetypal core. This archetypal core is mythical, i.e., the God-images are experienced as independent of the perceiving psyche.

I find that Sasportas' Types are a beginning point, but I feel that we must search deeper for the archetypal structures that animate the subpersonality. There are many ways of loving, and the Love Type may access any number of the archetypal experiences of loving. The Love Type can be represented by any number of deities.

For example, chart 2 is the chart of Dennis. Dennis is 28 years old. His birth chart shows a Sun in Pisces, an Ascendant in Scorpio, Mars in Cancer, and Neptune in Scorpio. There is an emphasis by Water element. He has a planet in each of the Water houses: Sun in the fourth, Mars in the eighth, and Neptune in the twelfth. Water emphasis by sign and house allude to Love Type subpersonality. The sign Pisces and the planet Neptune are also indicative of the Mystic Type. Furthermore, Venus, the planet of the Love Type is in Aries, a fire sign; fire signs are also indicative of the Mystic Type. We see here two subpersonalities, probably three if we include the Will Type (Uranus strong by aspects), pulling in different directions.

Conversations with Dennis brought to the fore these different subpersonalities. The Mystic subpersonality is very much involved in metaphysical studies, especially the so-called New Age emphasis on mind; this also provides an outlet for Uranus, who gravitates towards mind disciplines. The Mystic Type may have trouble with boundaries, and both Neptune and Neptune in the twelfth house point to boundary issues. Dennis has gotten into trouble, especially in work situations, because he has trouble defining boundaries. The need for relationship (Love Type) and freedom (Will Type) are especially at odds: Dennis's intimate relationships are fraught with difficulty as there are power struggles between himself and his partners as each subpersonality exerts its needs.

What was most striking in talking to Dennis was his rage at family and ex-partners. Much of his descriptions of current family relationships showed him to be using emotional black-mail with his parents. His feelings were that, basically, they had hurt him in his development and that they *owed* him something. He was working hard on developing boundaries between himself and his parents, and the rage seemed to be a necessary condition and resource to accomplish this. With the images of Neptune, Pisces, and rage in mind, I thought of the Neptune (Poseidon) God-pattern.

Bolen describes the Neptune God–pattern as having destructive emotionality, emotional instability, and low self-esteem.[51] I would say this describes Dennis. Bolen says that the Poseidon/Neptune mythology emphasized an eye for an eye feelings:

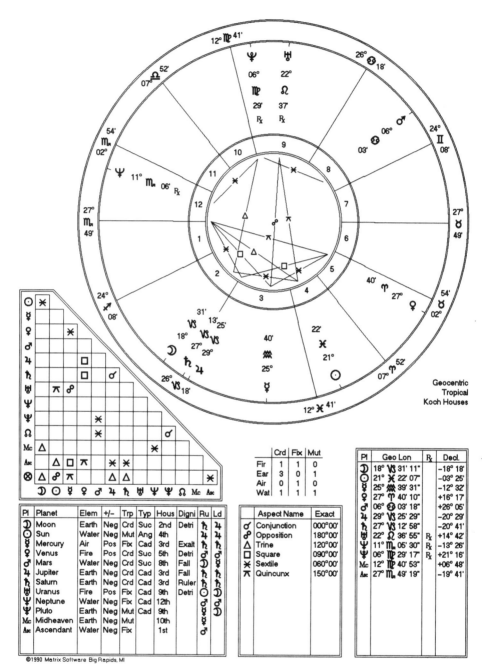

Chart 2
Dennis

As a negative emotional complex, Poseidon vengeance can become all-consuming, destructive to the personality of the man it takes over as well as toward whom the hostility is directed. A man so possessed plants bombs, attempts to ruin someone financially, or directs his efforts toward destroying another man's reputation–or may only obsessively fantasize doing so. But the inner situation is the same—he has been taken over by a powerful negative aspect of Poseidon.[52]

In fact, Dennis described a situation where he confronted his parents and in essence accused them of his pained and hurt feelings and his inadequacies in life; he seemed to take no personal responsibility for his current state of affairs. He felt that it was all *their* fault, and they should know it.

When a God-pattern is dominant within us, our awareness is limited by one particular viewpoint. The God Neptune had a history of engaging other deities in contests and then losing the fight. One example is his contest with Athena to become the patron deity of the city of Athens. Each God created a present for the people of Athens: Neptune a horse and Athena the olive tree. The Athenians voted Athena's gift the most useful, leaving a dejected and rejected Neptune. Dennis's current history is such a pattern of confronting all too powerful opponents; beginning with Mom and Dad, which I capitalize to emphasize the archetypal Mom and the archetypal Dad within him as opposed to the mere mortals that his parents really are. Against Mom and Dad Dennis cannot win because we can never personally absorb the totality of the archetype. This same pattern repeats itself in relationships and in work environments. Where Dennis picks a fight with someone with power (Neptune), his boundaries disappear (Mystic Type); yet he seeks persons (Love Type) with just such power over him. We see how the subpersonalities conspire within him and his as yet undeveloped self–awareness. As is usually true when an archetypal situation dominates a chart, these struggles are supported by other factors in the chart. Dennis' problems arise from dominant patterns coupled with an unawareness of these patterns.

Our last astrological perspective, psychological astrology as defined by Liz Greene and Howard Sasportas, clarifies an astrology of soul that can be used when working with Dennis. We have seen that Sasportas's subpersonalities are similar to psychological complexes, that the chart can give some clues as to their existence in a person's psyche. Psychological astrology looks to the birth chart to find the innate patterns and predispositions inherent within us, for the archetypal situations that are dominant in our lives. Greene and Sasportas write:

> Psychological astrology has, like the old Roman god Janus, a double face. It can provide a surgical scalpel which cuts through to the underlying motives, complexes, and family inheritance which lie behind manifest problems and difficulties which the individual faces; and it can also provide a lens through which can be viewed the teleology and purpose of our conflicts in context of the overall meaning of the individual's journey. Both faces ultimately turn toward a central mystery, the mystery of the human psyche of which astrology is both our oldest and newest map.[53]

An astrology that focuses on the mystery of the human psyche and engages the images within the individual through the tool of the birth chart is in essence an astrology of soul. We use the chart as a tool to invoke the archetypal situations and allow psyche the activity of imagining, or personifying. Face to face, person to person, we initiate a dialogue. We discover the dyad archetype in the realization that my reality touches me from without, *and* that I, in turn, elicit or seek specific archetypal situations in the world that ultimately reside within me.

We can end this chapter how we began, looking to the star–strewn heavens, either within or without. We have looked at psyche's ability to personify, sought for and found the Gods in the birth chart, and initiated our dialogues. Western dualism finds reconciliation within psyche's images. We cannot meet with the personages of existence, the personifyings of psyche, and remain untouched. The fate that comes with the image is the topic of our next chapter.

CHAPTER THREE

Psyche, Image, And Fate

We have found that fate is as liquid and elusive a word as love. Plato thought they were the same; and it is worth noting in passing that in Old Norse, the word for the fates is identical with the word for the sexual organs. Novalis wrote that fate and soul are two names for the same principle. Man's oldest image of fate is the image of a woman; so let us begin where we may first find her.

—Liz Greene, *The Astrology of Fate*

In this chapter we will elaborate upon the meeting of ego (consciousness) and image (collective unconscious). Soul speaks to us through its images. Through the images of soul we come to know fate. And the image of fate is the image of a woman. The archetype of the number three brings us to Binah on the Tree. For Qabalists, Binah is the sphere of soul, and in turn, the sphere of images. Binah means Understanding, and Hillman has said that archetypal psychology is a psychology of understanding.[1]

Soul, when we allow it to engage in imagining, or personifying, introduces us to the myriad Gods of existence. The Gods relate through their stories, each outlining an archetypal situation accessible by all of humanity. We know the archetypes to be collective, and that soul speaks to us through the images of the archetypes; it follows that *my* soul may not be *mine* at all. This leads us to view soul as a collective phenomenon. Meeting with an archetypal personage tends to disorient the ego, at least initially, because the *mine* can never totally encompass the archetype. Our human sense of ourselves, usually centered around the ego, becomes a limiting factor. Hillman writes about this limiting of the experiencing of soul when he discusses the concept of dehumanizing:

> That the soul is experienced as my "own" and "within" refers to
> the privacy and interiority of psychic life. It does not imply a lit-
> eral ownership or literal interiority. The sense of "in-ness" re-
> fers neither to location nor to physical containment. It is not a
> spatial idea, but an imaginal metaphor for the soul's nonvisible
> and nonliteral inherence, the imaginal psychic quality within all
> events. Man can never be large enough to possess his psychic or-
> gans; he can but reflect their activities.[2]

It is "the imaginal psychic quality within all events" that we are
pursuing throughout this book. We have been required to go step by
step "backwards" from soul's native activity, as it were, because we
are needing to rediscover soul. In Chapter One we acknowledged
the imaginal psyche with the help of the image of the Tree. In Chapter Two we began to invoke the persons that reside within the imaginal psyche, the Gods of existence, by using astrology, an art
which is, as Greene and Sasportas write, both new and old. In this
chapter we examine at close range what happens when we meet
with the imaginal psyche, when the ego encounters the Gods.

Living an imaginal life forces our sphere of being to expand,
but we must be careful not to identify ourselves with the archetype,
because the human ego cannot contain it. We then speak about psychosis, or to use Jung's words, an "inflation of the ego" occurs. A self
changed and transformed by the image is a dehumanized self, a self
approximating the Self, the totality of one's being as visioned by
Jung.

As in previous chapters, we will take some time at the beginning to explore image and archetype by first examining some of
Jung's concepts about the image. We will then look to the Goddess
Hecate for some imagining about image, moving towards an understanding of fate as it appears in the divisions of body, soul, and
spirit; beginning with spirit (Jung), followed by soul (an archetypal
encounter by Herta Payson), and ending with body (a case story).
What all three examples have in common is the archetype of the descent, the discovery of interiority. Hillman writes:

> The further we interiorize, the more our psychic necessities take
> on body. Then such aims as release, freedom, and transforma-
> tion fade as we become drawn to an attentive caring for (ther-
> apy) and imaginative understanding of the necessities that rule

the soul through its psychic body, its images deep inside, the mythic depths inside its fantasies.[3]

Archetype and Image

We know that however much individuals differ from one another in the content of their conscious minds, they become all the more alike when regarded from the standpoint of the unconscious. The psychotherapist cannot fail to be impressed when he realizes how uniform the unconscious images are despite their surface richness.

—C.G. Jung, *Symbols of Transformation*

Jung wrote *Symbols of Transformation* with the archetype very much in mind. He redefined Freud's idea of libido, feeling that libido should refer to psychic energy in general and not simply sexual energy. From an energy perspective, Jung recognized that libido, if it is fluid, must move in some defined manner. The means of that movement is the "imago" or primordial image (*Symbols* 1912), which Jung later changed to the word archetype (1919), while in the interim using "dominants of the collective unconscious" as a reference to the archetype in *Two Essays on Analytical Psychology* (1916).

The first occasion for the use of the word archetype came in July 1919 at a symposium presentation consequently published in the essay "Instinct and the Unconscious." Jung changed his usage from "imago" and "primordial image" because others interpreted this to mean a belief in the inheritance of representations—(actual) ideas or images. An editor's footnote explains:

The primordial image is, however, in the present text, clearly understood as a more graphic term for the archetype, an essentially unconscious entity which, as Jung points out, is an a *priori* form — the inherited component of the representational image perceived in consciousness.[4]

Jung always maintained that the archetype is itself irrepresentable. We are aware only of the archetype's ordering influence and the images that it constellates within our psyches. Included in the essay "Instinct and the Unconscious" are Jung's definitions of instinct and archetype. For instinct he writes:

> Instincts are typical modes of action, and wherever we meet
> with uniform and regularly recurring modes of action and reac-
> tion we are dealing with instinct, no matter whether it is associ-
> ated with a conscious motive or not.[5]

For archetype he writes:

> Archetypes are typical modes of apprehension, and wherever
> we meet with uniform and regularly recurring modes of appre-
> hension we are dealing with an archetype, no matter whether its
> mythological character is recognized or not.[6]

The word "apprehend" means to understand, to perceive. Jung
defines the image (representing the archetype) as the "instinct's perception of itself," a self-portrait as it were. We understand our instincts by means of the image. Liz Greene rephrases for us:

> Instinct and archetype are therefore two poles of the same dyna-
> mism. Instinct is embedded in, or is the living force expressing
> through, every movement of every cell in our physical bodies:
> the will of nature that governs the orderly and intelligent devel-
> opment and perpetuation of life. But the archetype, clothed in
> its archetypal image, is the psyche's experience of that instinct,
> the living force expressing through every movement of every
> fantasy and feeling and flight of the soul.[7]

Greene's reference to instinct and archetype as two poles of the
same dynamism occurs in Jung's essay "On the Nature of the Psyche" first published in 1946. In this essay Jung compares the instinct
to the color red and the archetype to the color blue: matter and spirit.
There is a psychoid component to instinct (the infra-red spectrum of
the color analogy) and a psychoid component to archetype (the ul-
tra-violet spectrum of the color analogy).

There is an energy movement, then, along the instinct/arche-
type continuum. This movement occurs by way of the image:

> Just as conscious apprehension gives our actions form and di-
> rection, so unconscious apprehension through the archetype
> determines the form and direction of instinct .... Thus the yucca
> moth must carry within it an image, as it were, of the situation
> that "triggers off" its instinct. This image enables it to "recog-
> nize" the yucca flower and its structure.[8]

Continuing with the color analogy, the active archetype is represented by the color violet, a merging of the red of instinct (matter) with the blue of archetype (spirit), which gives us our double aspect of the manifest archetype; the active dynamic component—behaviors and emotions, and the representational, formal component—the image.

Throughout Jung's writings we meet with the archetype under many guises: the primordial image, "imago," dominants, image, myth. Jung also states that the archetype "represents the authentic element of spirit" in his essay "On the Nature of the Psyche." Between the publication of *Symbols* in 1912/1913 and "On the Nature of the Psyche" in 1946 there had elapsed 34 years. The introduction of archetype as spirit appears to have been connected with Jung's scholarship in Eastern disciplines and their perspectives. Jung writes in 1933:

> The East is wiser, for it finds the essence of all things grounded in the psyche. Between the unknown essences of spirit and matter stands the reality of the psychic-psychic reality, the only reality we can experience immediately.[9]

This stated immediacy of the psyche and its images as *the only reality* is what Hillman refers to in his writings and a conclusion reached by Jung after many years (we will explore Hillman's views on the image in our next chapter).

In the course of Jung's life and work he used the word "image" in various contextual environments. This is not surprising when we remember that the approach to the image is rarely a straight line. In explaining his theory of the complex, Jung writes:

> What then, scientifically speaking, is a "feeling-toned complex"? It is the image of a certain psychic situation which is strongly accentuated emotionally and is, moreover, incompatible with the habitual attitude of consciousness. This image has a powerful inner coherence, it has its own wholeness, and in addition, a relatively high degree of autonomy ... [10]

In this context, "image" refers to a unit of psychic experience. A complex has an archetypal core that has become paired with a person's actual life experience, sometimes in the form of a trauma, and the goal of therapy is to help the person separate what is archetypal from what is actual. By finding the image which is the core of the complex, we can heal the conflict between the conscious attitude and the unconscious complex, this conflict being the neurosis.

Jung also writes about specific instincts, one of which he calls the reflective instinct. The root word is *reflexio* which means to bend back: the reflex that carries an instinctive discharge is interfered with by the psyche so that the discharge does not happen in the external world, but is reflected back into an endopsychic activity. Instead of an instinctive act, we have derivative states or contents that occur within the psyche. This reflection means that the compulsive instinctual response does not happen. The means by which we can gain a relative degree of freedom from compulsively acting out the instinct is the image:

> Reflection re-enacts the process of excitation and carries the stimulus over into a series of images which, if the impetus is strong enough, are reproduced in some form of expression.[11]

The expression can be speech, abstract thought, dramatic representation, ethical conduct, scientific achievement or a work of art. Through the reflective instinct a stimulus is transformed into a psychic content, into consciousness. The outer world of matter becomes the inner experience of psyche. Edward Whitmont explains:

> The structuring of our minds, then, makes us experience existence in the dualistic form of a world of "outer" objects which we are able to organize, and of "inner" impulses which we find hard to master. But in both dimensions we perceive by way of images. The same images which present themselves to us as representatives of the outside world are subsequently used by the psyche to express the inner world.[12]

In this instance, Jung uses image to denote representations of sensory experience. We perceive images transmitted via our nervous apparatus. Elsewhere, image and meaning are paired by Jung. He writes:

> Image and meaning are identical; and as the first takes shape, so the latter becomes clear. Actually, the pattern needs no interpretation: it portrays its own meaning.[13]

Image and meaning being identical, Jung trusted dreams and fantasy material to reveal the workings of the unconscious. Image as meaning is best illustrated by the symbol. Jung saw the symbol as simultaneously being the best possible formulation of an idea whose referent is not clearly known, and as representative of an unrecognizable tendency of the unconscious:

> If symbols mean anything at all, they are tendencies which pursue a definite but as yet unrecognizable goal and consequently can express themselves only in analogies. In this uncertain situation one must be content to leave things as they are, and give up trying to know anything beyond the symbol.[14]

A symbol is not a sign and its meaning can never be fully known. In other words, the symbol has power because the roots of its power-source, the archetype, remains in the darkness of the psyche's depth. A sign has a collectively accepted meaning and resides in consciousness. Traffic signs are an example: an eight-sided polygon colored red means stop, no more, no less.

The image as symbol carries meaning which is both static and dynamic, like the series of still frames (images) that make up a motion picture, or a myth, or a fairy tale. Symbols are whole in themselves, yet allude to a goal. A symbol is the best representation of the unconscious process *at the moment*. Image as meaning is fluid. Whitmont says about the symbol:

> The symbolic approach by definition points beyond itself and what can be made immediately accessible to our observation. While this approach is not abstract or rational, neither can it be regarded as irrational; rather it has laws and a structure of its own which correspond to the structural laws of emotion and intuitive realization.[15]

We have already said that the exploration of the image is like looking at a piece of sculpture. This is supported when we follow the use of the word image throughout Jung's writings. If we remember that the sphere of Binah is numbered "3" and that our physical world is a Cartesian universe centered around a set of three axes at right angles to each other, and we imagine the archetype to be the invisible center-point from which the three axes radiate out, we have a metaphor of how the image creates reality.

In Jung's psychology archetype slowly gives way to image, because image is really all we can immediately know. Hillman, in fact, simply refers to image, bypassing the need to continually reference the archetype. We will follow Hillman's lead in giving primacy to the image by turning to soul and its fate.

The Goddess Hecate and Psyche

It seems that fate, image, and soul belong together. When we turn to soul we meet with the images of fate. Soul is usually depicted as feminine. Liz Greene in *The Astrology of Fate* details how the images of Fate are also feminine:

> She may be met in the old, wild, barren places: heath and treeless mountaintop, and the mouth of the cave. Not always one, she is sometimes three, emerging out of mist or clothed in it.
>
> ....Daughters of Nyx the goddess of Night, or Erda the Earthmother, they are called Moira or Erinyes or Norns or Graiai or Triple-faced Hekate, and they are three in form and aspect: the three lunar phases.[16]

In mythology there were usually three Fates and we are looking to the Fates of the body, the soul, and the spirit as they express themselves in images which are not always easily discernable. Our fantasy of body and spirit mediated by soul, requires a God-consciousness to help us move and differentiate among images. Taking our cue from the number archetype of three, Binah, the Fates, we turn to Hecate, the triple Goddess of the Moon:

> Hecate is a goddess of roads in general and crossroads in particular, the latter being considered the center of ghostly activities, particularly in the dead of night. Thus the goddess developed a terrifying aspect; triple-faced statues depicted the three manifestations of her multiple character as a deity of the moon—Selene in heaven, Artemis on earth, and Hecate in the realm of Hades. Offerings of food (known as Hecate's suppers) were left to placate her, for she was terrible both in her powers and in her person—a veritable Fury, armed with a scourge and blazing torch and accompanied by terrifying hounds.[17]

Hecate is best known for being the patron Goddess of witches and sorceresses like Medea and is usually associated with the barrenness of the crone aspect of femininity. Yet, early in her history, she was considered to be one of the fertility Goddesses, cousin to Demeter, and attendant of Persephone in the Underworld. According to Hesiod, she was honored by Zeus above all other deities. Hesiod also attributes to Hecate power in heaven, earth, and sea bringing wealth and victory to her worshipers whether farmer, soldier, fisherman, or athlete. Later writers do not share Hesiod's enthusiasm for the Goddess, emphasizing instead her darker aspects.[18]

Hecate's parents were both Titans, brother and sister. She is therefore a second generation Titan, as were all the original six Olympians. Looking closely at her attributes she is at one and the same time clearly defined yet strangely elusive, for her attributes seem to point to other deities. She is first of all a Goddess of the Underworld, most likely predecessor to Persephone for she is of an earlier generation. She is not queen like Persephone, nor ruler there, but the Underworld is her home. Her association with Selene and Artemis must have occurred much later in history, Artemis being a later generation Olympian. It is therefore likely that her power in heaven, earth, and sea were original attributes given later form by the associations of Selene and Artemis. We can understand why Zeus would honor her, for she is the older and probably the more powerful, for she has the ability to navigate all realms easily. The triple power aspect of the deity is reflected in the later myths of Zeus, Posiedon, and Hades, for the three brothers divided heaven, sea, and earth, respectively.

Hecate shares the darker aspects of a Fury with the hellhounds. The Furies were born from the blood of the castrated Uranus falling upon Ge. In this respect, Hecate would embody some of the qualities of the Fates, for the Furies (also three in number) punished those who would act without the bounds of Nature. This is especially true of the symbolism of the scourge, and reflects the hounding quality of the image, whether in our dreams, our fantasies, or our art. Once we encounter our inner images we can choose to respond in any number of ways; but they hound us, like the Furies, until we come to worship at their alter, offering a sacrifice, usually our too worn ego views.

Hecate carries the torch, fire, and fire alludes to two other deities: Hestia, Goddess of the Hearth and Hephaestus, the smithy God of the Forge. Hestia consciousness, as we will examine in Chapter 4, is a consciousness of centering, the ability to turn our attention towards a singularity of vision. Hestia in Greek times was represented by the fire in the middle of the home or temple, the center of being for the individual, the family, and society. This is shown by the ritual of the new bride taking fire from her home of origin to light the fire of her new dwelling; only then was the house consecrated a home. The same was true when a group would move out to start a new settlement—the fire from home was carefully carried to the new location. Hecate carries her torch aloft, as if always ready to light a fire, to initiate a new focus, a new beginning, by invoking a new image. Hecate, Triple Goddess of the Moon, is a Goddess of Images (Moon), who, ever vigilant for images, illumines and animates (fire) whatever image is appropriate to the moment. Once the image is singled out, Hestia consciousness allows us to be centered within the image.

Hephaestus was the God of the Forge. We will be developing his God-consciousness more thoroughly in Chapter Four. Hephaestus used fire to create artifacts reflecting and replacing Nature. His fire is the fire of raw emotion and sexuality, the passions that burn us with their fierceness. Emotions animate us, for images come with their own affects. Hephaestus consciousness helps us create with these energies of raw emotion and not be overwhelmed by them. Hecate's fire is a contained fire, a torch which must be periodically replenished. Hecate consciousness can help us assimilate the affects within the image by containing them as the fire is restricted to the torch.

A torch reminds us that fire must feed or cling to something other if it is to endure. Hillman in *The Dream and the Underworld* states that the figures of the Underworld (the unconscious) are shades, ghostlike representations of everyday reality singularly other than that reality. The light that shines from the fire of the torch is bound to produce shadows. The brother of my dreams is not my real brother—he is a shadow—derivative of my actual brother, like the fire that is dependant upon the fuel of the torch. That we cannot take the figures of the Underworld literally would seem to be what is suggested by Hecate's torch, as the light of the torch produces shadows.

Hecate's hounds remind us of the hunting dogs of Artemis — Virgin Brutal Nature. As Goddess of the Night, Hecate's hounds guard the secret place from whence images emanate, for the power of the image comes from the Dark and to bring all into the light of the day is to kill the essence of the image. It is said of her that Hecate killed the Giant Clytius with her torches during the battle where the Giants, children of Ge and Uranus, attempted to take power away from the Olympians. She is a Goddess to be reckoned with, for like Artemis she guards the Sanctuary. A sanctuary is a sacred place, and only those who are prepared in advance may enter within.

Death was the result for the non-initiate who beheld the shrine. Similarly, if we are not prepared to encounter the image, or if we go it alone and inexperienced, there is the danger that the image might overwhelm us.

Hecate appears as stationary, standing at the Crossroads of the Dreamworld, guarding this sacred place with her hounds and her fire. She is Goddess of the Roads, the ever more intricate labyrinthian paths within the psyche: this road to Air (Sky) and Spirit, that one to Earth and Body, and this third one to Water and Soul. She points the way, maybe grandly, with torch, or subtly, with nod. She rarely speaks, melting into the ground and reappearing elsewhere, at a distance.

To contemplate Hecate is to contemplate the sacred nature of the image. One suspects that her many attributes are talismans—magical implements that allow her to travel wherever she pleases within the realm of images, the Underworld. She is a guide of souls by means of the image. She is neither a messenger nor a traveler—she stands at the crossroads pointing the way. She was never equated with a male deity, so she must be a Virgin Goddess with a one-in-herself quality. She neither cares how the Underworld is run or who runs it—that is up to Hades and Persephone to worry about. She is herself a shade, a two-dimensional ghostlike figure. Hillman tells us that the shades are reflective of ordinary life, but belong not to that life, but to the Underworld. The realm of images, the Underworld, must be fed with the stuff of life; the shades feed on the discards of ego life.

To get a feel for Hecate is to get a feel for the Underworld; she is the everpresent God-consciousness, in my own imaginings, of James Hillman's *The Dream and the Underworld*, where everything is literally turned upside down. The Underworld can be likened to the womb of the Goddess in her chthonian aspect, the place where images are born, live, and are reabsorbed; we can invoke here the image of Binah, the Sea, the Great Mother. We cannot always *see* Hecate for when we are with her we are equally *within* her and we are just another shade. Jung made reference to the dream-ego to differentiate it from the waking ego. Moving into the realm of the shades happens by approximation, each step closer means we too become shade-like. Hecate *manifest* points the way to Hades, the place, and Pluto, the God. Let us descend to the realm of images with Hecate as our constant companion.

Image and Fate

Jung defined the image as the means by which instinct was modified by archetype, this process being a spiritual quest of humankind. But Jung also recognized image as symbolizing body. Jung's contemporaries were sceptical of his ability to diagnose physical illnesses from a patient's dream. Hillman tells us that soul (psyche) tends towards pathologizing, that illness of the spirit, soul, or body is not abnormal nor is the fantasy material that psyche weaves around illness abnormal. Normal and abnormal are *equally* fantasies of soul. Pathologizing is a creating activity of the God-image, of any archetypal structure. When we study the myth of any God we come to realize that inherent in the story is the particular way that the God-consciousness manifests pathology. The Gods *are* our pathology. Through the symptoms of body, as Freud discovered, we come to know psyche, and if we know our stories we can suspect that a particular God-consciousness is about, by fantasizing from the symptoms.

Liz Greene reminds us that our first experience of fate is our mother's womb and by extension our own mortal bodies, which is to say the cycle of life and death.[19] The genetics of family, occurring over millennia, cannot be transcended no matter how hard we try for we are allotted a share: we inherit our parents propensity for illness/health and the family's psychological baggage to redeem. Through our bodies we are compelled to follow the urges of instinct and come to appreciate the "biology as destiny" dictum. Freud's psychology helps us to appreciate the fate of the body; Eros as instinct is prevalent in his psycho-sexual theories.

Humans also have a propensity to attempt the heights of spirituality, enticed by the far-off voice of Logos. Greene summarizes Jung's psychology of the spirit and how it relates to fate thus: "Fate is what I am, and what I am is also why I am and what happens to me."[20] Greene concludes that the ability to meet our fate from a creative rather than a fear-stricken stance, mediated by the strength of our sense of being an individual, is a viable alternative to either total denial of, or total surrender to, fate. This suggestion seems to follow from Jung's psychology of spirit as a psychology of personality. A weak ego finds it too frightening to engage the Fates in dialogue. But acknowledge them as Nature we must, if we are to travel the snowy peaks of spirit, which is why many spiritual disciplines emphasize that its adherents must *first* meet the responsibilities of life—a fearful and fragile individual will most likely be overwhelmed by the brightness of the snows.

Greene tells us that the Fates exact their price when, in our ascent to spirit, we ignore the bounds of our inheritance:

> This fate, which the Greeks called Moira, is the "minion of justice": that which balances or avenges the overstepping of the laws of natural development. This fate punishes the transgressor of the limits set by Necessity.[21]

Spirit, found in the pristine snows and rarefied air of the mountaintop can be the cause of illness because the Fates are retributive, that is, they punish those who would ignore them, as Greene so eloquently points out (in Chapter Two) when she references the "it" to be found in a birth chart.[22] Operating in the middle ground of soul that has access to the body, the images that are our fate will pull us down from the mountaintops: either through the illness of the body or the overwhelming pull of the unconscious, the illnesses of the soul. The Fates will not be ignored.

The images of fate as body or fate as spirit tell us that body and spirit are immutable. Through our bodies we are all the same: generic human beings having to respond to the body's fate. Through spirit, as varied doctrines tell us, we are all one and the same for we all share in the same ground of being. Soul takes the building blocks of body and spirit, and through its imaginings, allows us to become individuals.

When I think of the fate of soul, I equate its images with the images of fairy tale. Fairy tales almost always abandon the laws of the determinisms of body and spirit. Greene points out that the fate of fairy tales is never wrong nor is it ever ethically challenged:

> It seems to be fate, rather than accident, which accomplishes the strange transformations in fairy tales, and it is fate which above all else resents being unrecognized or treated without humility. Nor is this resentment ever questioned on a moral basis within the tale. No character in the story ever says, "But it isn't reasonable or humanitarian that the wicked fairy put a bad spell on Briar-Rose."[23]

The Fates of fairy tales, the witches and fairies, are the ones that conjure up all sorts of ingenious things like a frog-prince, or a beast that is transformed by love. Here, too, in the land of soul, there are immutable laws—only just such procedures will accomplish a certain goal. Greene points out that will alone can do little and where cleverness helps it is cleverness coupled with timing or just the right magical implement or some other strange assistance. Fairy tales with their images of the fantastic come closer to our dream images than many myths. These soul images have less to do with the instruction of collective myths, and more to do with the soul's joy and playfulness with itself. Greene feels that fairy tales, more than myths, seem to point to the secret collusion that the Fates have in the story—many times it is the same fairy who cast the spell that assists in its revocation. According to Greene, fairy tales "... suggest, where myth does not, that a bridge may be built between man and Moira, if respect and effort and the appropriate rites are offered."[24]

In the imaginings of soul we are free to become ourselves and come to know our own unique myth. Our soul images are the telling of this unique story, of how we respond to body, to soul, to spirit. The images can come in dreams, in fantasy material, in creative activities like art, dance, and science, and as the result of various spiritual disciplines. Always in the imaginings of soul we are just a little bit freer, and paradoxically, just a bit more constrained by our fate. It is this paradox which colors our three examples of the three Fates.

Jung and the Fate of the Spirit

Carl Gustav Jung first met with fate in the unconscious of his patients. For Jung, fate came from the outside, at least initially. According to Henri Ellenberger, Jung was impressed by the high frequency of universal symbols (archetypes) in the delusions and hallucinations of psychotic patients while he was working at the Burgholzli Hospital in Zurich with Eugen Bleuler during the years 1900 to 1909.[25] Jung could not ignore what he observed. He began to suspect that there was a quality to the unconscious that was different and beyond the scope of what Sigmund Freud had discovered. This led him to publish his work *Symbols of Transformation* in two parts in late 1911 and early 1912.

Jung first published Symbols under the title *Metamorphosis and Symbols of the Libido*. In his introduction to the Collected Works version of Symbols he writes:

> I have never felt happy about this book, much less satisfied with it . . . . The whole thing came upon me like a landslide that cannot

be stopped. The urgency that lay behind it became clear to me only later: it was the explosion of all those psychic contents which could find no room, no breathing-space, in the constricting atmosphere of Freudian psychology and its narrow outlook.[26]

Symbols was the first run, the first attempt by Jung to articulate the quality of the unconscious which he later elaborated under the concept of the archetype. In *Symbols* he began the journey toward the archetypes, making reference to the archetypes as primordial images.

Jung suffered through the writing of *Symbols* because he knew beforehand that what he had to communicate would not be understood. He also had to decide if remaining true to his observations was worth the sacrifice of losing Freud as a friend, which did indeed happen. The writing of *Symbols* was necessary for Jung: it was a creative work able to contain his new found thoughts, and foreshadowed his own descent into the unconscious. There is a loose and rambling quality to *Symbols* for Jung reaches anywhere and everywhere to get his main point across: that the energy of the psyche, libido, is moved and transformed by the primordial image (the archetype).

Having parted ways with Freud in 1913, Jung realized that he had to find his own footing. Thanks to his autobiography, *Memories, Dreams, Reflections*, we know just how difficult it was for him to find this footing. The years from 1913 to 1920 were years of intense turmoil and creative activity for Jung. Ellenberger refers to this time period as Jung's creative illness, a time when Jung was called by the unconscious, when he allowed himself to begin and complete his individual descent. What follows is a summary of this time period, beginning with early 1913.

From (approximately) Christmas of 1912 to Christmas of 1913, Jung struggled with some intense and startling dreams. One initial theme centered on the fantasy that "there was something dead present, but it was also still alive."[27] He gives an example of these fantasies: bodies placed in crematory ovens while still alive. Jung describes these fantasies as resolving themselves in a dream where he walks past human figures lying on stone slabs atop pedestals, figures that appeared to be mummified. Each figure was in period dress, from the 1830s down to the twelfth century. Each time Jung stood before a figure it would stir as if still alive. Jung writes:

Of course I had originally held to Freud's view that vestiges of old experiences exist in the unconscious. But dreams like this, and my actual experiences of the unconscious, taught me that such contents are not dead, outmoded forms, but belong to our living being. My work had confirmed this assumption, and in the course of years there developed from it the theory of archetypes.[28]

The collective unconscious clearly activated, Jung describes an intense inner pressure, a pressure so strong that he feared a major psychic disturbance. Jung twice undertook an analysis of his life, a review to see if there might exist a forgotten something—anything that might provide a clue to his psychic disturbance. Each life review turned up a blank:

Thereupon I said to myself, "Since I know nothing at all, I shall simply do whatever occurs to me." Thus I consciously submitted myself to the impulses of the unconscious.[29]

Voluntarily submitting himself to the impulses of the unconscious led Jung to the memory of his tenth or eleventh year, a time when he took great pleasure in building little houses and castles from stone. Jung realized that there was still some life in these things, that the little boy possessed a creative life that the grown man lacked. Jung struggled against the impulse:

This moment was a turning point in my fate, but I gave in only after endless resistances and with a sense of resignation. For it was a painfully humiliating experience to realize that there was nothing to be done except play childish games.[30]

And so Jung turned to finding appropriate stones from the lake shore and from the water, building cottages, a castle, a whole village including a church. He noted the ritual quality of this activity, finding time before and after his patients to work on the village. Jung's inspiration was the inner certainty that he was on the way to discovering his own myth. The building game, as Jung called it, yielded a string of fantasies that he carefully recorded.

Jung braved the onslaught of the unconscious that began with the publication of *Symbols*, was furthered by the playing of his building game, which had released a flood of fantasies, and culminated in a series of exercises in December of 1913. These exercises, conscious fantasies where Jung imagined himself dropping down-wards or undertaking a steep descent, produced some surprising discoveries. Ellenberger, summarizing from Jung's autobiography writes:

> On December 18, the archetypes began to manifest themselves more directly. Jung dreamed that he was with a young savage on a desert mountain where they killed the old Germanic hero Siegfried. Jung interpreted this dream as meaning that he had to kill a secret identification in himself with a heroic figure that had to be overcome. In the subterranean world where his fantasies now led him he met the figure of an old man, Elias with a young blind woman, Salome, and later a wise and learned man, Philemon. By conversing with Philemon, Jung learned that man can teach himself things of which he is not aware.[31]

Jung felt that the images were an important process without which he might have gone mad:

> To the extent that I managed to translate the emotions into im-ages—that is to say, to find the images which were concealed in the emotions—I was inwardly calmed and reassured. Had I left those images hidden in the emotions, I might have been torn to pieces by them .... As a result of my experiment I learned how helpful it can be, from the therapeutic point of view, to find the particular images that lie behind emotions.[32]

Reading in *Memories, Dreams, Reflections* we see that the two year period between the publication of Symbols and December of 1913 was only the beginning, truly an initiation. The chapter titled "Confrontation with the Unconscious" continues as Jung with-draws from the outer world, giving up his teaching post and relying on his commitments to family and patients as anchors in a turbulent sea. The inner journey continues to the year 1920. During this time Jung's focus was on finding his own myth. He discovered the an-ima, the feminine soul within himself. He received the "Seven Ser-mons to the Dead" in 1916, a work reflective of what was coming to birth within him, of his encounters with the figures of the uncon-scious.

During the years 1918-1919, Jung began to understand the symbol of the mandala—a Sanskrit word for magic circle—and for Jung a symbol of the archetype of the Self as psychic totality. Jung had begun to draw mandalas in 1916 after the "Seven Sermons" but he did not understand them. He began to draw mandalas again, almost daily, in 1918-1919. During this process of mandala drawing, Jung repeatedly asked himself, "What is this process leading to? Where is its goal?" The answer, as usual, came in a dream; from this dream Jung concluded:

> The center is the goal, and everything is directed toward that center .... For me, this insight signified an approach to the center and therefore to the goal. Out of it emerged a first inkling of my personal myth.[33]

Jung's realization of his own unique myth took many years, years that saw a psychic disintegration and eventual recentering evinced by mandala drawing and symbolism. Jung's personal myth and psychology is a psychology of centering, whether by means of the ego or means of the archetype (of the Self).

Jung's question to himself of what myth he lived, seems, in retrospect, to mirror the story of Parsifal who, in his quest for the Grail, had to ask the right question, hinting to us all that perhaps we too must ask the right questions of ourselves. Jung's lifework would seem to indicate that he asked the appropriate question *for him*: "What myth do I live in?" Jung concludes in the chapter titled "Confrontation with the Unconscious":

> The years when I was pursuing my inner images were the most important in my life—in them everything essential was decided. It all began then; the later details are only supplements and clarifications of the material that burst forth from the unconscious, and at first swamped me. It was the *prima materia* for a lifetime's work.[34]

Jung's fate came from within, from soul as the unconscious. If fate is a woman and soul is a woman and love is a woman and image is a woman, where, in the years of Jung's life we have just examined, do we find a woman? Jung's myth, his goal, was the process of individuation: the actualization of the potential within the personality to become what is within it to become. Jung's psychology is a psychology influenced by the element of spirit. For spirit, the unconscious as fate and soul appears to have a devouring aspect—the mother as dragon, which is essentially what *Symbols of Transformation* is about.

Jung's myth is the myth of the Son that must find his way to the Father as Spirit. The feminine must then be either Sister as anima, soul, or Mother, good and bad. For example: during the time period of his creative illness, 1913-1920, the anima appears to Jung as a female voice telling him that what he is doing is art:

> At first it was the negative aspect of the anima that most impressed me. I felt a little awed by her. It was like the feeling of an invisible presence in the room. . . . . What the anima said seemed to me full of a deep cunning. If I had taken these fantasies of the unconscious as art, they would have carried no more conviction than visual perceptions, as if I were watching a movie. I would have felt no moral obligation toward them.[35]

At its most extreme, spirit would ultimately ignore, replace, or simply use the feminine. This is the case where we find Father, Son, and Holy Ghost.

It seems to me that Jung gave voice to spirit, if I may so put it. For Jung, the archetypes were a matter of spirit even when he acknowledges that the right understanding of the feminine soul is lacking in the psychology of the Western mind. When he writes about his encounters with the feminine it is initially confrontational and for all his discourse on the anima, she is an image to be used in the descent towards the unconscious. This is a simplistic view because I am stating the case for Jung's psychology as being one of spirit. The greater reality is that Jung opened many doors; some rooms he explored and some he left untouched. He was a pioneer in the truest sense of that word.

The Quest for God is no idle activity. It is noteworthy that those individuals fated by being chained to God are identifiable by the way they lived their lives. I feel Jung was such an individual. In questing for and finding the center within, Jung found the face of God. May we all be so blessed.

The Fate of Soul

The fate of soul is seen when we look to the creative person who is concerned with the truest expression of the image. We can begin with a metaphor, borrowed from Western magic, to move into the realm of psyche. In Western magic the astral plane is the plane of plastic form and corresponds to the sphere of Yesod. Spirit can project image into the astral waters, clothing itself, so as to be accessible to us through image. The magician also projects into the astral from the physical. The astral plane, the plane of psyche, becomes the meeting ground between higher and lower, microcosm and macrocosm, the medium by which spirit and matter come to communicate with each other. On the astral plane, desire creates its own image. The magician, knowing this, pairs desire with visualization in order to move the astral light. The magician imitates Nature. This is not so very different from Jung's conceptualization of libido as being moved and transformed by the image; and the image, coming as it does from the archetype, manifesting spirit.

The artist and the magician both attempt to give form to images. Their association is not as foreign as it first appears. The Order of the Golden Dawn had many initiates who were creative artists: Florence Farr, actress, W.B. Yeats, poet, Arthur Machen and Algernon Blackwood, both writers. The Romanticism of Germany brought together individual creativity, the activation of the collective unconscious, and magic. The Golden Dawn supposedly received its charter from an initiate, an eminent Rosicrucian Adept who lived in Germany and was a member of a German occult order.[36] The Germanic occult lodges have had a history of emphasizing the creative genius of the individual, an emphasis on the inviability of the individual soul.

Pursuing the fate of the soul happens when we actively follow where the image leads: not because we wish to become individuated, not because we have no choice in the matter, but because there is a certain joy and need within to follow soul into the depths. It is a response to the call of the Gods, who whisper to us ever so lightly; the search for the God Pan as he plays on his windpipes. Whatever this call may be, we cleanse ourselves, consecrate ourselves, and, sweetly anointed, make our way to the Sanctuary guarded by Hecate. This a true magic, no matter what it is called in its native tongue, or what framework it develops from.

I here include part of the creative expression of one woman's response to the call from within. Herta Payson felt that the myth of Eurydice in the Underworld had not been given total justice, and that the account of the myth is from Orpheus's viewpoint. Eurydice was wife to Orpheus who was bitten by a poisonous serpent and died. He petitioned the Gods for her return. Hades granted this boon, on the condition that he not look back as he left the Underworld, assured in the knowledge that Eurydice was following behind. Orpheus could not contain himself and at the last moment looked back, whereupon Eurydice had to return to the world of the shades. We can note the willingness of Eurydice to find the images that speak deeply to her:

"I remember . . . stairs which ran away beneath my feet, going down so swiftly and so easily I scarcely noticed time retreating. Then the rocks which lined the walls grew large, closing carefully until they towered high; a valley opened out beneath, and my descending steps took me, it seemed, between great monoliths of stone. The light grew dim. Dark reached up to touch with first one finger, then with three; a fog so thick and close it softened rock and step. I could no longer feel my way. The world I'd known faded from sight and mind. Carefully I moved through black which carried hints of green and purple, hints which touched a memory that made me weep for pleasure. Descent compelled me, shadow enveloped me until, making the second choice, I gave myself down to the dark.

Eurydice, they called me, back in time. I sit, now, with a multitude. Names have no meaning here; what lies beneath the word is all we hear. The sun is far away and yet shines reflected from the back door of our minds—minds whose open windows let in air which blows clean breath, polishing the mirrors on the floor.

We sit and talk. Is talk the word? We share our images, our dreams.

"Once," I say, "I had a dream. I dreamed I lived in a world of trees and sky and water. Birds flew, and butterflies shone in the sun. Clocks ticked, music played, time passed."

The others murmur. Images hover in the air above our heads. "Ah," says one, and "Yes," another whispers. The shimmer of the images turns gold to green to rose as shapes of contentment, pleasure and delight join hands with shadowed greys and pale confusion.

"Within my sight," I say, "was joy and music. My husband played the lute and all things danced. Who could resist! Who would want to? The trees, the very rocks would move from long-grown habits, water flowed reversed, and separate paths entwined. His music taught the birds new songs. The wind would answer him in harmony."

"Orpheus," one says, in reverie. "I dreamed of him once, in the former days. Child of a Muse, he was, and reared in Thrace where music was a mighty worth. He sang more sweetly than the Sirens, saving Jason and his men to quest beyond the dangerous isle."

"He told me so," I say.

The shadows dip and dart about our heads. Hands reach to touch, weaving shade with glimmering light. We sit amidst the labyrinth. Forever is a moment, caught upon the glistening web. We listen to the shape of breath. Time without time breathes gladly in the lungs made frantic in a life of sound. Gratefully we hold the space within our cup-shaped hands and let the softened darkness take our ears.

"The day the serpent bit me," my voice slides in between the mesh of dark and dream, "the meadow grass was sweet. I tasted honey from new bees and walked through paths the deer invented. Trees brought down their shade."

In silence now the others listen. The labyrinthian, air-bourne shapes about us pause, collect themselves, and tumble, each reversing on the thread which spun it out.

"The snake was small. I had thought, you see, that I was happy. Life stood before me; young, in love with beauty—everything they said was good was mine. Yet, in the grass a little, finger-long green snake addressed me. No word, you know. I'd never seen the images before. A mountain big as mist grew up behind my eyes. A red light shone. From far away beyond the wind and stars which strangely showed at noon, great shapes came flying. My ears heard sounds I never knew before--deep questing murmurs in the trees. I saw beneath the grass the flower's roots, searching the ground for signs of hidden dew, and through my eyes the tears I wept turned green.

"And that is all there was. The snake revealed the answer to the question that I did not know I sought. Life without death is never life at all. Upon that tiny fang there hung a glistening drop of purest gold. I took the serpent's bite with joy."[37]

The Fate of the Body

Many times it is neither the quest for God nor the quest for creativity that brings us in touch with a client. It is the trauma of a life event or developmental milestone. Often we begin the therapeutic encounter from a crisis mode, the client seeking immediate relief for the stressors in their life. A psychology of soul being a psychology of understanding, we look to the images that spontaneously arise during this time. We seek the images that lie behind the emotions as we move deeper into the ground of soul.

I will be sharing the struggles of one man as expressed through his images. Understanding the image means we remain in the world of Hades. In Hades the shadows stand at the periphery, movement happens at the corner of our eyes for Hades comes from the root word for "Unseen." Every person creates and is created by his or her own unique part of Hades, his or her own little acre they tend and nurture, where myth and archetype is reality.

Hades is the land of images. Pluto and Persephone are King and Queen here and the Hecate God-consciousness is required. James Hillman believes that the world of images is a place in itself, a place we visit in our dreams, a place we go to create soul. The approach to Hades should be one of topography as we explore high and low, mountains and valleys. We can move in the realm of Hades, but this world is all upside-down. Death is constant companion, and the transformative image moves and lives. Hillman writes:

> . . . by the call to Hades I am referring to the sense of purpose that enters whenever we talk about soul. What does it want? What is it trying to say (in this dream, this symptom, experience, problem)? Where is my fate or individuation process going?[38]

When we follow Hillman's lead, we give the image primacy, immediacy, substance. We invoke instead of analyzing, we relate instead of distancing, we integrate instead of reducing, we acknowledge with our souls instead of rationalizing with our minds. *Then* we can analyze, distance, reduce, rationalize, if there is still a need. As in the following case story, we begin with image and utilize word. For the information on the astrological Pluto and the Pluto archetype I am indebted to Liz Greene's *The Astrology of Fate*; and for the topography of Hades, the place, I am indebted to James Hillman's *The Dream and the Underworld*.

Scot is thirty-seven years old and is HIV-symptomatic. He is also a Viet Nam veteran. His original letter to me reads:

> I have had experience in astrology for most of my life, having practiced as a counselor myself for several years in Los Angeles and San Francisco. I have learned however, that I cease to be objective when considering my own chart and have, therefore, decided to contact you due to dramatic configurations I noticed transpiring during this year which I am at a loss to understand,

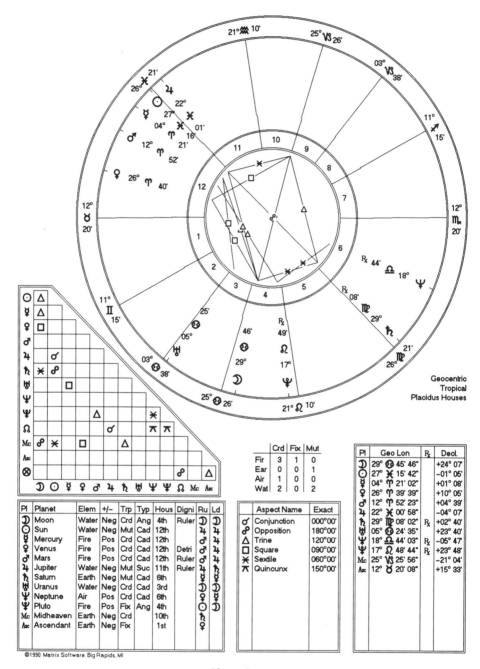

	Crd	Fix	Mut
Fir	3	1	0
Ear	0	0	1
Air	1	0	0
Wat	2	0	2

Pl	Geo Lon	Rx	Decl.
☽	29° ♋ 45' 46"		+24° 07
☉	27° ♓ 15' 42"		−01° 05'
☿	04° ♈ 21' 02"		+01° 08'
♀	26° ♈ 39' 39"		+10° 05'
♂	12° ♈ 52' 23"		+04° 39'
♃	22° ♓ 00' 58"		−04° 07
♄	29° ♍ 08' 02"	Rx	+02° 40'
♅	05° ♋ 24' 35"		+23° 40'
♆	18° ♎ 44' 03"	Rx	−05° 47
♇	17° ♌ 48' 44"	Rx	+23° 48'
Mc	25° ♑ 25' 56"		−21° 04'
Asc	12° ♉ 20' 08"		+15° 33'

Pl	Planet	Elem	+/−	Trp	Typ	Hous	Digni	Ru	Ld
☽	Moon	Water	Neg	Crd	Ang	4th	Ruler	☽	☽
☉	Sun	Water	Neg	Mut	Cad	12th		♃	♃
☿	Mercury	Fire	Pos	Crd	Cad	12th		♂	♃
♀	Venus	Fire	Pos	Crd	Cad	12th	Detri	♂	♃
♂	Mars	Fire	Pos	Crd	Cad	12th	Ruler	♂	♃
♃	Jupiter	Water	Neg	Mut	Suc	11th	Ruler	♃	☽
♄	Saturn	Earth	Neg	Mut	Cad	6th		☿	☽
♅	Uranus	Water	Neg	Crd	Cad	3rd		☽	☽
♆	Neptune	Air	Pos	Crd	Cad	6th		☉	☽
♇	Pluto	Fire	Pos	Fix	Ang	4th		☉	♄
Mc	Midheaven	Earth	Neg	Crd		10th		♄	♀
Asc	Ascendant	Earth	Neg	Fix		1st			

	Aspect Name	Exact
☌	Conjunction	000°00'
☍	Opposition	180°00'
△	Trine	120°00'
□	Square	090°00'
✳	Sextile	060°00'
⚻	Quincunx	150°00'

Chart 3
Scott

other than the strong Plutonian influences I'm experiencing now.

Using Scot's birth data to create an astrology chart for the birth moment, I discovered that at the time the planet Pluto by transit was several degrees away from the seventh house of Scot's natal chart. The seventh house is the house of long term relationships, the experience in life of two people coming together for a stated purpose, such as marriage, or a business partnership. Pluto can mean isolation, aloneness, death. Scot's partner of 10 years also has HIV, and in June had moved to Florida to be with his family. For Scot, a partnership had ended, and more, the fact of the physical death of a partner remains a near possibility. For someone so used to symbols when looking at a chart, I was taken by surprise.

There are many factors and symbols in a chart. The question is always where to start. If it is therapy that is to occur, I begin with a person's dreams. Scot's first dream, first session is as follows. The dream is situated in Viet Nam. Scot has just killed a Viet Cong who has gunned down four of his patrol mates. He is alone. He is about to kill himself. He draws a knife. But just as he is about to use the knife, he hears the call of a whip-poor-will, meaning that one other man is alive and needs his help. Scot is trained as a medic. He rushes to his friend's side. He finds Robert, dying. He gives him morphine to relieve the pain. Another call, this time of a moose. Another comrade approaches, it is Jimmy. Jimmy is covered in blood not his own. He seems fine.

> "Look into my eyes, Robert," I coax him; "look into my eyes and tell me what you see. Look, Robert, into my eyes ... " I say and he slowly calms down and does as he is bidden. "You are hurt, " I say, "my dear comrade, hurt bad," and he begins to sob again, uncontrollably. Knowing that Jimmy will surely not understand, but knowing the gravity of the situation, I reach out and slap Robert soundly across the face with an open hand and then pull his head into my lap and share his grief for a moment. "I will save you Robert, if I can," I promise.

> "Yeah, Scotty. I'm in pretty bad shape, eh? Well, it'll take more than these filthy scum to put the ol'Bruce down, eh?" he replied as he breathed his last breath and died in my arms. In anguish I cry out and almost in answer, a single shot rings out and Jimmy falls across us—dead—and I wake up .... "

We begin with the images. The dream-Scot faces isolation, aloneness, and fear. One of Scot's major fears is the fear of being alone. This initial dream seems to indicate that the experience of Pluto in the seventh house will be one of the agony of the feelings of being alone. His partner is no longer with him due to circumstances beyond anyone's control. Not being in control is another Pluto theme. We have no choices to make. Further, Scot found that through the worst part of his own diagnosis during the summer (1988), everyone he reached out to had gone on vacation. He truly found himself alone. It was around this time that he had this dream and that I began to work with him.

Our first two months of work saw the development of the Pluto God-image. The theme of aloneness has many levels for Scot. For instance, he outlived two platoons while in Viet Nam, the experiences of which have provided images for his dream. It must be especially difficult to face a seventh house Pluto transit that symbolizes aloneness if one is extraverted, which appears to be the case for Scot. Jung defines the extravert as someone who needs and responds to others as a primary mode—the situational context is important to the extravert. The introvert is always responding to internal processes and is cautious when interacting with people and events. Extraverts however, find it easier to respond to new people and new situations; they adapt themselves to the environment by actively pitting themselves against it. The introvert will feel alone even in a crowd of thousands.

Scot was trained as a medic during the war and has worked as a secretary since. Both professions require attunement to the needs of others and an acute awareness of environmental conditions. In this initial presenting dream, he is about to kill himself and only stops when he hears the whip-poor-will call and responds to the needs of another.

Another dream of this period is as follows:

> I was walking down a "Main Street" dressed in a tuxedo and carrying a briefcase. Inside that case, I knew, were bandages, syringes and other medical supplies to help "the village" (I don't recall why that was important). Everyone was looking at me; some of them were pointing. I didn't know any of them. I started running because I thought they were going to do something—I don't know what—I just felt very frightened of abuse or something. As my legs moved faster, I seemed to be actually

> slowing, and run as hard as I might, I just couldn't get away. Then I heard M16s and mortar firing so I dove into a doorway. The door was made of paper and I went right on through. When I got up to dust myself off and look out the window to see what was happening, my fingers began to dissolve. Then I heard laughter all around me. I looked up and around and my hair started falling out.

Hillman tells us that in Hades images of death and decay are standard. We begin to fall apart. Death and decay are Pluto themes, as well as confronting a hidden enemy. On the physical level Scot is confronting a virus he cannot see. On the psychological level the dream seems to say that only a shock, the mortar fire, can force him to go "inside" an image of Hades as the Unconscious. Pluto is the fear that forces us to confront a part of ourselves. For Scot, as extravert, only a shock will force him inside. Once inside, his hands dissolve. When I asked him, he replied that without his hands he could no longer work as a secretary, and by extension, he could no longer exercise his extraverted attitude. The dream says, after all, that the barrier between inside and outside is paper-thin, and if he is to be inside, he will need to let go (the hands dissolving) of his usual way of being, and creatively employ his extraverted mode of understanding.

There were many more violent dreams after this. The themes of death and decay continued. One motif that kept repeating was of Scot beginning high above the ground, and by dream's end being on the ground. Another dream is this: he begins in a helicopter, wounded, on a stretcher, but his stretcher falls out.

> As I fall, I notice a big azure light start to grow below me. As I fall I see I'm falling toward it. Inside that light is a very tall woman with red hair billowing around her as though in the midst of a great wind dressed in some sort of blue gown and white apron. Her arms are raised above her head as though she were a priestess. Lightening crackles from her fingertips and her voice is like a rushing wind . . . .

> Scot lands at her feet. She reaches down her hand and says "I must leave you now, my son, for I have much to do. You must rest before you can begin your journey home. You have become lost, but you will find yourself; only you can heal your gentle spirit—no one else can help you with that. You must learn to love yourself and give of self even more. Your compassion can

be a beacon for others and your lesson is nearly complete. You have to find your own way home—it has not been possible until now. You have chosen—you have strength to meet your task if you will use it. Look inward, my son. I will meet you at home when you have completed yourself." I open my mouth to ask her what she means by completing myself, but she has suddenly shrunk in size and has become a mourning dove. She has flown away and I'm all alone amidst the heather. My sense of loss is keen, cutting near the quick as I lay there, alone , sobbing."

The dream-Scot needs to be on the ground. The entrance to Pluto's realm is usually through a cave, Hecate's home, or a fissure in the earth. How can he begin the journey inward and down if he cannot remain on the solid earth? This Goddess image promises the possibility of healing, but only with Scot on the ground. *She* begins on the ground, then transforms into a dove, a role reversal since Scot begins in the air and ends on the ground at her feet.

When looking at Scot's chart, it is no surprise that the Goddess as guide and healer should figure so strongly for Scot. There are three ways that the Moon, which is traditionally seen as a planet along with the Sun, has emphasis in his chart: by sign emphasis, by emphasis as part of a planetary configuration, and by placement in the angular fourth house. Three key astrology signs in a chart are the Sun sign, the Moon sign, and the Ascendant. For Scot these are Pisces, Cancer, and Taurus respectively. The Moon rules the body area attributed to Pisces, is ruler of the sign Cancer, and is said to be exalted in the sign Taurus. This is emphasis by sign. The second form of lunar emphasis in the chart results from various planetary relationships all leading back to the one focal determining planet, the Moon. This is emphasis by configuration.

The Moon is in Scot's natal fourth house, an angular house, and angular houses are said to be more energized than the other houses because they define the cardinal points. The fourth house is the lowest or nadir point in the chart. It is the house of the personal unconscious, the house of childhood and the family, the house of origin and roots. The fourth house is the early home environment before the development of the discriminating mind and later personality. According to Liz Greene, planets in the fourth house are usually coincident with a difficult or broken home in childhood. Greene also feels that the experiences of the fourth house lie, like a subterranean stream, unconscious to the individual, later in life. In actuality,

Scot's parents were both killed in an accident when he was only months old, and he and his brother were adopted by another family.

Another strong Goddess inheritance for Scot is the fact that he is of Scottish descent, and the Goddess is strong in the Celtic tradition. The Moon is the Goddess, the giver of form, the mediatrix. In the above dream, as in Scot's chart, the feminine power mediates, earths, shows the way. She says in the dream, "Look inward my son."

After Scot's official HIV diagnosis, several weeks into our work together, he began to experience depression and fear, anger and rage, disgust, and suicidal thoughts. All these emotions were difficult for Scot to own. His dreams continued to be violent, but were concerned now with the disease. Scot's dreams progressed from the Pluto theme of the hidden enemy to dreams focused on his disease. In these dreams he is ill and looking for help and meets with violence instead. The dream Scot struggles to be anywhere but on the ground; there is much pain here.

Sometimes the call to turn inwards becomes difficult precisely because we experience a part of ourselves as violent. When Pluto beckons but we fly away, he can become a violent God, lest we forget that in myth he is a rapist. A painful dream with all the images of Pluto and the Underworld (a riverbed, dogs, cave, violence) is as follows:

> It begins with me running down a river bed trying to escape dogs that are chasing me. I found a cave that had a real small opening. I crawled in and collected sticks that were lying around and built a fire. In the firelight, I could see black spots growing on my arms, chest, and legs. I began praying for help and the dogs gathered outside the cave raising a real ruckus. While I was praying, I heard someone start to laugh. When I opened my eyes the dogs were changing into men and they thought it was real funny. When they were all people, one of them said, "You think a little fire is going to scare us off? Stupid Kid, we're here to show you what life can really be like." They crawled through the opening and started ripping off my clothes .... I woke up when they started raping me.

The Goddess image told Scot that he needed strength. We can understand why the dream-Scot has not wanted to be on the ground. At this point the firelight of consciousness is small compared to the assault of the unconscious.

The real Scot has faced many of his emotions. One dream was rather powerful. The images seemed to turn to the sacred. Pluto means riches, and usually the riches of Pluto are gotten to only after struggle, and only after we let go of our frustrated desires. Scot dreams that he is in a dark room within a circle of twelve candles, with one more candle lit behind his left shoulder. He is lying down, immobilized, and an unseen figure enters the room. He knows this figure to be male and that he is to be sacrificed. He is afraid. When I asked Scot what he thought, he responded that the number 13 for the thirteen candles, was the number of the Goddess as Matron. He was aware that this was some type of ritual happening. We talked about the idea of sacrifice: that it is usually a sacred act, that it is done with a purpose, and that consent is important. I asked him to think What and Who in this image desired the sacrifice, how the sacrifice was to be done, and when.

It is important to understand what the images mean to a person. The Lunar Goddess in almost every case, as shown by Robert Graves, has three aspects which Scot called the Virgin, the Matron, and the Old Crone. In the dream where he lands at the feet of the all-powerful feminine, the image stands firmly on the ground then flies away. We see two aspects of the Goddess, the earthly one and the heavenly one. In the dream of the magic circle, the dream-Scot is to be sacrificed to an invisible aspect of the Goddess, an aspect to do with Hades and the Underworld. Between these two dreams, we have a sense of who the Lunar Goddess is within Scot's psyche.

The following week Scot reported variations on the magic circle dream, one in particular where he is above his bed looking down at himself. Again he is in the air, an image we both found amusingly poignant. One of the most painful experiences of a planetary Pluto transit is the need for a voluntary death, a death where consciousness participates. The magic circle would seem to point to this.

There are other dreams. Scot is either in an ambulance or in a hospital. In each case, he argues with the medical personnel. With the thought "... if you won't let me do it my way," he unplugs himself from the life-support machines. Again the Pluto archetype emerges, this time in the form of rage, for in these dreams Scot is going to show them—he would rather kill himself than rely upon the help offered by others. These dreams led us to discuss rage. We could now focus on the feelings of rage as we weaved back and forth within the sacred circle of the Goddess.

Not long after this, Scot was hospitalized due to depression and auditory perceptions. We can look to his chart to help us understand. He has four planets in the twelfth house, the house associated with prison and other public institutions. This may appear frightening, until we realize that the twelfth house is the house of the collective unconscious and denotes boundary loss issues. When a person cannot take care of himself or herself, or needs added collective support, then a hospital is the appropriate place. Scot's Sun sign is Pisces, and Pisces also denotes a thin-skinned quality to the ego that allows too much to filter through. Pluto by transit conjoins the seventh house, but simultaneously opposes the Ascendent, the end of the twelfth house. Pluto has been opposing the twelfth house planets for a long time, so that hospitalization would seem to indicate a final release of tensions. Scot's lunar emphasis, four planets in Water signs, four planets in the twelfth house, all show someone very close to the collective unconscious most of the time. The Moon and Pluto in the fourth house, a water house of the personal unconscious, also supports the theory that the boundary between and ego and archetype is, as in an earlier dream recounted, "paper thin."

The shock of having HIV is an incredibly complex problem. It is truly amazing that Scot has so far absorbed this turn of fate in his life given his propensity to get lost in the collective unconscious. He has shown the Taurus rising stubbornness to survive. May the Goddess keep him in her protective embrace.

We leave the sphere of Binah knowing that inherent in the image is the fate that it bestows upon us. The Fates are three in number, the number of Binah, the sphere of the initiated soul, and remind us of the interplay of body, soul, and spirit. A broad knowledge base is important in sorting out the Fates, one from the other, as Jung taught us in his own life's work.

The study of the Qabalah is one method that I personally use to sort out the Fates. When we examine any complex system of images such as mythology, religion, magic, astrology, Qabalah, or archetypal psychology, we cannot but be impressed by the attention given to correspondences between heaven and earth, body and spirit. Each system has ways of healing the body through its images since each system has discovered that many times it is an incorrect relationship to the image that constellates the disease. For examples:

astrology has assigned a sign and a planet to each part of the body; the Tree of Life is said to be mirrored in our own bodies; certain Native American healing ceremonies use elaborate sand paintings to reflect the unity of body, soul, and spirit in healing.

It may be necessary for those of us with the disposition of the Western mind engaged in a typically Western situation called Psychotherapy to possess a broad knowledge base; however, access to the collective image is available to all. The little old lady down the street with her glass of water for divination and her Tarot cards is no different in her approach than the Jungian analyst, or the archetypal psychologist, or the Shaman of Native American rites, or the Santero of Latin America: they all engage the image that defines our fate. Image is the base material that allows us to sculpt the stuff of life. It does not matter what preference one has to gain access to the images. There is an old saying, Roman I believe, that the Fates will gladly lead those who will follow, but drag along those who would resist. The choice is ours.

CHAPTER FOUR

The Heart-mind: Hearing The Call

One way of giving value to personality is to connect it with transcendent factors, especially God. By doing so the Jungian idea of personality is in keeping with the Greek, Roman, and Judeo-Christian tradition. Each personality is potentially a self that embodies and reflects something more than itself. It is not self-sufficient, but in relation with others, both other persons and "the other" which is not personal and not human. The very word personality from the Greek, *persona*, implies a mask through which sounds something transcendent. Without this "other" which stands behind ego-consciousness, independent of it, yet makes personal consciousness possible, there would be no individualized personality, no subjective center to which events relate and become experiences. This inner conviction in oneself as a personality Jung also calls "vocation."
—James Hillman, *Archetypal Theory*

This chapter is about psychotherapy as an attentive caring for and nurturing of psyche, soul. We have so far walked the paths of Kether, Chokmah, and Binah completing our Supernal Triangle. In Western magic the magician, bathed, robed, and consecrated, stands at the center of his/her universe, the temple, protected within the magic circle. At the corner of the temple is the triangle of art into which the magician evokes a spirit of choice. Evoking means to materialize, to make real, and to evoke a spirit into the triangle of art is to make that spirit appear on the material plane. The triangle as symbol implies the ability to bring into being, to manifest what is latent.

I will describe a process of manifesting what is latent, of evok-

119

ing "the other" behind ego-consciousness. Jung described the Self as both the fullest extension of the individual and as the experiences of the transcendent and other, implying a transcendent supreme value beyond the ego-personality.[1] I would like to suggest the idea of an ego-Self to bring together the apparent and the transcendent simultaneously. Then Jung's naming of the ego as the "ego-complex"[2] clearly encompasses the archetypal reality behind consciousness. Ego and archetype being necessary complements to each other, together afford us the experience of being and becoming. I would like to further suggest by the wording ego-Self that although at times in therapy work as therapists we lend our strength to ego, or emphasize archetype, if we remain within the realm of psyche, soul as the middle ground between conscious and unconscious, then the needs of both ego and Self appear to be met as if by magic. Marie-Louise Von Franz[3] describes this middle ground as a dimming of consciousness, ego moving to meet archetype at the fringe between day and night, the twilight zone where stars first become visible. This is the realm of the ego-Self, an imaginal place accessible through active imagination.

Moving into the twilight zone of awareness, we can see the star-strewn sky within. We are attentive to the call of the Gods, the true meaning of the word vocation. And if there is silence and the Gods are nowhere to be found, we evoke them; it is we who summon. We establish an inner congress, we give voice to psyche; and by voice I mean the broadest possibilities of making real. We real-ize the dream.[4]

This chapter is also about what I call the heart-mind. The concept of heart-mind is suggested by this chapter being dedicated to the sphere of Tiphareth. Tiphareth is the archetypal quality of the Son/Sun and of the Element of Air. It is said that the Hebrew Ruach, variously translated as mind, spirit, or intellect, as a quality in man or woman resides in Tiphareth. We are therefore needing to examine mind even though we have been dealing with the trinity of body, soul, and spirit. Let us give to mind the definition of the ability to engage in intelligent activity that supports soul's ability to psychologize or deepen events by means of the ideas present in its images. As therapists we encourage an environment where the psychologizing of soul through its ideas is given free reign: we stay very close to story and to the images within story, images that bring to us soul-ideas, and, with repetition of this process, spiral ever deeper into soul.

Tiphareth is the sphere of the heart chakra of the Eastern Tantra traditions; it is the sphere of the archetype of the Christos (not to be confused with the actual person of Jesus), the dying God. When we look at the Tree we see that Tiphareth is the center and that eight other spheres are directly connected to it. In Hebrew Tiphareth means Beauty/Harmony; it is a sphere of centering. Tiphareth centering, considering mind and heart as belonging to this sphere, is what I call heart-mind.

Mind has been briefly defined. But what do we mean by heart? Mind has a common intuitive meaning in our Western culture; heart however, is said to be the rambling of the mystic. Let us look to the images that appear when we contemplate the heart.

Tiphareth as the heart-center is the sphere of compassion. Compassion is usually defined as the ability to identify with others and to find the possibilities of their weaknesses within yourself.[5] This seems an ego axiom. If we remove the negative connotative word "weakness" (an ego word), and replace it with the word pain/ sorrow, the definition of compassion moves us to something deeper: compassion is the ability to recognize the potential of another's pain/sorrow within yourself and to respond to another's pain/ sorrow as if it were your own. This suggestion is not to imply the loss of boundaries, a catastrophe in a therapy setting; however, we do not stay clinically removed from the other person's sorrow, nor do we value negatively another's pain. At the very least, with this definition of compassion we become a silent but present witness. When we recognize that we too have pained, have sorrowed, have felt, then the compassion of the mystics is not a stagnant nor idyllic condition - it moves us to action; even the Buddha, who found nothing in this material plane but sorrow, chose to remain incarnated for the benefit of others.

We can borrow astrological images to help us value the concept of heart. The heart-center is ruled by the astrology sign of Leo, the Lion. Leo is said to be the sign of creativity, of children, and of love affairs. Leo is the sign of personal generativity, and is equated with the archetype of the Grail myth, the quest for the Self. The Sun rules Leo. The Lord of Light and Life on this plane, the Sun, rules the heart. Both the heart in the body and the Sun in a birth chart provide a focus, a center; the Sun sign in particular affords us with an archetypal structure as a center. These astrological images tell us that

Sun/heart/center help define one another.

Western magic offers its own ideas concerning the heart. All true systems of initiation have as their center the Sun of Tiphareth, the heart-center, although different systems use different frameworks and therefore have different images. The heart quality, however, is consistent because Qabalistically Tiphareth is the center of the Tree. On the Middle Pillar, the unawakened virgin soul is the Daughter, Malkuth. God on this plane is represented by Kether, the Crown. Tiphareth reconciles the distance between Malkuth and Kether by marrying soul (Malkuth), Malkuth also being known as the Bride. The lower alchemical marriage happens between the qualities of Son and Daughter, Tiphareth and Malkuth. This marriage brings soul upwards and God downwards to center in Tiphareth. The archetypal and the conscious come together; this is the idea of ego-Self and why systems of initiation, especially Western magic, make the heart-center the locus of their activity.

Psychologically, the image of Tiphareth as heart-mind provides a focus for the wanderings of soul. It affords us with an image of centering within our suggested ego-Self through the activity of psychologizing: the ability of soul to deepen events into meaningful experiences through its reflective activity. This reminds us of Jung's use of the reflective instinct, the root word *reflexio* meaning to turn back upon. The ability of soul to turn back upon itself happens through its use of ideas, which Hillman qualifies as soul-ideas, ideas that help soul to interiorize, deepen, and subjectivize impersonal data and events. It is important to remember that not just any idea will do.

An extreme example is the advertisement that I read recently about a periodical newsletter which said "facts that could change your life." One of these facts was a discourse on wheat bran versus oat bran, which I translated in my mind as the question of whether one would have Cheerios or oatmeal for breakfast! It all seemed so absurd. But this is a good example of psychologizing. What another would take *literally as important* provided me with a way of contemplating, of thinking about important versus unimportant activities in my own daily life. Through this heart-mind activity I was able to reinforce what I already knew: I value what I feed soul more than what I have for breakfast. I know that bran fiber is supposedly good for you, but that is the extent to which I want to know. I can act upon this knowledge, but any more time spent contemplating the virtues of various brans seems to me rather trivial. What is really frightening is that our American culture is saturated with such useless data—it seems people take their bran quite seriously.

Deciding what ideas are important for soul is not an ego decision; soul does the choosing through the images it presents to us. We retain this relative importance of ideas by consciously following a path with a heart, an instruction that the Yaqui warrior-magician Don Juan gave Carlos Castaneda, adding further that the literal path was unimportant, even inconsequential.[6] To soul, it is the movement and the heart quality of the path that is of paramount importance: a path with a heart quality implies that the awakened heart is the locus of imagining,[7] soul's native ability *par excellence*.[8] An ego-Self centered in Tiphareth intuitively knows what soul is needing because the numerous voices contained within soul are never far away. Giving primacy to images implies that mind (Tiphareth) resides in the imagination and not the other way around.[9]

Qabalists say that the higher a numerical value the more complexities it secrets and the farther away from the unity of Kether. The number of Tiphareth is six. One times two times three equals six and implies Kether, Chokmah, and Binah. We can understand how a higher number could contain greater mathematical permutations. Our task in this chapter consequently proves both more complicated, because like the activity of mind we attempt to bring ideas together, and less complicated since our previous chapters have provided us with all the images necessary to assist us in evoking the ego-Self. We will utilize the centering quality of Tiphareth or mind as being anchored in the imagination later on in the chapter. What we seek are the implications for a therapy that defines a center somewhere between ego and archetype.

Psyche as Soul, Psyche as Mind

The word "psyche" is variously translated from the Greek as either soul or mind. Consciousness psychologies in particular seem to prefer the psyche as mind translation. Consciousness psychologies, psychologies that have as their locus of activity consciousness and that do not posit a transcendent *a priori* ground upon which the personality is based I broadly label as ego psychologies. During the time that I was mentally preparing to write this chapter, I was given two books within days of each other. The first book, *Object Relations Therapy: Using the Relationship*[10] by Sheldon Cashdan was recommended reading by a clinician friend of mine. The second book, *The Velveteen Rabbit or How Toys Become Real*[11] by Margery Williams was a gift. Together they give us a way to contrast a psychology based on soul and a psychology based on mind. The ego psychology of object relations theories recognizes the importance of right relationship as does a psychology of soul. The main difference is that object relations theories are concerned with actual, outer others only, while archetypal psychology is equally concerned with the imaginal inner others of existence.

The story of *The Velveteen Rabbit* at first seems a simple children's story. It certainly begins simply:

> There was once a velveteen rabbit, and in the beginning he was really splendid. He was fat and bunchy, as a rabbit should be; his coat was spotted brown and white, he had real thread whiskers, and his ears were lined with pink sateen. On Christmas morning, when he sat wedged in the top of the Boy's stocking, with a sprig of holly between his paws, the effect was charming.

At first ignored by the Boy, the Velveteen Rabbit is befriended by the Skin Horse, who had lived longer in the Nursery than any of the other toys. The Skin Horse was bald in spots so that the seams could be seen underneath. The hairs on his tail had been pulled out. He was wise. The Velveteen Rabbit asked the Skin Horse one day, "What is REAL?" The Skin Horse replied that being Real is not so much how you are made, but what happens to you; when a child loves you for a long time not just to play with but really loves you, then you become Real. The Velveteen Rabbit asked if it hurts to become Real and the Skin Horse replied that it did sometimes, but when you are Real you don't mind being hurt. Next the Rabbit asked if becoming Real happened all at once or little by little to which the Skin Horse replied:

> "You become. It takes a long time. That's why it doesn't often happen to people who break easily or have sharp edges or who have to be carefully kept. Generally, by the time you are Real, most of your hair has been loved off, and your eyes drop out and you get loose in the joints and very shaggy. But these things don't matter at all, because once you are Real, you can't be ugly except to people who don't understand."

The Velveteen Rabbit could tell that the Skin Horse was Real and he too longed to become Real, to know what it felt like; he wasn't at all pleased with the idea of growing old and shabby and he wished that he could become Real without these things happening to him. After a time, the Rabbit became the Boy's favorite toy. He began to sleep with the Boy in the Boy's bed: he found this to be uncomfortable at first, the Boy hugging him very tight, sometimes rolling over on him, and sometimes pushing him far under the pillow so that the Rabbit could scarcely breathe. The Rabbit missed his talks with the Skin Horse but gradually became used to his new life with the Boy.

Time went on and the Rabbit was very happy. His fur got shabbier and shabbier, his tail came unsewn, and all the pink had rubbed off his nose where the Boy kissed him. One day the Rabbit was left outside on the lawn until after dark and the Boy became upset. The Boy's Nana could not understand all the fuss over a toy: "Give me my bunny!" he said. "You musn't say that. He isn't a toy. He's REAL." Upon hearing this the Velveteen Rabbit knew that what the Skin Horse had said was true at last, the nursery magic had happened to him, and he was Real because the Boy had said so. That night he could not sleep, there was so much love stirring in his heart.

It was a wonderful summer. That summer, while out in the woods with the Boy, the Velveteen Rabbit was chanced upon by two flesh and blood rabbits, who challenged him to leap like a bunny. The Velveteen Rabbit had no hind legs however, the back of him was made all in one piece. When the other rabbits realized this, they cried "He isn't real!" Just then the Boy returned and the other rabbits disappeared.

Weeks continued to pass, and the Boy loved the Velveteen Rabbit very much. He began to lose his shape, the pink lining in his ears became grey, his whiskers were loved off and his brown spots began to fade. But to the Boy, the Rabbit was always beautiful, and that was all the Rabbit cared about. He knew that nursery magic had made him Real and when you are Real shabbiness doesn't matter.

One day the Boy became ill with Scarlet Fever. As part of the doctor's advice, all the boy's toys, including the Rabbit, were gathered up to be burned. In a sack outside among the other toys, the Rabbit wriggled bit by bit and got his head through the opening and looked outside. Sad, he remembered the Boy and the shared mornings, the long hours in the garden; each hour passed before him, each more beautiful than the one before, as the memories of his time with the Boy returned:

> He thought of the Skin Horse, so wise and gentle, and all that he had told him. Of what use was it to be loved and lose one's beauty and become Real if it all ended like this? And a tear, a real tear, trickled down his little shabby velvet nose and fell to the ground.

And then something strange and wonderful happened. Where the tear had fallen a flower began to grow, with slender green leaves of emerald and a blossom like a golden cup. Its beauty made the Rabbit forget to cry and he just watched. When the blossom opened, out of it stepped a Fairy. She was the nursery magic Fairy. She gathered him up in her arms and kissed him on the nose, the nose still damp from crying. She introduced herself:

> "I am the nursery magic Fairy," she said. "I take care of all the playthings that the children have loved. When they are old and worn out and the children don't need them any more, then I come and take them away with me and turn them into Real."
> "Wasn't I Real before?" asked the little Rabbit.
>
> "You were Real to the Boy," the Fairy said, "because he loved you. Now you shall be Real to every one."

With this the nursery magic Fairy took the little Rabbit and flew with him into the woods to find the wild rabbits. She instructed the wild rabbits to be very kind to their new playfellow and to teach him all he needed to know. And she kissed the little Rabbit and placed him on the grass. "Run and play little Rabbit," she said. The Velveteen Rabbit, scared, did not move. He did not know that the second kiss from the Fairy had changed him all together. Something tickled his nose and before he knew it he lifted his hind toe to scratch it. Realizing he actually had hind legs, brown soft fur, ears that twitched by themselves and whiskers that touched the grass, he gave one leap and the joy was so great that he sprang high off the turf. When he looked for the Fairy, she had gone. He was really a Rabbit at last.

The friend who gave me *The Velveteen Rabbit* had read it when he was 14 years old, a sophomore in high school, and had been touched by it. Rereading it before giving the book to me, now at age

30, he made one comment: He did not understand why the rabbit was so "passive." I asked what he meant by this. My friend felt that the Rabbit could have done something more active to better his situation; that yes, he deserved to be Real, but this was bestowed upon him. Yes, he had shed a real tear, but it seems like the tear *had* to fall to the ground in *this* particular place. What my friend disliked the most was the "bestowing" power of an outside agency, the Fairy. My friend said, "He should have shed a real tear and then he should've found out that he could move his legs or something." Not totally convinced that he was right and feeling that this was probably a standard adult response, I spent several days replaying the story in my mind because I felt there to be a different way of interpreting this children's tale.

My friend's comment seemed strange in light of the fact that as a boy he had liked the story. "What happens to us as we become adults?" I thought. My response came as I fantasized about the hero ego-attitude. The solar hero/heroine attitude, or hero consciousness, is an archetype of our Western ego-culture. The hero attitude refers to the ego in both men and women as Jung demonstrated in *Symbols of Transformation*. It is one of the masks of the adult in our Western culture.

It is a paradox of the Greek inheritance that they worshipped their heroes in myth, yet many hero myths contain the story of the hero and his tragic flaw, usually excessive pride. *Hubris*, pride, leads the hero to perform acts against Nature which is to say the Gods. The Greeks were aware both of the necessity of the heroic attitude to life and of the excesses of such an attitude. Many Greek hero myths tell of individuals, replete with their pathologies, committing violence against Nature.[12]

One hero myth that many people remember is the myth of Heracles, the Hercules of the Romans. Most of us remember the twelve labors performed by Heracles but few of us remember his pathology. His twelfth labor was to retrieve Cerberus, the hellhound who guards the gates of the Underworld. In preparation, he went to Eleusis to be initiated into the Eleusinian mysteries, the most sacred of the ancient Greek ceremonies. Prepared thus and guided by Hermes and maybe Athena as well, he descended into the Underworld. He proceeded to wreck havoc in the Underworld, finally demanding of Hades that he be permitted to carry off Cerberus. He fought with Hades, wounding him, took Cerberus into the light of day, and then returned the hell-hound to his rightful place.[13]

Heracles, as a reflection of an ego attitude, betrays and does violence to the Underworld, the realm of psyche. He becomes an initiate of the mysteries only to betray them, using his initiation for the aggrandizing of himself. He spreads chaos in the Underworld, wounds Hades, and takes Cerberus. The myth of Heracles is one of the most extreme of the myths of the alienated and dysfunctional hero ego-attitude.

Heracles's relationships to women are atrocious and he projects his violence everywhere; killing and maiming are standard activities. His relationship to the feminine and thence to soul is lacking. His relationship to the environment is one of conquest. The Greeks immortalized him in the constellations and at the end of the myth he is made immortal by what seem to be some rather disconnected machinations. The Heracles mythology is important to the Western inheritance, and describes some aspects of the Western ego-attitude. Let us develop this further.

A recent supporter of the heroic attitude is the late Joseph Campbell. He was the author of such volumes as *The Hero with a Thousand Faces*. In the book *The Power of Myth* which is a transcript of a conversation with Bill Moyers, Campbell says:

> People say that what we're all seeking is a meaning for life. I don't think that's what we're really seeking. I think that what we're seeking is an experience of being alive, so that our life experiences on the purely physical plane will have resonances within our innermost being and reality, so that we actually feel the rapture of being alive. That's what it's all finally about, and that's what these clues [myths] help us find.[14]

If this is true, if we are seeking the rapture of being alive, why is this so important? Does not the need to be or do a thing imply that it holds meaning for us? Campbell continues with the example of Buddha who expressed that the mind has to do with meaning, and then asks, what is the meaning of the universe, of a flea? The conclusion is that there is no meaning, "your own meaning is that you are there."[15]

Looking in the index of *The Power of Myth* there is no "soul" under the S's. However, we find psyche listed twice, the first reference is as follows:

The psyche is the inward experience of the human body, which is essentially the same in all human beings, with the same organs, the same instincts, the same impulses, the same conflicts, the same fears. Out of this common ground have come what Jung called the archetypes, which are the common ideas of myth.[16]

The second reference to psyche has to do with the troubadours discovering a motif of the *human* psyche.[17] In my opinion, Campbell's views appear to be mostly from a heroic ego stance. Psyche is nothing more than the experience of our bodies, archetypes nothing more than motifs to help us experience being alive. Meaning is relegated to mind and mind is ephemeral. *Life is action, we have to make it happen.* Myths are ways of making life happen, instructions to be taken literally. The archetype does contain ideas as we have seen, but Campbell focuses mostly on the ideas contained in myth.

Archetypes are "ground ideas" according to Campbell.[18] Literalness, the aloneness of the individual, the lack of faith and trust that life happens anyway, as opposed to *making* it happen, psyche reduced to body, myths reduced only to instructions are all hero ego stances. Most instructive is Campbell's description of "human" before psyche. The transcendent quality of psyche beyond the body's literalness is downplayed. One of the most influential men of modern times, who utilized the myth, did so more from the perspective of the Enlightenment, the Age of Reason, than from the Romantic viewpoint. It is evident that Campbell valued relationships, but I would say that he valued relationships from the heroic stance. The point I am making is that the heroic journey is only one of many, that our culture values the heroic stance, and that the hero personality gets lost in the ideas of soul, but does not necessarily ever wed soul. Soul as psyche is much more than the experience of our bodies, or the ideas found in myths.

The question I started to answer was whether the Velveteen Rabbit was passive. The answer is yes if we view the Rabbit's story with heroic eyes. Viewed from the perspective of soul, the Rabbit was quite active. The Velveteen Rabbit knew from the Skin Horse that becoming Real means you are loved for a very long time and that it hurts. The first active thing the Rabbit did was to wish to become Real. Secondly, when presented with the opportunity to be loved by the Boy, it *allowed* itself to be loved no matter how uncomfortable it was sometimes and no matter that he knew the price he might have to pay. Allowing oneself to be the recipient of love is no passive activity, as the Rabbit was soon to learn. The love relationship between himself and the Boy transformed them both. The third active thing the Rabbit did was shed a very real tear. To love and be loved means we are vulnerable. The little Rabbit did not judge why it found itself alone and hurt, he chose instead to remember the magic of that special relationship. There is magic in the ability to feel and in the ability to shed a real tear; this is soul's ability to deepen events into experiences that hold meaning for us. Soul is represented by the Fairy. The magic happens the moment we can shed a real tear; in therapy this is a truly momentous occasion for the client.

The appearance of the Fairy is of the utmost importance, for psyche mediates. The ego as hero finds himself alone because he refuses to learn right relationship. He intuitively knows that right relationship takes effort and makes us vulnerable: love as a quality of soul has a transcendent aspect that takes ego beyond its narrow boundaries. The hero negatively values relationship, but he expects to be loved. To truly love would require that he step outside of himself and in doing so acknowledge the others who share his world. The hero as ego finds himself alone because in his world everything is literal, the imaginal persons of soul are non-existent; and if he cannot find right relationship within, how can he expect to engage in functional relationships without? In other words, there is no room for the mediating function of the Fairy. The tear needing to be shed *here* exactly and at this time is annoying to the hero, who has his own agenda and wants nothing to do with anyone else's, least of all that of souls.

The Velveteen Rabbit was a creature of soul. The Rabbit shares with soul an emphasis on the magic of love and loving, of allowing oneself vulnerability, and of becoming REAL. This becoming real by way of soul's deepening of life experience is perhaps what Campbell means by the experience of being alive; however the ego, literally following myth, is not what accomplishes this, even though the ego is obviously instrumental. The thrill-seeking activity of ego makes us feel alive, but this is temporary. It is psyche as soul through its psychologizing activity that brings with it the experiences of being alive that transcends the ego.

The implications for a therapy based on soul means that therapist and client engage in soul's process of becoming real by allowing what is authentic for soul, namely its images which reside deep inside, the nonhuman "other" behind consciousness. When we allow ourselves to become the recipient of soul's ability to love us, we can become Real. Soul has a two-faced quality, like the Roman God Janus, one face turning to the archetype, one face turning to ego. Soul can teach us that the image can love us if we but allow it. Then our sense of being alone gives way to the voices deep within. We are not required to be active in the hero ego sense of that word, but we are required to be active.

The Velveteen Rabbit teaches us how we become Real through the process of relationship. The Skin Horse, the Boy, Nana, the other rabbits, and the Fairy all helped define who he was, yet once each definition by way of relationship was achieved it became a permanent possession of the Rabbit. At first the Rabbit was Real only to the Boy; this would be soul's initial movement from the sphere of Malkuth towards Tiphareth, when we first come to know our images deep inside and begin to listen to them. The images are real only to us. Moving from Malkuth to Tiphareth means that we find mind in image, that heart becomes the locus for imagining, and that ego moves to meet Self. When we actively create the middle ground of the ego-Self we become Real to everyone. Becoming Real to everyone is the true magic of soul mediating between ego and archetype.

Turning to a different understanding of the importance of relationship, we find object relations theories that have as their antecedent, Freudian psychology. In *Object Relations Therapy* by Sheldon Cashdan there is an overview in chapter one of the history of object relations theories; what follows is based on this historical summary of early theorists. The premise of Cashdan's book is that if we examine the early theorists of ego-object relations, there are points of agreement amongst them. Cashdan reworks the common threads of ego-object relations theories into an object relations therapy.

One major conclusion that Cashdan sees within early object relations theorists is the following:

> The 'stuff' of which mind is made has less to do with libidinal impulses and psychic energy than with the internalization of relationships. To understand what motivates people and how they view themselves, one needs to understand how relationships are internalized and how they become transformed into a sense of self.[19]

These internalized inner images of early relationships are the focus of object relations therapy. Cashdan proposes that the therapeutic relationship then becomes an in vivo expression of what is pathological in a person's life, and is consequently the base material for doing therapy work. In other words, the therapeutic relationship itself is the focus. What object relations theory emphasizes is the importance of right relationship and in this it agrees with a psychology of soul. But there are some differences.

Object relations theories have evolved from Freudian psychology where the ego, the mind, psyche, and personality can at times be equivalent variables. Object relations theorists use the word self, referring, it seems, to a more all-inclusive concept than ego: they view individual development as centered around the concept of self (not capitalized to differentiate this concept of self from Jung's archetypal Self) which is the result of *internalized* relationship experiences. The raw data for these internalized relationship experiences are objective and out there; W.R.D. Fairbairn felt that internalized badness within the child comes from parents that were actually depriving and rejecting.[20] Many early object relations theorists assumed the child to be a blank slate acted upon by the environment, especially by mother.

Object relations theorists see splitting as key in development: mother, for the child, becomes split into good mother and bad mother and these images are internalized. As the person, develops an integration of these two images hopefully occurs. Psychopathology is the lack of integration of these split internalized images. Therapy attempts to remedy this split within the self by means of the therapeutic relationship, the therapeutic relationship absorbing the projections of the dysfunctional self.

We begin to see where a therapy of psyche as soul and a therapy of psyche as mind diverge. Archetypal psychology looks to the inborn inner images that are found in the collective unconscious and asks how these are projected onto the environment. Early object relations theorists had no room for the archetypal, imaginal realm of soul. The only object relations theorist who believed in an inherent inborn predisposition in the neonate was Melanie Klein, who believed that the child experiences constructive and destructive urges. She never used the words collective unconscious, even when she felt that the child's expectation of what mother should be like begins in the womb.

For object relations theorists, splitting is a key developmental problem. In contradistinction, archetypal psychology might view splitting as the result of the child experiencing the archetypal Mother. As we have seen, the archetype has a positive and a negative pole; the child's experience of good mother versus bad mother might be the child's projection of the two poles of the archetype. Integration is still necessary, but viewing the situation with an archetypal stance we do many things. One, ego is no longer the only locus of activity; two, we realize that maybe there is nothing to be fixed only something (or someone) to be understood; three, archetypal psychology does not view the ego's experience of an archetypal structure as belonging to the ego, i.e., this is not my emotion, my fantasy, my idea. The experience of emotion and fantasy and idea comes from the archetype. It is not mine in the usual ego sense. And four, by limiting the ego's ownership, we remove the pressure on ego to be what it cannot become.

Jung saw personality as critical, but he was able to integrate the archetypal background of personality. The main differences between consciousness psychologies and archetypal psychology are that the latter does not take ego's literalness literally, and that the idea of self contains a supraordinate dimension. We try to sort out what might have been the actual experience of say, mother; who mother really was. We allow ego to retain that which it has lived, aware that archetypal structures color our ego experiences. With this awareness, we move to discover what contribution archetypal structures have had in a person's development.

When we are dealing with major psychopathology, the object relations theories and other ego psychologies are beneficial; persons who are near to psychosis, the chronic mentally ill, and most of us when in a crisis mode would not benefit (directly) from a psychology based on inner images. In these instances work with ego psychologies, especially supportive ego therapies, are most useful, for sometimes we want to *stem* the flood of inner images.

There comes a time when functional individuals, after having approached and gained assistance from an ego-based therapy, or psyche as mind, find a need for something less constricting and more all encompassing. They are seeking to place a value on personality that does not rely on ego, but on a transcendent reality. Archetypal psychology as a psychology of soul can answer this need.

Evoking the Ego-Self: A Magic

I have taken the liberty of rewording Cashdan, for I define ego psychology more broadly than the current usage. Cashdan does not label his therapy an ego psychology. Any psychology that does not posit a trancendent *a priori* imaginal quality to psyche I broadly term ego psychology. Fantasy when used, as Cashdan does in his therapy, is the result of internalized images based upon conscious experience. This is true of object relations therapy, or Freud's psychosexual framework, or the many other therapies in existence. Jung's psychology can also be seen as an ego psychology in that he spent time addressing the problem of ego and the field of consciousness; but his is really an archetypal psychology. Jung bridged the distance between ego and archetype. If we follow Hillman and simply give primacy to archetype we reach the extreme end of the ego/ archetype continuum because we begin with image and then move towards an understanding of ego. We try to understand all of existence as fantasies of soul, and this includes the masks worn by the ego.

I have said that the numeration of Tiphareth contains within it the numbers of the Supernal Triangle Kether, Chokmah, and Binah. Each of these spheres has a path connecting them to Tiphareth. We will now tread these paths using Western magic as developed in the Tarot, especially the work of Paul Foster Case; use myth to elaborate a psychotherapy of soul; and weave all this heart-mind activity with Hillman's ideas. The three paths that connect Tiphareth to the Supernals are The High Priestess (Kether to Tiphareth), The Star (Chokmah to Tiphareth), and The Lovers (Binah to Tiphareth). Three being the number of making visible, we will make apparent the philosophy of a therapy based on the primacy of the image.

The High Priestess
The Path between Kether and Tiphareth

The High Priestess is the image of the Tarot for the path connecting Kether and Tiphareth (see illus. 10). The Hebrew letter is Gimel, which means camel. According to Paul Foster Case[21] the letter-name suggests travel, communication, and commerce; and also suggests association, combination, coexistence, and partnership. Gimel as a mode of consciousness is called the Uniting Intelligence. Gimel is the path of the Moon, and the color attributed to this path is the blue of water. The direction given to Gimel is Below as subordinate, dependent, subject to command, and obedient. Case employs his own brand of psychology, attributing to the High Priestess the realm of the "subconscious," what I equate with the image producing stratum of the unconscious.

Case states that the High Priestess is a Virgin Goddess, the First Matter of the alchemists. She sits between the pillars of affirmation and negation, black and white:

> The High Priestess sits between the pillars, because she is the equilibrating power between the "Yes" and the "No," the initiative and the resistance, the light and the darkness.[22]

She sits on a throne before a veil:

> Only when this veil is rent or penetrated by the concentrated impulses originating at the self-conscious level may the creative activities of subconsciousness be released and actualized.[23]

Her robe flows out beneath her for it is the water of the stream of consciousness, and all subsequent bodies of water in all the other Tarot trumps have as their source the robe of the High Priestess.

To summarize Case, the High Priestess is the Uniting Intelligence between Kether and Tiphareth. She is one of the three paths that crosses the Abyss between the Supernals and the sphere of Tiphareth below. That the image producing stratum of the psyche has high importance is seen by the appearance of the High Priestess so early in the sequence of Tarot and by the way she connects two spheres on the Middle Pillar. Case also suggests that the power of the imaginal realm can be awakened if we "concentrate impulses originating at the self-conscious level," thereby releasing the creative activity of the image. Early occultists, as we know, employed image extensively in their work, and their first task was to awaken the powers of the imagination.

In archetypal psychology terms, Tiphareth receives the influences of the collective unconscious of Kether. The High Priestess unites the psychoid aspect of the archetype with the perceptible image in Tiphareth. To tread the path of Gimel is to activate the image,

Illustration 10
The High Priestess

to impregnate the Virgin Goddess with focused attention. A different image is the Velveteen Rabbit's desire to become Real by invoking soul through love; in astrology the planet Neptune which resides in Kether is known as a higher octave of Venus, the Goddess of Love.

What the High Priestess shows us is how to invoke the image by loving it, by our learning right relationship to soul. The ego-Self in Tiphareth has direct access to the archetypal background of existence; we have only to turn our focus there to find image.

The datum with which we begin in archetypal psychology is the image.[24] The constitution of soul is images (The High Priestess) and soul's prime activity is imagining. We find image most natively in our dreams where the dreamer is in the dream and not the other way around. Image does not mean an after-image, the result of sensation and perception, nor does it imply mental constructs symbolic of ideas and feelings which it expresses. The image has no referent beyond itself—image is irreducible. To be visible does not mean that the image has to be seen. We cannot confuse the act of perceiving images with imagining them. An image is not what one sees but the way in which one sees. "An image is given by the imagining perspective and can only be perceived by an act of imagining."[25]

Hillman summarizes Edward Casey who delineates a process of coming to understand image.[26] First, one believes in images as hallucinations or things seen; second, one recognizes them as acts of subjective imagining; and last, one becomes aware that the image is independent of subjectivity and of the imagination itself as mental activity. Images claim reality by their authority, objectivity, and certainty. Hillman writes:

> When "image" is thus transposed from a human representation of its conditions to a sui generis activity of soul in independent presentation of its bare nature, all empirical studies on imagination, dream, fantasy, and the creative process in artists, as well as methods of *reve dirige*, will contribute little to a psychology of the image if they start with the empirics of imagining rather than with the phenomenon of the image—which is not a product of imagining.[27]

In other words, soul engages in imagining because of the image, not vice versa; it is the image that affords imagining.

The implications in therapy, or any work with the image, is that we have to stick to the image as a golden rule. The image as source is complex. Being imaginal it retains a virtuality beyond its actuality:

> An image always seems more profound (archetypal), more powerful (potential), and more beautiful (theophanic) than the comprehension of it, hence the feeling, while recording a dream, of seeing through a glass darkly.[28]

In work with clients we can never forget that we are seeing through a glass darkly, that even as we try to understand the image through dreamwork we are simultaneously limiting its depth and breadth.

The meeting place between client and therapist is the image. As the influence of Kether flows into Tiphareth via The High Priestess, something happens for we must remember that the primal fantasy in Tiphareth, and therefore our postulated ego-Self, is centering. Barbara Kirksey, in her article "Hestia: A Background of Psychological Focusing,"[29] addresses our need for centering.

Kirksey begins her article by describing an event. This is the appearance of an imaginal figure that connects our fantasies to the on-goings of our individual lives. This is no intellectual acquaintance:

> When this occurs, a pattern of images, a certain preference for an imaginal landscape, and a personal random history of images suddenly emerge as "making sense." There is a focusing, and the connection to that figure becomes the occasion of awakening to psychological experience.[30]

The idea of focusing leads Kirksey to the ideas of gathering, weaving together, and centering randomness as resulting from the impact of our encounter with an imaginal figure. Jung wrote much on centering, as his personal history shows, using the image of the mandala, and the concept of the archetype of the Self. Kirksey concludes that, though some recent authors have wanted to rid us of our fantasies of centering, the movement to find a center is not so easily dismissed from the psyche's concerns, and that the desire for centering manifests itself in diverse and insistent ways. This is especially true in a therapy setting, for many times the client is seeking a means by which seemingly random events can have a meaning in their lives.

Kirksey then asks if there exists a style of consciousness that has to do with centering. Examining the Greek myths, one such God-pattern emerges: the Goddess Hestia. Hestia was the eldest of the Olympian Gods, choosing to remain virgin. Hestia was usually represented as a heap of hot coals; and a heap of hot coals at Delphi was known as the *omphalos*, or navel, and was the Greek center of the world. She is therefore associated with centering and focusing.

Hestia had no literal image, indeed her myth resists the taking on of body. She was the fire at the center of both home and shrine. Her temple was round and domed, and Kirksey states that her image is architectural, one of sheltering. Her value to psychological life is her ability to mediate soul by providing a place to congregate, a focus, a gathering point. Kirksey writes:

> And through this point the psyche and world merge. Hestia allows *spaciality* to be a form of *psychological reality.*[31]

The sacred meeting place between client and therapist is precisely this idea of space as psychological reality.

Hestian metaphors are spatial metaphors: "off-base," "off-center," "spaced out," "off the wall." Without Hestia there is no home and consequently no homecoming:

> Without Hestia there can be no focusing on the image, and there are no boundaries to differentiate the intimacy of the inner dwelling and the outer world.[32]

Hestia provides for a cohesive function in the soul, preserving the element of wholeness, and allowing the individual to image in peace.

This need for boundaries is important. When we work with clients it is imperative that the contact with the archetypal realm be given limits, for the ego can never contain the totality of the archetype. Occult traditions caution against the obsessive quality of the image. We help the client create a bounded space, to claim only so much of the archetype as is permissible. This bounded space is necessary for the existence of the ego-Self.

With Hestia consciousness we can focus on the image once we have found a bounded space. To focus is to bring into sharp alignment, and Kirksey reminds us that it is the camera lens that adjusts to what is being photographed; Hestia consciousness teaches us that it is we who must shift in order to see the image clearly. The focus in theater is the part of the stage that is the best illuminated, and Hestia consciousness allows us to illuminate psychological experience. In this regard we can appreciate the Goddess Hecate's torch, as the one who carries this ability to illuminate from dwelling to dwelling, or archetypal structure to archetypal structure. Hestia helps us create the Sanctuary for the image while Hecate guards its entrance. Kirksey leaves us with one final thought: the focus is also the center of the most intense activity and not necessarily a place of harmony or integration. The forms of this *massa confusa* are our pathologies, the psychic storms that demand we move from center stage so that other characters may enter.

Kirksey well describes what hopefully happens initially in a therapy setting that begins and ends with image. The process, continuing the Hestian metaphor is one of circularity, of finding a center in random events once we have activated the path of Gimel. A consciousness residing in the middle ground between ego and archetype, the heart-mind of Tiphareth, creates a home for the images, so that the Hestia consciousness can burn brightly.

The Star
The Path Between Chokmah and Tiphareth

There are varying opinions as to what Tarot trump represents the path of He, the path between Chokmah and Tiphareth. Paul Foster Case and A.E. Waite follow early traditions of assigning to He the figure of The Emporer, but Aleister Crowley saw He as being The Star. I will use Crowley's attribution of He as being The Star. In Waite's deck, The Star is numbered seventeen even though by following Crowley's lead The Star should be numbered four (see illustration 11).

The Star connects Chokmah to Tiphareth. Chokmah if we remember, is the sphere of dynamic energy and Logos as Divine Will; spirit is found here. It is the sphere of Nous. Nous is variously translated as reason, order, intelligibility, and mind.[33] Chokmah as the Father imparts the mind quality of heart-mind to Tiphareth. From Chokmah the ideas contained within the personifications of psyche emerge and the dynamic energy of the archetype is realized. Chokmah is also the sphere of the creative word, and it is on the creative word as used in therapy that we now focus our attention.

Looking at the trump known as The Star we see a naked woman, the Egyptian Goddess Hathor or Mother Nature, the fertile mother. According to Case,[34] she kneels before a pool of water which represents universal consciousness. Universal consciousness

Illustration 11
The Star

is another way of saying the collective unconscious and as all bodies of water flow from the robe of The High Priestess, we can say the pool corresponds to the image producing stratum of the unconscious. We can note that about her shine the stars of the firmament of Chokmah.

The Hebrew letter-name for He means window, and sight is the function attributed to He. Vision, inspection, reconnaissance, watchfulness, care, vigilance, examination, inquiry and investigation are all suggested by the attribution of sight and the letter-name of window. He is known as the Constituting Intelligence. To constitute is to frame, to make up, or to enact as law.

Looking at the trump, the stars shining above the woman in the image of The Star remind me of a saying. It is said that a star shines in the firmament for each individual here on Earth. The fixed stars of Chokmah might then allude to individual allotments, each star representing a quanta of cosmic fate as *daimon*, or ruling intelligence. Through the agency of He, each individual soul experiences its allotment of fate as a *daimon*, or God.

This picture of a ruling intelligence that imparts order and links us to the cosmic sympathy is comforting. This might be another way of describing the archetype. We see the archetypal feminine in The Star trump mediating between Father and Son, Chokmah and Tiphareth. The Divine Will flows into our sphere of the heart-mind by way of soul-images, the pool of The Star as the collective unconscious. The dynamic upwelling of energy contained within the archetype moves us to action, and by acting we give shape to its image.

This comforting picture begins to change when we are compelled by the incessant upwelling of energy of the archetype to act against our conscious wishes; when we are hounded by the fate of our lives, the compulsions and obsessions that will not and cannot be made to go away. We are compelled as the daimon-ic quality of the archetype overwhelms us and indeed becomes a ruling intelligence. Our ruling intelligence no longer seems orderly but chaotic and instead of following we hesitate at the threshold.

We should not forget that in Greek myths the Gods appeared to unwary mortals and overwhelmed them. The pain of being overwhelmed by the Gods as archetypes can be seen in the myth of the hero Orestes. Orestes is commanded by Apollo to kill his mother, who had murdered her husband, his father. The consequence of his obedience to the God is that the Erinyes, the Furies, who avenge mother-right and blood-guilt hound him mercilessly. Driven finally to the Areopagus, the high court of Athens, he is tried by a jury. The jury is to decide his fate. The ballots cast are equal until the Goddess Athena intervenes and persuades the Erinyes to spare Orestes's life. Athena offers a sanctuary to the Erinyes and an alter where these powers may reside and be honored. From hence forth they are known as the Eumenides, or Kindly Ones, and referred to as the "resident aliens."[35]

With Hestia consciousness we found a center. But the center point is also the place of greatest activity. Finding the Gods at the center means we are caught in the web of the Gods; our experience is that of drowning in the pool of The Star. Orestes is caught in the impersonal struggle of cosmic forces. Apollo demands he avenge his father's death, sealing his fate to a certain death at the hands of the Erinyes, or be punished at the hands of Apollo. These daimones wrestle for the fate of his soul. The struggle of Orestes is not a personal one. It is the Gods who wrestle over his fate. The stars in the firmament of The Star point to the multiple consciousness aspect of the collective unconscious. Which star rules, which daimon will have center stage?

Orestes is caught between contrary forces. He is powerless. The only thing he can do is to plead his case. He is caught by the power of the Goddess Necessity. Psychologically, Necessity translates as that area of experience that is unable to be persuaded by or subjected to the rule of mind.[36] This implies a conflict for the heart-mind of Tiphareth. The ego-Self is caught between the order/chaos dichotomy of the image.

The import of the Orestes myth according to Hillman is that through the power of words, Necessity as the Erinyes, is given a rightful place in the cosmic order.[37] They become resident aliens, honored and attended to. The power of words to reconcile the decree of Necessity as the blind compulsion of the archetype is very much utilized in therapy. Freud's talking cure, the analysis, begins to take on an archetypal dimension:

> An analysis repeats the struggles in the soul of Orestes between reason and compulsion, and it repeats the speech of Athene, who persuades to reconciliation by finding place and giving image to the driving necessities. In the mouth of Athene speech

becomes a curative *hymn*, a word which etymologically means "spun" or "woven words."[38]

The dyad of Chokmah resurfaces as the poles of reason and compulsion, and the word becomes the means by which we inspect, care for, examine, watch for, inquire, and investigate—the suggestions of the letter-name window of He.

In Waite's trump, the woman (soul), kneels between two pitchers, equally attentive to both. One pours forth water into the pool of the collective (the archetype) and one pours forth water on the land (the ego). One of the rivulets in the right hand pitcher finds its way back to the pool. There are several suggestions here. First, the ego (the right hand pitcher) must have a connection to the underlying "other" that makes its existence possible; this is the rivulet that finds its way back to the pool. Each individual contributes to the experiences of the collective, giving back a portion of what it has taken. It is a transformed portion—the water flows over the land, bringing with it nutrients from the earth. Second, the woman shows us how to balance ego and archetype: she is equally attentive. This an act of balancing by means of inspection, vigilance, framing, etc. In our therapy work we sit within the creative tensions of the archetype. Out of this tension comes a response, what Jung called the Transcendent Function of the unconscious.[39] This is not a solution, because then we destroy the complexity of the image. What we derive is a right understanding of the image: Who it is, What it wants, How it affects us, Where it is going. There is nothing to be done but wait, as first the fire of focusing (Hestia) burns through us and thence the cooling of the water (The Star) heals us.

This sounds poetic. But to sit with our necessities is a pain not lightly wished upon anyone. We tend to wander like Orestes, hounded, trying first this solution and then another. Finally we come to the high court of our peers, and this too fails us. It is only by appealing to the Gods, the ones who inflict us with our necessities, that we can come to be reconciled.

The process of finding a center and then staying there takes time in the therapeutic journey. We help the client prepare for this by delimiting what is rightfully theirs and what is archetypal. Together we fan the Hestian coals until they glow. From the light of the fire the shadows are illumined and the water of the very real tear is shed; the ultimate libation to the Gods. Together all the tears find their way back to the universal pool of The Star enriched with the salts that allows organic cells to live. This is the heart quality of the heart-mind, which we will examine in our next section.

We see in The Star two levels of conflict portrayed. The first is the realm of the stars, the multiple consciousness aspect of the collective unconscious, different Gods vying for dominance. Once we come to know which God is the ruling intelligence, then we must deal with the archetype's native ambivalence. This is the second level. One of Jung's many contributions was the realization that we do not have to act out all the aspects of the archetype; we do so only as long as we are unaware of what the image demands. Orestes's fate is decided while he is off-stage, but he has stopped running. This is often the case when a client first comes to us. He or she has decided to stop running, to face the Gods. It often happens that a client will appear for only two or three sessions then disappear, not being ready to sit at the center point of greatest activity. And it is not up to us as therapists to decide whether a person stays or leaves. We too must sit and wait off-stage as the Gods engage in rhetoric.

Rhetoric is Athena's power. The Goddess Athena resides in the sphere of Chokmah. She was born fully armored from Zeus's head. She carries the masculine quality of mind. Hillman says of her that she has a connection with the Goddess Necessity: she is the patron Goddess of the arts of pottery and of weaving; also of measuring; she is the creator of the bridle, the yoke, and the harness.[40] Athena has to do with containment and limitation. It is instructive that she was referred to as *Meter*, mother, and what she mothered were the non-religious secular brotherhoods.[41] Hers was the battle cry. She uttered the will of her father.

Utterance, the magic of words, cannot exist if we view the world as materialists, when the world is composed of things. Dead things do not respond to the word. But when the universe is populated with the voices of others, when the powers and principalities and angels are acknowledged then the word creates and destroys reality.

> Through words we can alter reality; we can bring into being and remove from being; we can shape and change the very structure and essence of what is real. The art of speech becomes the primary mode of moving reality.[42]

This is a reminder of the basic premise of the Golden Dawn: through names and images are all powers awakened and reawakened. As therapists, we must know this and be careful of how we use words.

The word is powerful, especially when uttered for the benefit of another's ears. Freud learned that secrets tend to fester. The lance that drains the wound is the shared word. We no longer feel alone. And by uttering the word the pain we feel begins to change. We give voice to the necessities that rule our lives; we build an altar within the soul and honor them.

Hillman also says of Athena that she stands for the idea of normalcy.[43] Athena's normality is objective and collectively defined. Objective is normal and normal is objective. She has a strong connection to the ego: she was a counselor to many heroes. She is the internal mentor. She is the moment when we stop to take counsel with ourselves: "Athene's counsel presents the norms of this world, and its necessities, in close cooperation with the ego's interests."[44] As therapists we must remember that normal and abnormal are equally fantasies, and that what is normal for one may not be normal for another. This is why archetypal psychology is a psychology of values and we must be aware of our own values if we are not to thrust them upon our clients. This becomes more complicated when we keep in mind that each God has its own morality; then we are dealing with three different value systems. The use of the word becomes even more important.

There are two final considerations while we are treading the path of He. These are the functions of reflection and of teaching that as therapists we bring to the therapeutic relationship. The dyad of Chokmah stands for reflection; so too the pool in The Star. We reflect back to the client what is happening. This is vital in most therapies. If we are confused, and our own house is in order, then the confusion probably belongs to the client. We listen to our bodies, our own fantasies. We take on the projections of the client and reflect them back. The therapeutic relationship is one of image meeting image, our images and the client's. We utilize Athena's weaving skills through the use of words and help the client see the pattern of the fabric of their lives. We are centered in our own hearts and our compassion moves us.

We are also teachers. We too take on the curative hymn of Athena, imparting knowledge. We too give counsel to the interests of the ego. We become The Star, poised between ego and archetype, mediating one to the other. Our greatest tool as therapist is our own person, our own self-knowledge. We teach, but in turn are taught. We help find the words of power that unlock the mysteries of the soul. Ours is a logos of psyche; we give word to soul.

The Lovers
The Path Between Binah and Tiphareth

> The healthy or mature or ideal personality will thus show cognizance of its dramatically masked and ambiguous situation. Irony, humor, and compassion will be its hallmarks, since these traits bespeak an awareness of the multiplicity of intentions embodied by any subject at any moment.
> —James Hillman, *Archetypal Psychology*

The power of Athena is the ability to contain conflicting and ambivalent feelings. Through the power of words we maintain ourselves at the center of greatest activity. The multiplicity of soul is given a creative outlet; Athena was a craftsperson. We engage in rhetoric with our clients and mediate the dynamic tensions of the image. We differentiate among various daimones, giving voice to one then to another. Constantly we refocus, moving between Hestia consciousness and Athena consciousness, taking counsel first with image then with ego. But this is not a complete relationship; we have yet to speak about Eros, or the erotic element of our therapy work. Eros represents affects and images afford us with an affective relationship. We need the heart aspect of the heart-mind.

The path between Binah and Tiphareth is the tarot trump of The Lovers (see illus. 12). Binah is the sphere of Eros/love; the ability of the image to love us. Binah corresponds to the fate of the soul as the ruling intelligences of Chokmah take center stage, each in turn. It is the sphere of soul-making. Binah imparts heart to the heart-mind, and the activated heart is the locus of imagining. With Binah our triangle of art is complete and the ego-Self becomes the mature personality able to contain a multiplicity of selves.

Binah brings us to Eros. Eros is synonymous with drive and with Jung's redefinition of libido. Eros appears in the transference, the unconscious projections of the client onto the therapist. Archetypal psychology, residing in the sphere of Binah makes use of Eros in its workings. Hillman writes:

Illustration 12
The Lovers

The imaginal, mythical transposition implies that all erotic phenomena whatsoever, including erotic symptoms, seek psychological consciousness and that all psychic phenomena whatsoever, including neurotic and psychotic symptoms, seek erotic embrace. Wherever psyche is the subject of endeavor or the perspective taken toward events, erotic entanglements will necessarily occur because the mythological tandem necessitates their appearance together.[45]

Hillman adds further that since love of soul is also love of image, then the transference, even its strongest sexualized demonstrations, are a phenomena of the imagination. The transference becomes the means by which literal and personal relations are reconciled with their impersonal and imaginal ground. The tarot trump of The Lovers, connecting the sphere of Binah and Tiphareth, and the myth of the God Hephaestus, will help us to examine Eros and affect as it appears in work with the image.

The Hebrew letter-name of The Lovers is Zain, which means a sword or weapon.[46] Diversity, contrast, antithesis, distinction, discrimination, nice perception, acuteness, sharpness, and sagacity all are suggested. Zain is the Disposing Intelligence and to dispose is to place apart, to arrange, to distribute, to organize, prepare, and adjust. All these suggestions appear not to have a connection with the idea of love as union; the Tarot trump is after all called The Lovers. Something is amiss, and as usual we must search deeper.

The card shows a man and a woman, both naked, standing apart. The man looks to the woman, the woman to the Angel. There is much activity represented, but all is orderly. There is a teleology to this image, a goal, a circular movement. And, for the first time, distinctly human as opposed to archetypal figures appear. Case writes that the man is self-consciousness and the woman subconsciousness, adding further that the relationship between self-consciousness and subconsciousness should be one of loving intimacy; both human figures are naked.

This is clearly a relationship oriented card. The suggestion is of our ego-Self, poised somewhere between conscious and unconscious. We are attentive to image, and image is attentive to us; the Angel as archetype looms large. We can remain within the tension of opposites: consciousness (the man) looks to soul (the woman) and soul brings us to the image (the Angel). Each is distinct, yet related. The focus is sharp.

Right relationship happens because there is proper discrimination. Boundaries remain intact, roles are differentiated. We are not the image, but we relate to it. The roles of the therapist and of the client remain separate and clear. This is the import of The Lovers.

Keeping boundaries intact is not easy, either between therapist and client, or client and archetype. The former of these two relationships is known as transference, and the latter was called by Jung inflation. When a client projects internal unconscious psychic contents onto the therapist we say that a transference has occurred. This was one of Freud's contributions. For Freudians, the therapeutic relationship was not effective unless the transference process happened; one even fosters the transference. Jung saw the transference as unnecessary, a situation that had to be handled with the utmost care when it did happen.[47] Jung was able to realize that the projected contents were archetypal, belonging neither to therapist nor to client. He looked to the images to differentiate the projected contents, and helped the client understand the nature of the projection.[48] In other words, he turned the attention to the Angel in the trump of The Lovers.

Inflation occurs when the individual takes the power of the image as his/her own, when the ego absorbs the energy. Whitmont calls this state one of identity with the archetypal energy;[49] what we have described as the compulsive power of the image. When we are identical with a drive and never question why we are moving or where we are going, when we feel that we are being carried by a tremendous force, when we are blown up by an unknown force that is not our own, not of our own judging and choosing, we are experiencing inflation. We are "swept up," "swept away," "not ourselves," "outside of ourselves." The feeling is one of moving fast, of spinning like a top. Once the dust settles and we take stock we are surprised. We have literally been out of control.

The power of the archetype can also have a creative aspect as we have seen. In the transference, it allows us to give form to image and therefore to the underlying archetypal structure. And since images have a story, we can come to know right relationship to the image. Inflation is another matter. If the client can stop long enough to question the motive force behind his or her actions, then the image can be given form in a different way. Inflation is different than being hounded by our necessities. With inflation we are so unconscious that we simply "act out." Orestes was well aware that his necessities were external to him; they were impersonal forces. One who is possessed by the image usually realizes this after the fact. This is the nature of the image. We are always at all times giving shape to the archetypal structures of psyche; archetypes are fields, ordering our experience. One way of becoming conscious of the archetype is as described by Barbara Kirksey under our section of The High Priestess. Here an imaginal figure orders a random pattern of events. To be possessed by the image is in the nature of things. We therefore use Athena consciousness. Athena consciousness would have us reflect and pause and contain. But what are we to do with the Eros or drive of the image, once contained?

The myth of the God Hephaestus can be of assistance.[50] Hephaestus was the son of the Goddess Hera, wife to Zeus. Hera, angered that Zeus should give birth to Athena without benefit of the feminine, gave birth to Hephaestus to counter this insolence. But something went wrong when she birthed Hephaestus. He was homely and crippled: his feet were on backwards. Enraged, she flung him off Olympus. Succored by nymphs on the island of Lemnos, he grew to adulthood embittered and angry. In his early years Hephaestus showed amazing ability with his hands. He was able to fashion works of art so like nature that no-one could tell the difference. In his anger, he fashioned a wonderful throne which he sent to his mother, the Goddess Hera. Upon sitting down, the throne held her fast and levitated off the ground. Helpless, Hera floated. The God Dionysus retrieved Hephaestus from his home deep in the earth by getting him drunk and brought him to Olympus. He was persuaded to release Hera, but not before he asked for Aphrodite's hand in marriage. The ugliest God was wed to the most beautiful Goddess, a situation that displeased Aphrodite intensely.

Hephaestus was rarely home, however. He spent his time under the earth in his smithy working. Hephaestus was the only Greek God who worked. He was a fringe person, never at the center of activity in Olympus. This suggests that the Eros contained in the image seeks its own gradient of expression; it seeks a new centering which forces us to refocus. Hephaestus was a clown, entertaining the other Gods so that quarrels were quelled. Humor and levity is important in therapy work. Hephaestus was powerful, but nonbelligerent. His keynote was his fire, and he cannot be separated from his fires. His craftsmanship was impeccable. He fashioned the first woman, Pandora, after Zeus ordered him to create her. Pandora was an artifact. Hephaestus's creations resonated to the ground of nature in such a profound way, according to Murray Stein, that there is a kind of confusion between nature and culture, nature and art.[51] His is the creative fires of the Great Mother, and Hephaestus was never far from the feminine ground, the earth, the imaginal realm of the psyche. His craft is one of mimicry and imitation of the feminine creative process.

Hephaestus is the perfect complement to the Goddess Athena. They are both hermaphroditic; Hephaestus is hermaphroditic masculinity and Athena hermaphroditic femininity. They both represent the contrasexual aspect of their single parents, never straying far from the source of their power. Athena is mind and Hephaestus is affect. They are both craftspersons.

Hephaestus represents the creative aspect of the emotions as Athena represents the creative aspect of the word. Once we center in the image, it requires us to work. Hephaestus was a laborer. Therapy work is a labor of love, of carefully attending to and nurturing psyche. Images may be the *a priori* ground of existence, but we must invest time and energy. Hillman writes:

> Although an archetypal image presents itself as impacted with meaning, this is not given simply as a revelation. It must be *made* through "image work" and "dream work."[52]

Hephaestus consciousness is a consciousness that remains close to the feminine imaginal realm. We focus our energies as he did, using the fire of emotions to craft the narrative that is our lives. We use rhetoric or write, dance or sing, sculpt or paint. We dream the dream onwards. The creativity of Hephaestian consciousness is not artificial or contrived. The motive power is the image. The sexuality of Hephaestus is that of the Son/Lover of the Great Mother, an incestuous relationship wherein the energies of the imaginal feminine are made fertile by the unrelenting attention and intensity of the smithy-God.

There are two final aspects of therapy that come to mind when contemplating the path between Binah and Tiphareth. One is the meaning that we help the client make from the image as Hillman states. The second, is the ability to care that comes from the therapist, the compassion of the heart-mind. The therapist invests his or her own Eros to the work at hand, caring for and nurturing the unfolding creative process within the therapeutic relationship. Together client and therapist make meaning of and find love for the never ending images of psyche.

Our goal has been the creation of the mature personality as viewed from a therapy that gives primacy to the image. We center in the heart-mind of Tiphareth. This process is a creative one fraught with any number of difficulties for the client and the therapist. The nature of the image requires many qualities from us as therapists: the ability to reflect, the ability to teach, the ability to impart meaning and the ability to care. Our goal, if there is one, is to "stick to the image." Over and above, down and under, left to right, we follow the image where it leads. We have as our locus of activity the middle ground where ego and archetype meet. This place of centering, of greatest activity, is represented by the mountain in the trump of The Lovers that is pictured behind and between man and woman. We utilize the God-consciousnesses of Hestia, Athene, and Hephaestus; centering, voicing, and feeling the contents of the image as given by psyche. We help the client to dream the dream onwards and to realize the dream. We help the client become Real.

CHAPTER FIVE

Through The Gate

The soul sees by means of affliction. Those who are the most dependent upon the imagination for their work—poets, painters, fantasts—have not wanted their pathologizing degraded into the "unconscious" and subjected to clinical literalism .... The crazy artist, the daft poet and mad professor are neither romantic cliches nor antibourgeois postures. They are metaphors for the intimate relation between pathologizing and imagination. Pathologizing processes are a source of imaginative work, and the work provides a container for the pathologizing processes.
        —James Hillman, *Re-Visioning Psychology*

Our final chapter is titled "Through the Gate" because Malkuth, the sphere of the Daughter to which our last chapter belongs, is referred to in Qabalistic tradition as The Gate, The Gate of Death, The Gate of the Shadow of Death, and The Gate of Tears,[1] implying, as Hillman suggests,[2] that death is the ultimate metaphor of the soul. I have suggested that the pathologizing activity of soul belongs to the sphere of Malkuth. Pathologizing means to find death—to decay, to fall apart, to dissolve. Pathologizing also implies the archetypal experiences of hatred when we tear something apart and is the guilt we feel when we are "sick."[3]

Psychopathology has to do with the initiation of the individual into life through the fantasies that soul weaves around its afflictions. These are the singular moments of despair, decay, and decomposition in a life: the death of a loved one; the death of an idea; the death of an emotion; the death of an aspiration; the death of an intimate relationship; or the death of an illusion. These are but a few examples, for death exists all around us in the manifest world.

155

The archetypal structure of Death resides deep within the soul as well. This means that images have the potential to destroy as well as to build. Building (life) and destroying (death) are the complementary movements of the image that give rise to the creative activity of soul.

Image, soul, pathologizing, and creative activity follow one after the other. For soul, movement is all important. There are no summits, as spirit would have us find, no ultimates, no absolutes, all of which imply rest; for soul there is no rest because everything is relative. Even the landmark that we rely upon in our dream changes; the mountain of our dream is really a dragon asleep who wakes and disappears. When we are in the realm of soul, person responds to person, image interacts with image, dreams court life, life provides fuel for soul's activities, soul dialogues with us through its afflictions, and our afflictions lend power to our creativity.

I am stating the case for a description of soul as "eternally going." The sphere of Malkuth is the sphere of the four elements. Four is the number of concrete manifestation. When we evoke into the triangle of art, as we did in Chapter Four, we make manifest what is invisible, but once our attention wanes, so too does the apparition. According to Western magic, whatever becomes manifest on the material plane through the archetype of the number four must, by natural law, die, and in dying give rise to a new birth. Four is therefore the number of the *potential for going*, the idea that in every death there is a future seed of life. This fantasy of movement is found in Egyptian depictions of the Gods who are usually shown grasping the ankh, or Egyptian cross, that symbolizes love, life, and eternity. This is how the early Egyptians made reference to the eternal going of the Gods. The ankh was the (literal) key to eternity. It is in the nature of the Gods to go, to move in eternal dances through the landscapes of the soul. The Gods tell us of the soul's going.

Four as the number archetype of Malkuth is seen in Hillman's four activities in a psychology of soul and in the four Qabalistic qualities of the elements known as Father, Mother, Son, and Daughter. The archetype of the number four implies completion or stasis. The alchemists spoke of the squaring of the circle, so that stasis or equilibrium (the square) and movement (the circle) complemented each other. The squaring of the circle alludes to balanced motion. Balanced motion is Malkuth as the Earth, and we can remember here that the symbol for the planet and element of Earth is a circle with a an equal-armed cross within it. What the symbols of Western magic suggest, what the alchemists alluded to, and what I see within Hillman's four activities of the soul, is that balanced motion is an archetypal experience. Balanced motion, is the result of the "four" interacting within the circle—whatever the "four" might be, whether the four elements or Hillman's four activities of soul. Balanced motion however, does not mean we live without struggle, and it certainly does not imply a world without Death.

There are many definitions for the word balance, and most imply a movement towards equilibrium. But the "four" interacting within the circle can never reach total equilibrium, for stagnation and not creation would be the result. One definition of balance that I prefer is: "To move toward and then away from one's dance partner."[4] If we fantasize that an individual's dance partner through life is soul, then we have a feel for the balanced motion between ego and archetype, including the pathologies that come with images.

The Western fear of death and of the psychopathologies of soul make us inert as individuals. To be inert is to be totally unreactive, a condition of the Western man and woman that has been addressed variously by social scientists, artists, and politicians, among others. The denial of death is also the denial of soul. This is unfortunate because if we listen attentively soul teaches us that we are not alone, that we are loved by it's images and that death is essential if there is to be life. This is no glib statement and cannot be understood with words. We must first desire to become Real, we must first desire to grasp the ankh which is the eternity of the Gods. The ankh implies eternity, but only as long as we realize that eternity is not even conceivable without the reality of death. To dance with soul means that we are responsive, that we cannot remain inert; we are forced to rediscover what the meaning of death is really about.

The images that are the structures within soul bring with them death. The metaphor of death is a valid means of gaining knowledge for the soul.[5] The little deaths that are found in the pathologizings of soul are creative; all four activities of soul are creative. It follows, then, that images as the structures within soul, are creative. Images represent balanced motion, even when they bring us decay, even when what they offer us is a way of falling apart.

The creative process of soul was given a form in our fourth chapter of the heart-mind. Chapter Four, like the whole of this written work, are the creative processes of my soul, the movements to find a center point for my imaginings and the way these reflect my philosophy of the therapeutic process. One of the figures attributed to Malkuth is the circle. On the circle there is no beginning point or ending point, and all points on the circumference of the circle are equidistant from the center. We all must begin the journey of soul-making from somewhere on the circle and every point of initiation on the circle is equally valid.

Western magic teaches us that there are two equal and complementary movements on the Tree of Life. The influences of the Supernals descend across the Abyss, bringing to us the experience of grace that is centered in the heart-mind of Tiphareth. Equally important is the initiatory journey of the soul that begins in Malkuth. The soul strives upwards to find a center in Tiphareth. Kether is in Malkuth and Malkuth is in Kether after another manner; this is an axiom of Western magic. If Kether is the point and Malkuth the circumference then together they describe the mathematics of the circle and together they absorb the whole of the symbolism of the Tree. The Romantics expressed this union of Kether and Malkuth differently, by saying that the individual soul is also the world soul.

This final chapter will be succinct. I wish to present a case story to illustrate all of the concepts that we have explored, concepts that have to do with soul-making and the pathologizings of soul. I purposely have not included conclusions to this case story for to do this is to rob the images of their power. Hillman warns us that to identify our behaviors with God-images and then dismiss the Gods as understood is an injustice perpetrated against the images.[6] We simply replace one ego means of classification with another means of classification. Having stated that we cannot take images literally, we can begin to empathize with one starting point upon the circumference of the circle, the case story of Michael.

Michael: A Case Story

Before we can enter into the valley of soul-making, we must first find the Gate; the circle may have infinite points for a beginning, but there is only one Gate which is Death. The reasons that lead us to the Gate are many: sometimes we come to the Gate out of exhaustion, like the wandering Orestes; sometimes we are dragged to the Gate by the threats of loss of one's sanity or one's significant others; sometimes we seek the Gate out of spiritual aridity. Whatever the reason, we stand before the Gate. And how painful is the realization that this is just the beginning! We must cross the Gate into the valley of soul-making, we must prepare to shed the very real tear.

This preparation for the journey into soul-making is seen in the following dream images of Michael, who will provide us with the case story that is the centering point of this chapter. In this dream there is a suggestion that the journey will be one of travel by means of a boat. The unconscious is many times represented by bodies of water, the ocean being a common motif.

> Boston? I am helping my grandfather who is a small, dark, Italian man. I bring him metal hooks to help him repair and or make a new boat. At the moment, the boat's bottom is uppermost and the old man is waterproofing it with tar and pitch. I must help him because my father refuses, as he has lost touch with his ethnic roots and is a lawyer in Boston. The boat we are repairing is the same boat in an earlier dream this night. In the earlier dream, a small boat, with a torn out bottom lay upside-down in the shallows of a beach. There were many men and we needed to get the boat. A young man, handsome and strong, volunteers to retrieve the boat. He undresses and dives into the surf and recovers the boat.

Michael is in his early thirties. He underwent Jungian therapy several years ago and kept recorded all of the material generated from his eighteen months of therapy. Our agreed upon work together was to re-examine all the materials, his dreams and his sketches, looking for the God-images which he felt strongly influenced his work and his psychology. Our goal together was to bring into sharp focus the archetypal structures that have influenced his life.

We began by each of us assuming a task. I generated a copy of his birth chart and studied it while Michael read Jean Shinoda Bolen's *Gods in Everyman*. I set out to identify the possible subpersonalities and archetypal structures that might be alluded to in his chart, and he was to find which of the God-patterns he most identified with his psychology. I also went through his sketches and his journals looking to find evidence of the God-images that might be found there. What I present now is the result of our work together. This narrative stands on its own merits, as it is a story, and a story in images has no right or wrong, only immediacy of experience.

The Birth Chart

Michael's birth chart is rather complex (see chart 4). We see that the ten planets are widely distributed throughout the wheel. The planets occupy eight of the twelve houses and eight of the twelve signs. The total planetary distribution is difficult to identify as it has aspects of the locomotive type, the splay type, and the splash type.[7] The locomotive type represents a personality that moves through life with focused energy. Michael's locomotive configuration has Mercury as the leading planet which implies someone who initiates new activities using the mind first and foremost. The splay type indicates that the planets do not form any kind of recognizable pattern and that the personality tends to push out into life along very definite lines; a glove with its five fingers each moving in a different direction is an analogy for the splay type. The splash type indicates a personality with a universal outlook, a personality capable of appreciating the varieties of life experiences.

The planets, when we view aspects, are all involved in configurations of one type or another (illus. 13). A chart with these many aspects, or planetary relationships, indicates a personality that is both fragmented and synthetic. There are many archetypal structures vying for center stage within the personality and as the person matures and comes to understand the many voices within, a synthesis can occur. Astrologers believe that it takes the first thirty years of life for the chart patterns to become manifest in a person's life. This means that the God-patterns manifest themselves over time. In a chart such as Michael's there is indicated the pain of Orestes, as each God-pattern gains ascendency within the life, struggling with the other *daimones*. Each God-pattern takes center stage for a turn, until they give way to the next God.

The first step is to identify planetary groupings, and the second step is to find the possible archetypal structures within these planetary groupings. One planetary grouping that can be seen in Michael's chart is the T-square configuration (see illus. 14). Here the Sun is opposite Neptune, square the Ascendent, and square to Uranus. A T-square configuration indicates that a large amount of energy is generated because the planets, and therefore the archetypal structures, are in mutual conflict. The personality experiences an inordinate amount of internal tension when the configuration is activated. In Michael's case the Sun, the center point for the chart and a man's identification of his masculinity, is opposed by Neptune,

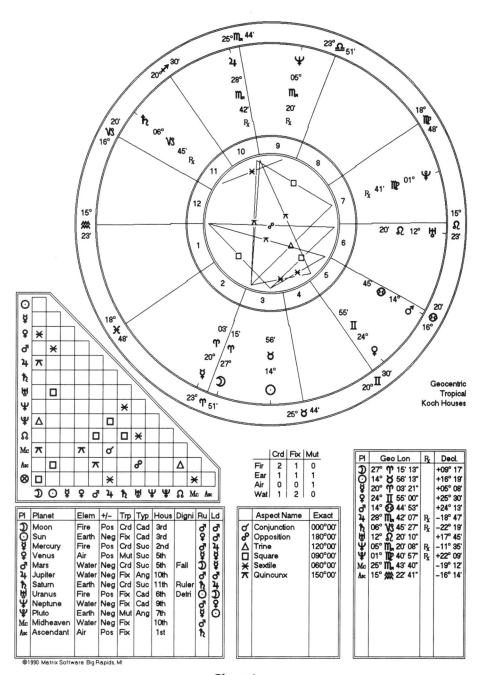

	Crd	Fix	Mut
Fir	2	1	0
Ear	1	1	1
Air	0	0	1
Wat	1	2	0

Pl	Geo Lon	Rx	Decl.
☽	27° ♈ 15' 13"		+09° 17
☉	14° ♉ 56' 13"		+16° 19'
☿	20° ♈ 03' 21"		+05° 08'
♀	24° ♊ 55' 00"		+25° 30'
♂	14° ♋ 44' 53"		+24° 13'
♃	28° ♏ 42' 07"	Rx	−18° 47
♄	06° ♑ 45' 27"	Rx	−22° 19
♅	12° ♌ 20' 10"		+17° 45'
♆	05° ♏ 20' 08"	Rx	−11° 35'
♇	01° ♍ 40' 57"	Rx	+22° 09'
Mc	25° ♏ 43' 40"		−19° 12'
Asc	15° ♒ 22' 41"		−16° 14'

	Aspect Name	Exact
☌	Conjunction	000°00'
☍	Opposition	180°00'
△	Trine	120°00'
□	Square	090°00'
⚹	Sextile	060°00'
⚻	Quincunx	150°00'

Pl	Planet	Elem	+/−	Trp	Typ	Hous	Digni	Ru	Ld
☽	Moon	Fire	Pos	Crd	Cad	3rd			
☉	Sun	Earth	Neg	Fix	Cad	3rd			
☿	Mercury	Fire	Pos	Crd	Suc	2nd			
♀	Venus	Air	Pos	Mut	Suc	5th			
♂	Mars	Water	Neg	Crd	Suc	5th	Fall		
♃	Jupiter	Water	Neg	Fix	Ang	10th			
♄	Saturn	Earth	Neg	Crd	Suc	11th	Ruler		
♅	Uranus	Fire	Pos	Fix	Cad	6th	Detri		
♆	Neptune	Water	Neg	Fix	Cad	9th			
♇	Pluto	Earth	Neg	Mut	Ang	7th			
Mc	Midheaven	Water	Neg	Fix		10th			
Asc	Ascendant	Air	Pos	Fix		1st			

©1990 Matrix Software Big Rapids, MI

Chart 4
Michael

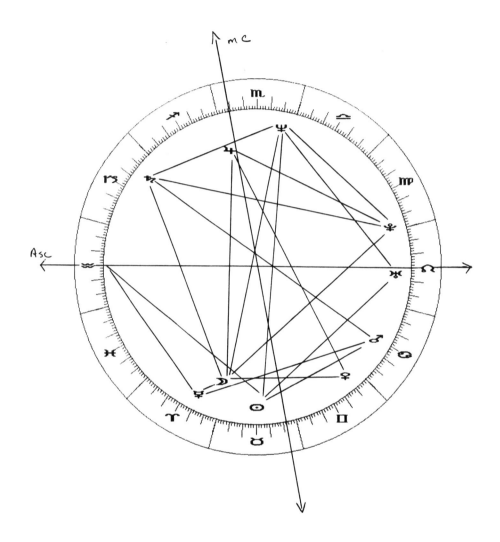

Illustration 13
Michael's Planetary
Configurations

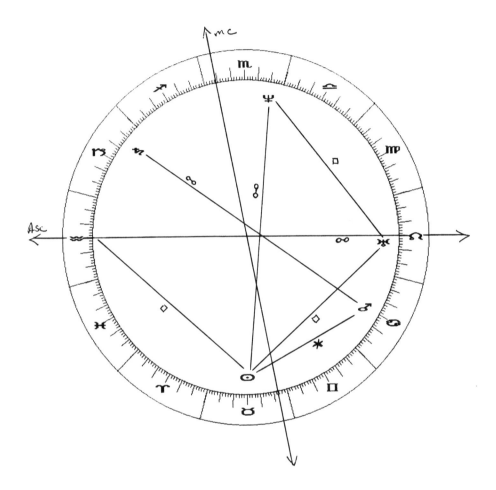

Illustration 14
Michael's T-Square

while Uranus is in square aspect to both.

What I look for are the possible archetypal structures that color Michael's sense of self through his Sun sign, which is Taurus. The Taurus archetype has a strong affinity to Venus, its ruler, and the Moon, the planet exalted in Taurus; these are essentially archetypally feminine energies. Neptune as a planetary energy is also feminine.

Neptune aspecting the Sun gives us the potential for what Sasportas calls the Mystic Type who seeks escape from the mundane aspects of life. We need to search deeper for the possible God-pattern or archetype of the mystic. Liz Greene suggests that within the Neptunian urge for self-transcendence we can find Dionysus:

> There is a breath of Dionysian madness in Neptune although he is generally masked by a mild and self-sacrificing quality. The moment of ecstasy is the moment of self-transcendence, and the individual experiences one of those rare flashes of oneness with life which is called the mystical vision. This is a deeply personal experience which is perfectly real to those who have experienced it and perfectly meaningless to those who have not.[8]

Uranus is in relationship to the Sun through the mentioned T-square configuration. This suggests a totally different energy value than Neptune. Neptune, representing the collective unconscious is feminine. Uranus is essentially a masculine archetypal structure. Uranus is in conflictual relationship not only to the Sun, but also to Neptune. Sasportas feels that a strong Uranus influence indicates a Will Type or a Change Type. The Change Type in particular, driven by the need for progress and transformation, suggests a possible archetypal structure coloring Michael's Sun, his center of personality. This is the *puer aeternus*, the eternal youth. Mercury as the leading planet in the locomotive type configuration, combined with the heavenward focus of Uranus, and Uranus's home sign of Aquarius on the Ascendent (labeled "A" in illus. 14), would suggest that the puer quality is very strong within Michael's personality.

The puer fears the embrace of life's responsibilities. The story character of Peter Pan who did not want to grow up illustrates the possibility that a man will remain essentially an adolescent personality all his life. The puer as image has a positive side as well; it represents the possibility for newness, for beginnings, for a fresh perspective to life. The puer is always on the lookout for the new opportunity, brings to us the flash of insight, and blesses us with the joy of discovering new things.

The T-square tells us that Michael experiences moments of "drowning" in the unconscious (the planet Neptune and the God-pattern of Dionysus), while simultaneously struggling to remain airborne which is the puer archetype (the planet Uranus and the planet Mercury). At one moment he is swallowed up by his emotions; the next moment he is speeding along, moving very fast, for both Mercury and Uranus are quick and facile God-patterns. There is a suggestion here of movement between elation and depression which is supported by a sextile, or flowing aspect, between Sun and Mars. Mars represents the principle of initiative and of physical vitality. Mars supportive of the T-square means that when Michael's internal tensions require action, he moves quickly, whether to the depths or the heights.

Looking again at illustration 14, we see three-quarters of a square formed by the Ascendent, the Sun, Uranus, and Neptune. Mars is supportive of the Sun, but is himself opposed by Saturn. All the energies of the T-square become directed via Sun to Mars to Saturn. Saturn is in his home sign of Capricorn. A strong Saturn and Capricorn emphasis indicate the Pragmatist Type and the Maintenance Type according to Sasportas. These types are conventional, stubborn, maintain the status quo and are too down to earth, i.e., they lack vision. The archetypal structure here is that of the *senex*, the old man. The senex is the complement of the puer. The puer is the beginning, the senex the end. The puer is the spark of spirit, the senex the constriction of matter. The puer is eternity, the senex is time. The puer is anarchy, the senex is agreed upon social customs. Together, puer and senex represent two poles of one archetypal structure.

Saturn as senex leads us to a second planetary configuration. This is the kite pattern (see illus. 15). The kite is formed by Saturn, Neptune, Pluto, and the Moon. Saturn, Pluto, and the Moon form a grand trine or triangle. Trines are spoken of as flowing aspects, while squares are conflictual; however, aspects between planets are colored by the planets involved as well as by the quality of the aspect. In the kite, the Moon is opposite Neptune and part of the grand trine; the Moon therefore is the focal determinator in the kite figure. This kite pattern, combining the earth element, the Moon, Pluto, Saturn, and Neptune, would indicate archetypal God-patterns of a subterranean nature, i.e., of chthonic, unconscious energy patterns.

I would suggest here Dionysus, Hades, and Hephaestus. The Moon as the planet of the ability to perceive images would suggest someone who can gain access to the images in a very deep-seated emotional way, "from the gut," to use a colloquialism. Both the Sun and Moon in Michael's chart have relationships to planets that represent aspects of the collective unconscious: Saturn, Uranus, Neptune, and Pluto.

This a short synopsis. The central idea is that Michael has many archetypal God-patterns operating through his personality structure. The Moon being focal, he has the ability to bring into consciousness the images of the collective unconscious. Implied here is a struggle between day forces (the planets in the T-square) and night forces (the planets in the kite). This is the struggle between consciousness (day forces) and the unconscious (night forces); the struggle of the ego to remain separate from, and not be absorbed by, the archetype. There is a general conflict for Michael between wanting to remain the puer in the realm of the Sky, the realm of the Father; and wanting to be baptized in the waters of the unconscious, the Underworld of the Mother. In whatever direction he moves, the senex aspect of Saturn as the planet that unites both T-square and kite requires a practical and concrete result.

The God-patterns

After meditating on Michael's chart, I developed the following possibilities of archetypal structures: the puer/senex polarity, Hermes, Dionysus, Hades, Hephaestus, and a strong feminine lunar archetypal structure. The influence of Luna in Michael's chart I left open-ended until I examined his dreams, for as I pointed out in Chapter One, Luna is a complex image to understand. Overall, the pulls between light and darkness, day and night, feminine and masculine, are evident in his two planetary groupings. This conflict is seen in one of Michael's dreams:

> I am flying away from a young woman, a powerful lady. She has light skin and long dark hair and she reminds me of a Gypsy woman. She is furious with me and I am in danger. This is why I decide to fly for flying is the only way that I can stay out of her reach. As I fly away, just above and in front of her, I turn and say in a heartfelt way, "I am sorry." I get the sense that I must not confront this Lady alone. I need to find X [Michael's therapist].

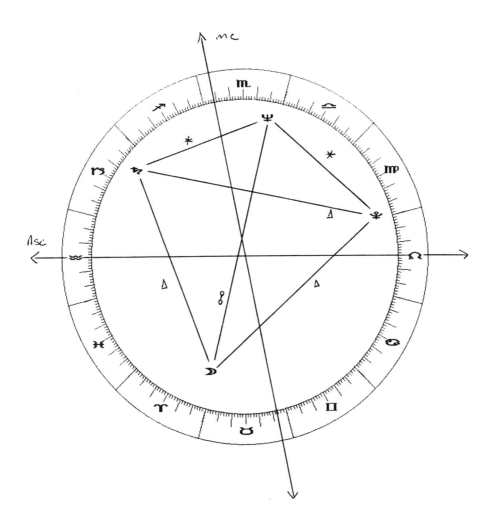

Illustration 15
Michael's Kite

The archetypal drama operating within this dream seems to be that of the puer (Michael flying) struggling to remain without the embrace of soul (the Gypsy woman). Hillman writes about the relationship between puer and soul, a theme strongly indicated by Michael's chart and the above dream:

> It [puer] can search and risk; it has insight, aesthetic intuition, spiritual ambition—all, but not psychology, for psychology requires time, femininity of soul, and the entanglement of relationships .... The puer in any complex gives it its drive and drivenness, makes it move too fast, want too much, go too far, not only because of the oral hunger and omnipotence fantasies of the childish, but archetypally because the world can never satisfy the demands of spirit or match its beauty. Hungering for eternal experience makes one a consumer of profane events.[9]

This conflict between the Sky and the Underworld is consistent throughout Michael's journals and sketches, and it is important to keep this in mind as we proceed.

Michael identified the following God-patterns as consistent with his psychology: Hades, Hermes, Ares, Hephaestus, and Dionysus. To this list I added the archetypal feminine as indicated by the strong lunar emphasis in the chart. Let us examine briefly these archetypal God-patterns, beginning with Hades.

Greek mythology tells us that after the Olympians fought with the Titans, the three brothers Zeus, Poseidon, and Hades drew lots for the rulerships of Heaven, Ocean, and Underworld. Zeus retained rulership of Heaven and Earth, Poseiden received the Ocean as his home, and Hades won rulership of the Underworld. Hades was greatly feared by Gods and humans alike. He made appearances only twice in Greek myth. The first time was to seek a wife, Persephone, whom he abducted and took to the Underworld. The second time he left the Underworld was to nurse the wound inflicted by Heracles; he went to Olympus to be healed.

Hades is the name given to the God and to the domain he ruled, the Underworld. Hades as a place represents the world of images, the unconscious. Hades as a God had no images, he was known as the invisible one. He fathered no children. He was a violent God, taking what he wanted.

The Hades personality is a recluse, a loner, mostly concerned with subjective experiences and perceptions; this is known as introversion. An introverted person tends to value subjective inner dynamics over outer objective events. This can be a liability, as objective reality can be distorted by one's inner responses. On the positive side, the introvert can be in touch with soul's inner images, and can take counsel from soul's subjectivizing activity. The Hades person is aware of the subjective subtleties of a situation. This ability to know subjective experience can be a source of creativity, for images find their way into this subjective realm.

Hades as a place indicates the archetype of the descent, for only by descending can we find the Underworld. The archetype of the descent is sometimes accompanied by the experience of depression, when our psychic energies seek a gradient of movement downwards. Depression as a manifestation of the descent can bring us to the shadow side of our personality.

The shadow is the archetypal structure for the repressed contents of the psyche. As an archetype, the shadow is the center of Jung's concept of the personal unconscious. The personal unconscious also contains the positive potential of the personality making its way to consciousness; it is here that contents from the collective unconscious, that have never been conscious, first appear. Our sense of inferiority is contained in the shadow realm, and the Hades personality may be identified with these feelings of inferiority.

The poles of the Hades personality are many. On the one hand, the Hades person is aware of subjective experience, or images. These are the inner voices, the intuitive reactions, and the dreams of psyche. The Hades person can take counsel from soul's images and can be creative with these images. On the other hand, the Hades person may distort the reality around him, may tend to be depressed and cut off from his emotions, may be isolated from his peers, and can have poorly developed social skills. Bolen suggests that the God- pattern of Hermes can be helpful for the Hades personality. The Hades man who has activated the Hermes God-pattern can descend to the world of images at will without becoming a prisoner of his own subjectivity.[10]

This brings us to elaborate on the God-pattern of Hermes. Hermes was the winged messenger of the Gods. He was the youngest son of Zeus and carried out his father's wishes. He is usually depicted as eternally youthful, wearing the cap of invisibility, and wearing sandals with wings. He carried the caduceus, or wand. This wand had twin serpents entwined about it with two wings at the top. The caduceus was a kind of magic wand that attested to his sovereignty as messenger and as a guide of souls. Hermes was the guide of souls to the Underworld after a person died. He could travel all realms at will. Hermes was thus identified with the realm of the Sky as well as the realm of the Underworld. He was a mediator between high and low, the crosser of boundaries

Hermes represents quickness of movement, agility of mind, and facileness of word. He can shift levels easily. The Hermes personality is a good communicator; he is a consumate traveler, if not of space then of the mind. Hermes was also known as the God of Thieves; as such he is the con-man with questionable morality, for the Hermes personality does not necessarily question the rightness or wrongness of his or others' behaviors. The Hermes personality shares with the God the ability to shift levels; Hermes as Guide ruled the liminal or transitional spaces of life experience. Hermes was present in the mythology of the other Gods and of heroes during the times of significant rites of passage.

The negative manifestation of this God-pattern shares the qualities of the puer. There is impulsiveness of action and a certain lack of the reality of limits. At its worst, the Hermes personality shows traits of the sociopath who never questions the morality of a given behavior. There can also be a lack of emotional commitment and intimacy. Hermes is always on the move and the man who manifests him is often described as difficult to "pin down."[11]

The third God-pattern identified by Michael was the God Ares. Bolen[12] makes reference to Ares as the Warrior, the Dancer, and the Lover. This is in reference to the God's passionate nature, shown by Ares being the God of War. Ares was usually depicted in full battle armour including sword and spear. He was the only son of Zeus and Hera and was the least liked by the other Olympians. Zeus especially, valuing the use of the intellect, scorned Ares, for Ares the God represented emotionality, masculine physical power, intensity, and immediate action. Ares acted and reacted from his heart and from his instincts; he used his body and was unmindful of the consequences of his actions.

Ares above all else represents physicality. Ares was originally trained as a perfect dancer and reminds us that in tribal cultures the warriors are also the dancers. The Ares personality is in touch with his body and with his emotions, especially anger and rage. The positive Ares attributes, therefore, are the ability to take initiative, and the kind of creativity that is given body, literally, as in dance. The interactions of the body, instinct, and emotion is given value by the Ares God-pattern.

On the negative side, the Ares man may become the abused abuser. Ares was often the scapegoat for Zeus's negative valution of him and the other Gods followed his lead. Being the scapegoat on Olympus, Ares personifies the cycle of the abused child that reaches adulthood and in turn abuses others. The Ares physicality turns into self and other abuse through the vehicle of the body. The emotional scars of the rejected son find their expression through the passion of the body, and in Olympus, like in our own culture, someone who acts from instinct as opposed to reason is found suspect. We can, in retrospect, understand how the Greek mind obsessed with the aesthetics of things, would find the God Ares a dissonant image: Ares, who shouting from his chariot and accompanied by his sons Fear and Panic, enjoined the battle, delighting in bloodshed.[13]

Michael's fourth choice was the God Hephaestus. Hephaestus shares with Ares the description of the rejected son, for Zeus intensely disliked Hephaestus. As we explored in Chapter Four, Hephaestus the God was a loner, like Hades. He was content to remain in his workshop fashioning objects that were both beautiful and functional. He was an outcast, a fringe person who harbored the wounds of faulty parenting.

The Hephaestus man tends to be silent about what he feels. His passions are hidden. The God was an unsuccessful lover, and Bolen suggests that the disappointments of unrequited love fuel the creative fires of the Hephaestus man. Unrequited love is in keeping with the emotional wounding that the Hephaestus man guards deep within him. It is of paramount importance for the Hephaestus man to find a medium for his creativity, for then the fires of emotional wounds are given an outlet. The Hephaestus God-pattern also contains the feelings of low self-esteem and inadequacy: Hephaestus was rejected by both parents and by his wife Aphrodite, who preferred to have an affair with Ares. He was a social outcast who had few successes in the world of the Olympians. His physical deformity was a literal reference to his emotional wounds.[14]

One of the positive aspects of the Hephaestus personality is the ability to create from the basic stuff of unconscious life: instincts and archetypes. The Hephaestus energy pattern requires that emotions and images be given plastic form. It can also suggest the Wounded Healer archetype, the process of which is described by Bolen:

> Hephaestus the craftsman is very much like the wounded healer whose motivation to heal comes from himself having been wounded, and whose wound heals as he heals others .... He couldn't be beautiful, so he made beauty .... Through his work, Hephaestus and men (and women) like him can see themselves reflected intact and functioning; through this reflection flows self-esteem and self-respect as well as the respect and esteem of others. Thus are healed the wounds that motivated the work.[15]

The last God-pattern identified by Michael was the God Dionysus. The mythos of Dionysus is rather complex, having many levels. His story is dramatic. Dionysus was the youngest Olympian. His mother Semele was mortal and beloved by the God Zeus. Hera, jealous of Zeus's affair with Semele, determined to bring about the death of Semele who was pregnant with Zeus's child, the God Dionysus. Hera appeared to Semele in the form of her aged nurse, and persuaded Semele to make sure of Zeus's divinity by insisting that he appear to her in all his divine glory. When Zeus next visited, Semele requested a favor from Zeus which he swore to grant by the river Styx, an oath that was irrevocable for any God once made. Zeus had no other alternative but to appear to Semele in all his divine glory which resulted in her death. At the moment of Semele's death, Zeus took Dionysus from his mother's womb and sewed him into his own thigh, which served to protect Dionysus until he was born.

Dionysus then was taken to Semele's sister who raised the God disguised as a girl to hide him from Hera. Hera soon found out, drove his caretakers mad, and they attempted to murder him. Zeus interceded again, saving the young God and finding new nurse-maids for him. As he grew, Dionysus was tutored by the God Silenus, who taught him the secrets of Nature and the making of wine.

The worshipers of Dionysus were predominantly women. They sought the God in the wildest parts of the mountains, where they consumed wine and engaged in the invocation of the God that included frenzied music and rhythmic dances. The God then possessed the women, and at the height of the ceremonies a sacrificial animal was torn to pieces and eaten raw as a sacrament. This description of the worship of Dionysus brings into sharp focus the God's mythos as being intertwined with the themes of life and death, and of the central role of ecstatic experiences for his worshipers.

Dionysus was very close to Nature. He was comfortable with the realm of the feminine and the realm of the mystical. As a God-pattern he indicates the ability to experience both the most ethereal and the basest of human feelings. More than any other God, he stands for the tension of opposites. Dionysus mediates between two worlds—the invisible world and the visible world. His is a psychological androgyny, the ability to feel the polarity of masculine and feminine within the same personality. Dionysus, when present, brings with him both beauty and fatal danger.[16]

There are overlaps of the Dionysian God-pattern with other archetypal images. Like Hermes he is the divine child within us; he is also the eternal adolescent. These are images of the puer. As a psychological process he also represents the archetypal experience of dismemberment. Hillman writes:

> Dionysus was called *Lysios*, the loosener. The word is cognate with *lysis*, the last syllables of *analysis*. *Lysis* means loosening, setting free, deliverance, dissolution, collapse, breaking bonds and laws, and the final unraveling as of a plot in tragegy.[17]

Dionysus has to do with the lowering of consciousness to the archetypal level, the twilight zone described in our fourth chapter.[18] This lowering of consciousness is seen in psychosis, and the Dionysus God-pattern predisposes a man to live the dismemberment experience; in this myth dismemberment is the prerequisite for gaining access to the world of the unconscious.

The five God-patterns as identified by Michael are Hades, Hermes, Ares, Hephaestus, and Dionysus. We can guess that with so many God-patterns there is an initial fragmentation of the personality structure, as the various God-patterns vie for center stage. What is consistent with all the God-patterns recognized by Michael is that the patterns (except, in certain instances, Hermes) are all patterns of behavior that are devalued in our current patriarchal culture.

The pain of being an outcast, including the motif of the Wounded Healer, is shown by the following entry in one of Michael's journals:

In the past month I have been walking around looking and analyzing what I see. I have always, always, always fought tooth and nail against being a collective man. Play by no-one else's rules. Run, run, run from the collective. Weed, till, plant seeds in my garden and watch them grow. Guard the seeds of your labor from the collective, they do not understand and would grind the seeds into collective fodder without saving one kernel to sprout again. I have been afraid. I have cried and been overwhelmed by my own sorrows and the pain of others. I have healed others when possible; performed surgery when necessary. Given because it is right. Taken because I found no other way. Always assuming that what was human about me was human in everyone else. I thought that if I could heal myself, *he* might heal himself; if I understood, *she* too could understand. Of course this is a limited view.

I have run from the collective man because he is a beast. Maybe collective man is a beast. I cannot say for certain. But the collective man within me never had chance. Until the age of twelve any attempts to reach out and trust were met by betrayal. To be a collective man one needs to trust enough to belong.

The Sketches

Michael's sketches are numbered sequentially one to six, in chronological order, from earliest to most recent (illustrations 16 to 21). The time span is February 1984 to November 1988. The pencil drawings were photocopied and do not fully reflect the original subtlety of the sketches. Having described the identified God-patterns, we can look at the drawings and end the case story with Michael's dream images. Images simply are, as in dreams. Michael and I viewed the sketches together, and the following descriptions include his additions to the images.

The illustration labeled "Michael 1: Image of the Puer" shows a blond youth reaching towards a serpent atop a column. The youth has a wing attached at the ankle. This is reminiscent of Hermes, who is a God-image of the puer. The youth in the drawing is standing firmly on the ground, fascinated by the serpent that seems to be just out of reach.

The sketch labeled "Michael 2: Image of Dismemberment" was drawn in the same month as that of "Michael 1." This drawing shows the face of a man in agony, his dismembered body above the

Illustration 16
Michael 1: Image of the
Puer

Illustration 17
Michael 2: Image of Dismemberment

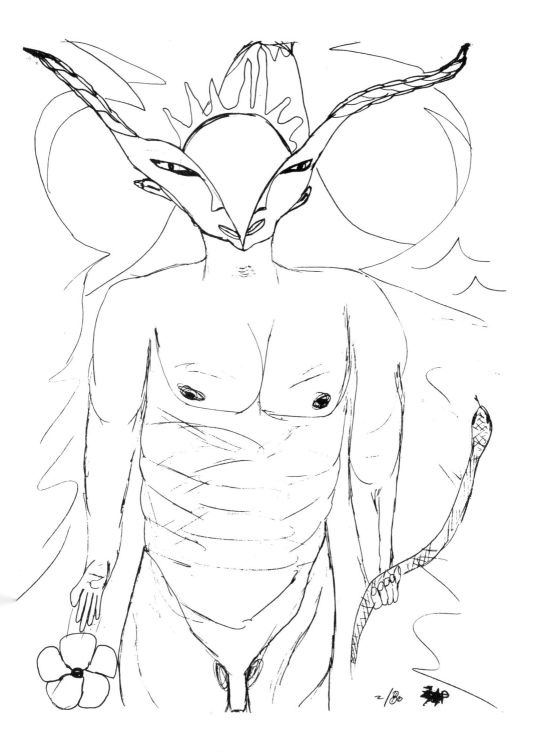

Illustration 18
Michael 3: Image of Dismemberment

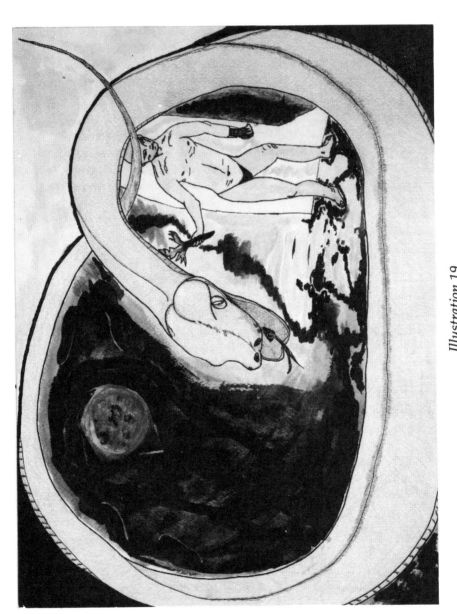

Illustration 19
Michael 4: The Descent

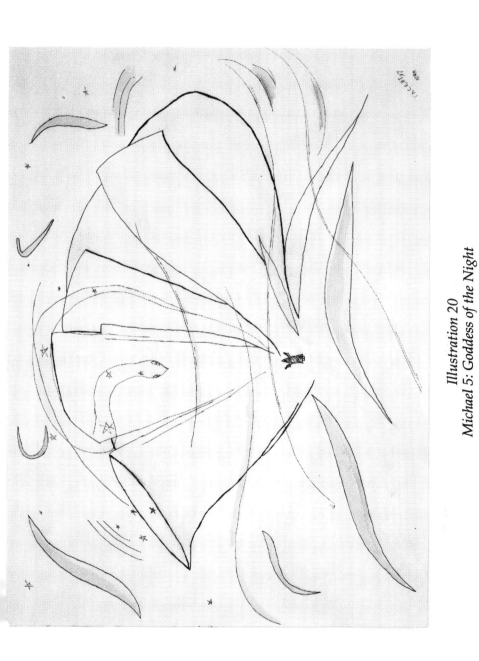

Illustration 20
Michael 5: Goddess of the Night

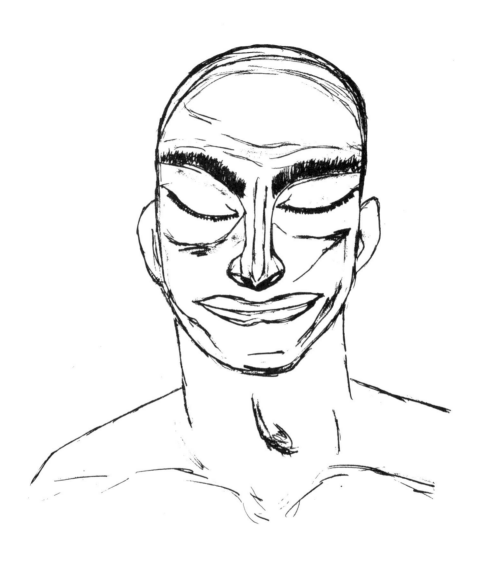

Illustration 21
Michael 6: A Guardian

face. The man's two cupped hands push through the cranium, holding a sphere. The circle may imply wholeness and intactness, the antithesis of the experience of dismemberment. This drawing seems to indicate the agony of the tension of opposites, a typically Dionysian motif, as is the image of dismemberment. The movement from the first drawing to the second appears to be the agony of the puer, who, fascinated by the serpent, is pulled into the waters of the unconscious.

The third drawing is labeled "Michael 3: Image of Dismemberment." This sketch was done two years later, several months before Michael entered Jungian analysis. In this drawing the opposites seem to have reached total separation. The mountain in the background is the antithesis of the valley below; there is a body of water of some sort wherein stands the central figure. It is difficult to know if the waters are parting or coming together. The central figure is distinctly non-human. It seems to have one female breast (on the left) and one masculine breast (on the right). The figure has horns, and it is difficult to know whether the head is splitting apart, releasing the Sun; or whether the head is fusing together, enclosing the Sun. The figure holds the serpent of the first drawing, and a five-petaled flower. Both of these suggest the Dionysian attribute of being close to the creative processes of Nature. Again we see dismemberment, but the agony shown in the previous drawing is gone. Instead we have a non-human other, an image of power and intensity.

The next two drawings are in color and were drawn two years after the previous sketch. These were Michael's first drawings in watercolors. "Michael 4: The Descent" brings us back to a human figure. Michael stated that this drawing heralded what he felt to be the unleashing of his creativity. He felt as if he had finally broken through to his creative center. Here we see the motif of the serpent once more. Michael identified this serpent as masculine and as a guardian. The serpent separates the outer world of the Sun and the inner world of the Moon. "Michael 3" showed the opposites in dynamic tension; in this drawing there is less tension and one gets the feeling that the opposites are in right relationship.

Looking at the human figure, I realized that the left foot, as we view the drawing, is on backwards. I asked Michael about this. He replied that it took several hours of work on drawing the foot before he finally gave up, aware that it was anatomically incorrect, but unable to consciously correct the problem. This male figure appears to combine the image of the puer with that of the God Hephaestus. The figure appears rather androgynous, having what appears to be undeveloped breasts and smoothness of body, references to the puer. The figure carries a torch, fire, and fire was Hephaestus's implement of creativity. The figure also has a deformed foot, a clearly Hephaestian reference.

The second color drawing titled "Michael 5: Goddess of the Night" shows a small figure looking heavenward. I have included it because Michael identified the serpent in this drawing as feminine. For Michael, the masculine mediated the descent, and the feminine is found in the heavens above. This is a reversal of the Greek inheritance, where the Earth is feminine and the Sky is masculine. I would suggest that the reversal is reflective of Michael's psychology and his God-images. This reversal is understandable in light of the God-patterns Michael identified, as will be explored in our next section; and is a creative way of synthesizing the hermaphroditic aspects of several God-patterns, notably Hermes, Hephaestus, and Dionysus.

The last and most recent drawing is titled "Michael 6: A Guardian." Here we have the head and shoulders of the male figure found in the color drawing labeled "Michael 4." There are no symbols. The image is distinct and clearly defined. The features are strong and proportional. One gets the sense that there is intense activity occurring within, as the figure has his complete attention focused inwards. There is a grace and presence to this image; although attentive to the inner world, the figure imparts an immediacy that is present in the here and now.

Meditating on these drawings, it would seem that the chronological sequence shows the gradual descent and dismemberment of the puer. At first fascinated by the serpent, the puer is dragged down into the waters of the unconscious where dissolution occurs (Michael 1 and 2). The image that appears after dismemberment is that of a non-human other (Michael 3). This is followed by images of both non-human (the serpents) and human together in the same drawing (Michael 4 and 5). There seems to be a gradual separation of these opposites, which is at first tense, after which the opposites appear as clearly defined. All this precedes the final frontal view of a male head and shoulders (Michael 6). It is interesting to note that Michael had little to say about the final sketch, except that he considers the image a guardian which he keeps framed near his personal work space at home.

The Dreams

Michael's journals span a period of two and one-half years, from June 1986 to December 1988. He was in Jungian analysis from August 1986 to December 1987. Michael's six drawings have a time span of approximately five and one-half years, from February 1984 to November 1988. The journals detail the last two and one-half years of a process that seems to have started with the first drawing, "Michael 1." The journals and the sketches come together in time at the end of 1988. It will be helpful for us to juxtapose the reproductions of the drawings with the times of the journal entries, as the two complement each other.

We end the last chapter as we began the first, with word and image complementing each other. What we have learned since Chapter One is that the image does not have to be seen in order to be experienced. The direct experience of the image is known through the affects, the moods, and the intuitive realizations that come to us from soul; in these instances the use of the word is one means of describing the image as internal process. The image as structure (formal representation) is a different experience than the image as content; usually, both aspects of the image are present. This is why Michael's sketches and Michael's words complement each other, even when each is experienced in different ways.

The archetypal structures within Michael's personality can be reduced to two major headings: the realm of the Sky-Father as mediated by the polarity of the puer and the senex; and the archetypal realm of the Great Mother, the feminine unconscious. We can identify Michael's struggles as the theme of the puer searching for the quality of time, the femininity of soul, and the entanglement of relationships. In other words, the journey of the puer to find psychology, or right relationship to soul.

Michael begins an early journal with the following dream, which for the narrative's sake we can refer to as Dream 1:

> I am in a large house. I am on the third floor with my mother. I want to leave but I am afraid she will hurt me if I try to go downstairs. She seems very angry. Next, I am downstairs in the living room. My mother is on the opposite side of the room, standing in the doorway to the kitchen. To my right, as I stand in a doorway, on the couch is X [Michael's therapist]. I know she is trying to help me get out of the house. She is talking to an unknown

man on the sofa as part of her rescue effort. He is telling her about cutting moulding, like that used for picture frames. He tells her that I should be learning how to make the shapes of the hexagon. The unknown man seems retarded somehow, but a craftsman.

This dream persuaded Michael to call X, who he had seen for therapy some years previously. He stated to me that he knew he needed assistance, so he called X. The timing of this dream was several months after the drawing labeled "Michael 3."

Dream 2 was recorded by Michael several weeks after Dream 1:

My grandmother, my mother, and myself sitting on the kitchen floor, which is white linoleum and immaculately clean. They are talking Italian which I marvel at, but cannot understand.

Michael writes about Dream 2:

This dream is unique in that I feel I should not be in it, that my sister should be the one to complete the three generations of my family. Yet on an emotional level, I feel happy, amused at the fact that they are speaking Italian, and very comfortable in the kitchen.

Dream 3 follows chronologically:

I am flying with my mother and grandmother. It seems that my grandmother taught my mother how to fly, who in turn taught me. The three of us flying through the air was exhilarating, and I felt safe with them.

Dream 4 is as follows:

A woman is inspecting a three story Victorian house she intends to buy. The house is in need of repairs. Inside, the ceilings are falling apart, the stairs need repair, and there is water leaking from the ceilings. The woman realizes that she needs a craftsman. She would like the house to be reconstructed exactly like it used to be.

This dream is significant in that Michael is an outside observer and not part of the drama. And the final dream in this sequence, Dream 5:

> I am talking to a youth, about 16, awkward. He seems retarded. I am speaking to him. He has applied for a job and he is worried that he may not be good enough for the job.
> "Are you strong?" I asked him.
> "Yes," he replied.
> "Are you quick?" I asked.
> "Yes," was his reply.
> "Then I am sure you will get the job," I reassured him.

Dream 1 was recorded on August 12, 1986 while Dream 5 was written down on August 13, 1987, a year and a day between the two. There are many more dreams during this time period, but I felt these five detailed a process. Michael in Dream 1 is trapped by the archetypal Mother. The dream Mother is angry. The angry Mother is suggestive of Hera, and when I realized this, these five dreams began to take on a certain cohesiveness. Suddenly a peripheral figure in Michael's God-patterns seemed to take center stage, and I found a focus.

Hera was the wife and sister of the King of the Gods, Zeus. She was chronically angry at her husband, who engaged in countless affairs and sired numerous progeny. As in the myth of Dionysus, Hera vented her anger on Zeus's lovers and his children, and never directed her anger at her husband. The few times when she did challenge Zeus, she met with dire consequences. Hera was enraged when she gave birth to the lame God Hephaestus; and pleased with the birth of Ares. She tried to murder Dionysus. We can make an educated guess that the Hera Goddess-pattern is strong for Michael. Dream 1 has the image of the "retarded craftsman," a reference to the God Hephaestus. The angry Mother, as the other central character in the lame God's mythology, would then have to be Hera.

Michael has yet to form a direct relationship to the Hephaestus God-image in Dream 1. The dream tells Michael that he will need X, because it is X who in the dream engages the wounded God in dialogue. The God- image in the dream tells X what Michael should be doing. The lame God is saying that Michael needs to develop his identification with the God by learning how to be a craftsman. Michael is trapped within the archetypal drama (the house) of the angry Hera and her lame son. He cannot leave the house without assistance, and the God-image tells him, indirectly, that he must learn to be a craftsman in order to be free. The ego must face the archetype.

Dreams 4 and 5 are a continuation of the Hephaestus image. Dream 4 shows a woman inspecting a house in need of assistance. She is fully aware that what she needs is a craftsman. The Hephaestus myth, as we saw in Chapter Four, tells of the final reconciliation between mother and son. In this dream the feminine seeks the masculine, and the dream itself would seem to indicate the archetypal drama of Hera and Hephaestus, especially their reconciliation. What eventually happens in the myth of Hephaestus is that the lame God is persuaded to release Hera from the Golden Throne, and he is reunited with his mother and with his divine heritage. Mother and son, both, let go of their anger towards each other.

Dream 5 suggests that Michael's dream self has made a direct relationship to the God-image of Hephaestus, the retarded youth. In this dream, Michael's dream ego values and supports the retarded youth. Michael can now value the image of the lame God within. This could not happen before the archetypal images of Hera and Hephaestus themselves resolved their conflict in the dream of the Victorian house needing repair. We can note that the combination of the puer and the smithy-God is consistent throughout Michael's images, for in this dream the youth (Hermes and Dionysus) is retarded (Hephaestus). As noted already, the drawing labeled "Michael 4" seems to show the puer and the smithy-God combined.

We are left with Dreams 2 and 3 which show the dream Michael as successor in his family's female lineage. Logically, Michael is correct when he writes that his sister should follow his mother. This sequence of grandmother, mother, and Michael was odd to me at first, but when I thought of Hera in the other three dreams, I thought about Dionysus. Hera tried to murder him twice. The second time she tried was when Dionysus was still a boy disguised as a girl. In Dream 2, Michael is metaphorically disguised as a woman. This is in keeping with the myth of Dionysus. Michael is in metaphorical disguise for this is his protection from the angry Mother; and, Dionysus being strong within his personality structure, we have an allusion to a certain closeness within Michael's personality to the hidden world of women's mysteries.

Dream 3 has the dream Michael flying with his grandmother

and his mother. This too is odd, as the realm of the Sky is usually that of the Father, but in this dream it is clear that it is the feminine that teaches Michael how to fly. This is consistent with the drawing "Michael 5" where the Goddess is found above. The interplay between Hera, Hephaestus and Dionysus is strong. But what are we do with images that show shifts of polarity? There is nothing in the myth of Hera that says she was a teacher to her sons.

The consistent polarity shifts in Michael's dream images are also seen in the activity of the God Hephaestus, who mediates the feminine sphere of the Underworld within Michael's psyche. We are literally "up in the air" with the feminine archetypal structures; we need to descend in order to find the masculine structures, the polarity of puer and senex.

We saw this polarity in the dream, noted earlier in this chapter, of Michael preparing for the journey; his grandfather (senex) is teaching him how to build a boat. One dream that Michael recorded is as follows:

> I am the Captain of the USS Enterprise. I am standing before a doorway to a room that is all dark and I know that each crew member has entered the room and extracted knowledge that only they can individually access. It is my turn. I am paralyzed with fear; an unknown woman is standing next to the doorway, gesturing to me to enter. It is important because the knowledge in the room is somehow decaying, and if we do not do this it will be lost for all time.

This dream makes reference to the television series *Star Trek*. At the beginning of each episode there was an announcement that began, "Space, the final frontier. These are the voyages of the Starship Enterprise." The last part of this prelude was that the Enterprise was to "boldly go where *no man* has gone before [italics mine]." The enterprise is a "ship" and men are usually depicted as being builders of ships. The word captain comes from the Latin *caput*, head. A captain is "head" of the ship. These are clearly masculine references.

These Sky images remind me of the God-pattern of Hermes, with his winged sandals. Hermes is one of the images of the puer, for Hermes executed the will of Zeus, the Sky-Father, who in turn was fathered by the God Uranus. Hermes has a direct link to the Sky realm via his father Zeus, and his grandfather Uranus. We see how the senex appears, complementing the puer, for Zeus and Uranus are strong father figures in mythology. Hermes was also able to access the Underworld; in astrology, Mercury represents the mind. Hermes' identification with the Egyptian Thoth tells us that he is the imparter of knowledge, hence the naming of Hermeticism. In this dream of the Enterprise, the dream Michael is in the realm of the Sky (Uranus).

Michael's images tend to show polarity shifts, however, and in the realm of the Sky we find a dark room. The dark room that contains knowledge is an image for the collective unconscious, which is a feminine place, and to which Hermes can gain access. In this dream the masculine Sky realm affords the dream Michael with access to the feminine through his identification with the God Hermes.

The following dream includes Michael's comments:

> J. in charge of cultivating a white rose bush. He is standing in front of a white rosebud that is opening, and I remind him that he learned to cultivate the bush from G. who learned from C.

Michael comments:

> This dream is a succession of spiritual fathers and sons. C. to G. to J. to me. The garden is the symbol of our lives, the little acre allotted to us by God to grow what we will.
>
> As I read back over the last few months, it becomes clear to me that the masculine component of my psyche is slowly awakening, blooming so to speak. For me, the salvaging of the internal masculine image is an accomplishment indeed.

A final dream that I include to illustrate the puer/senex interaction occurs midway through the journals.

> I am on my way to the "mainland." It seems that I am either at the Cape or at Newport, Rhode Island. In any case, it appears that I must cross a bridge in order to get to the mainland. There is an older man who I know can give me directions to get to the mainland, but I ignore him and get lost. I finally seek him out, he smiles, and points me in the right direction.

There are two God-patterns that Michael identified that we have not addressed, the God Hades and the God Ares. Hades was an invisible God, so the experience of Hades is direct as experienced through depression. Hades as a place, and as the archetype of the descent, is present throughout Michael's materials. Depression and despair, especially, are evident as he struggled through his therapy process. One journal entry is as follows:

> So. Where am I now that the dust is settling? Thirteen straight months of change is, I think, enough for awhile. The most difficult part of all this is that I find it difficult if not unbearable at times to simply sit with myself. It is like a new set of clothes that do not quite fit or are simply uncomfortable. There is a certain despair that comes with it, like I am giving something up instead of gaining—what—Myself! I do not like myself enough. Or sometimes it is a feeling like a hollow victory.

The God Ares was the least evident of the God-patterns. Michael stated that he identified with the Ares personality's access to rage and anger. For Michael, the experience and demonstration of anger come easily; he is not destructive with this emotion, but he is not afraid of feeling it. Michael also stated that he had always wanted to be a dancer, but that his parents were adamant that this was a "girl's" activity; he has never had formal dance instruction. As we spoke, I remembered that several of his dreams contained dancers. One dream is this:

> An island of some sort, but it is really some sort of stage. It is round. Trees on the outside, followed by a Stonehenge type structure all around. Within it a fire burns some old staging so that the new staging can be built. There is a waterway between this stage and where I am. A light shines, seeking someone to play Saturn, but he must be a dancer. The light stops upon a handsome man who is muscular. He dances within the spotlight.

Another dream is as follows:

> I am watching a young boy/man, he must be around 16, blond, attractive, dancing. I know I just watch for awhile and then I am talking to him.

Both these dreams include a dancer with another attribute. The first dream is that of a dancer dancing the role of Saturn, the senex. The second dream is that of a young adolescent dancer, the puer. It is fascinating when in Michael's dreams several God-images become combined.

One other strong theme throughout Michael's journals and

drawings is that of dismemberment, reflective of the God Dionysus. We have seen the dismemberment motif in Michael's drawings. Several months after he initiated therapy with X, Michael wrote in his journal:

> So, can the personality really be overcome? Is it really just set in stone by the age of 5 as Freudians would have us believe? Dismemberment, psychic dismemberment, that is what happened in September. Imagine a center. Imagine looking out of that center and perceiving all the pieces that together are called I. See all the pieces and drop the puzzle. Watch it fall apart. Pain and despair. Despair and pain.

If we remember that images do not have to be visual, that the archetype affords us with a certain kind of experience, then the dismemberment of the God Dionysus can be felt rather than seen. This is the case as Michael continues to write in his journal about dismemberment:

> It feels as if all my identity pegs are doors in "Let's Make a Deal." I can choose to become what is behind any one of those doors but I am not really any one of those doors or the sum total even. I am just on some stage and it does not matter who walks by or what the stage directions are. It was easier when I was driven and playing the martyr, much easier. They never told me that the price for greater clarity and greater consciousness is less stage directions; you get to ad lib a little more and take the rap a little more. But in some ways responsibility is still new territory since I have avoided it.
>
> Of course, a part of me is saying, "You are carrying this to extremes as usual. What is really happening is that you are questioning; no, you are asking more appropriate questions like "So what? To what end? To whose end? And then you wonder why doing and going through this should lead to feelings of depression?" Tra la la . . . . .

The dismemberment of Dionysus leads Michael to experience the separate parts of his personality. This is accompanied by feelings of despair and depression. Appreciating the parts that comprise the whole requires, from the puer aspect of Dionysus, that Michael begins to assume responsibility for who he is in the world, even when he recognizes the many voices within that are separate from him. The above quote illustrates the form that the many voices assume within Michael's experience, ending with his need to stop the voices by making light of them.

It seems conclusive, and Michael agreed, that the descent of the puer into the unconscious resulted in the experience of dismemberment as the first step before the puer could find psychology or soul. I continued to look in his journals as they spanned the two and one-half year period and what I found was a process of the gradual healing of the Dionysian madness. Eighteen months after the above journal entry, Michael has the following dream:

> I am in a building. I am aware of my bedroom and a long hallway. The shape of my bedroom and hallway from an L-shape thus:
>
> I can see a light at the end of the hallway, but there is a figure standing in front of me. I cannot make out the figure, it may be male or female, partly my mother and MOTHER. I go back into the bedroom, throw myself onto the bed and cry in agony and despair!

His comments to this dream are as follows:

> It seems to be as if I am on a hospital ward, in my bedroom, wounded. Three days ago I asked myself the question, "What will it take for me to heal?" I am in a hospital ward. Am I there because I cannot leave or will not leave, or both? Does MOTHER hold me prisoner or is she the nurse that is trying to heal me? A hospital can contain because the person is unable to take care of themselves or it can be a place where one goes to be healed. The hospital is also a place where we go to die. This dream is oddly reassuring.

The native ambivalence of dream images is shown by the fact that Michael cannot quite tell what is happening. He feels it to be a hospital setting of some sort, a place of healing. He knows there is an exit out of his bedroom, and that there is light at the end of the hallway. But it seems that he needs to remain here for awhile, to heal. Six months later there is a journal entry that reads:

> You know! Do you ever get to the point of asking one simple rhetorical question, directing it up to heaven? It goes like this, "What is going on?" You know you will never get a response. Or if you do, the answer will be something like slipping on a bar of soap in the shower and almost killing yourself, but the real annoying thing is having to buy a new shower curtain. Not that

you grieve for some little bit of petroleum product destroyed. It is the image of being naked before your God and then you drop the soap and then you are so embarrassed you step on it only to slip and kill yourself. Then the drum roll.

Well, the last few weeks have been golden. I will not say this too loudly for fear of slipping on a bar of soap. X refers to this as "serenity," having the sense of something within that seems to know what it is, where it is going, and why. Even through the most crazy times. In my earlier years, I was saddled with what I used to call the burden of being myself. Now I seem to be blessed with the burden of being myself. I feel as if I missed something, some sleight of hand, because when He said I could pick one of those closed fists, and He opened his hand to let me see what was inside, it was still me. What is surprising is that I accept the gift. What the hey, if it was good enough to nurture within His strong and graceful hand, it is good enough for me.

The Dionysus God-pattern is the reconciler of opposites, and as Michael found his serenity after the descent and dismemberment, he also found his God. This final quote shows what Hillman refers to as the mature personality that is able to show cognizance of its masked and ambiguous situation. Irony, humor and compassion are its hallmarks for these show an awareness of the multiplicity of intentions embodied by any subject at any moment.[19]

A Few Last Words

We end with image. Michael's case story illustrates the fate that accompanies our experiences of archetypal structures. Archetypes exist everywhere and at every moment for they are the ground of the psyche's existence. Images, therefore, are primary, whether we speak of the arts, the humanities, or the sciences. When we turn to the image we are face to face with a wellspring of creativity. As individual lenses for image we each color the archetypal expression, this is unalterable; but we can consciously participate in becoming better lenses, allowing the image to manifest in its purest form.

The Western dualism of spirit and body has co-opted the realm of psyche, soul. We do not dare to dream for dreaming's sake, or sculpt for sculpting's sake, or love for love's sake; instead we are taught to become consumers of profane events. It is as though the archetype of the puer runs rampant in our Western culture, flitting to and fro, mocking the offered embraces of psyche. One aspect of the archetype of the puer is the puer's wound. Let us not forget that the puer in all of us has a hidden wound, some imaginal place where the passions of psyche find expression. I am unable to venture a guess as to what the collective Western puer wound might be. However, through a psychology of soul, we can come to know the individual puer wound. This is the place where the waters of life, which is death, moistens the sometimes arid flight of the puer. Together, water and air allow for the formation of rain which falls to Earth. So too the puer as spirit, to be whole, must know what it feels like to have mud between his uncalloused toes.

In ending, I will refer us back to the Tree of Life. The journey of the virgin soul begins in Malkuth as it seeks the Gate of Death. For some, actual physical death is the only death they come to know. For some, the Gate is found after much searching. And a rare few begin life before the Gate. It is difficult to know who will draw what lot in life; but easier to know once the fate is drawn. So, in one sense, the journey of the individual soul should begin in Malkuth, as it seeks the world soul of Kether.

The usual course of events would have been for me to present the case material (Malkuth) and then proceed to tear it apart, ending with theory (Kether). This is artificial at best for the image is primary, and we must have soul in order to know image—they are inseparable and happen together. The approach to the image is circular; we can begin and end anywhere. I have therefore reversed the order of expected academic events. Since image is immediacy, I have wanted to end our journey with this immediacy. The order I have chosen challenges us to work a little bit harder.

Notes

ABBREVIATIONS

CW   *Collected Works of C. G. Jung.* Bollingen Series XX. Translated by R. F. C. Hull and edited by H. Read, M. Fordham, G. Adler, and Wm. McGuire (Princeton, N. J.: Princeton University Press and London: Routledge & Kegan Paul, Inc., 1953-1973), cited by volume number and paragraph of text.

INTRODUCTION

1. CW 9, pt. 1, par. 5.

2. Edward C. Whitmont, *The Symbolic Quest: Basic Concepts of Analytical Psychology* (Princeton, NJ: Princeton University Press, 1978), 42.

3. Ibid., 42.

4. Ibid., 73.

5. See Robert Graves, *The White Goddess* (New York: Farrar, Straus and Giroux, 1987).

6. James Hillman, "Archetypal Theory," in *Loose Ends: Primary Papers in Archetypal Psychology* (Dallas, Texas: Spring Publications, 1975), 186.

7. James Hillman, *Re-Visioning Psychology*, Harper Colophon Books (New York: Harper & Row, 1977),

8. Jim Tester, *A History of Western Astrology* (New York: Ballantine Books, 1987), 18.

9. Ibid. 23.

10. Hillman, *Re-Visioning Psychology*, x.

11. Ibid.

12. Ibid.

13. CW 6, pars. 789-791.

14. Henri F. Ellenberger, *The Discovery of the Unconscious: The History and Evolution of Dynamic Psychiatry* (New York: Basic Books, Inc., 1970), 515-516.

15. Ibid., 199-202.

16. James Hillman, "Peaks and Vales: The Soul/Spirit Distinction as Basis for the Differences between Psychotherapy and Spiritual Discipline," in *Puer Papers*, James Hillman, ed. (Dallas, Texas: Spring Publications, Inc., 1979), 58.

17. Herta Payson-Joslin, "The Transformative Image: A Feminine Approach to Therapy" (Submitted in Partial Fulfillment, Degree of Master of Arts, Goddard Graduate Program, Vermont College/Norwich University, November 1981), 3-4.

18. James Hillman,"A Note On Story, " in *Loose Ends: Primary Papers in Archetypal Psychology*, 3.

CHAPTER ONE

1. Herta Payson-Joslin, 7-8.

2. *The American Heritage Dictionary of the English Language*, William Morris, ed., 1976.

3. For the history of the Jewish Qabalah to the Middle Ages I am indebted to Charles Poncé, *Kabbalah: An Introduction and Illumination for the World Today*, 2d ed., Quest Books (Wheaton, IL: The Theosophical Publishing House, 1980). What follows is the history of the Qabalah summarized and extrapolated from Ponce's text.

4. Ibid., 53.

5. The early history of Western magic summarized from Francis King, *Magic: The Western Tradition* (New York: Avon Books, 1975), 7-16.

6. The "Emerald Tablet" is the revelation of Hermes Trismegistus, Thrice Greatest Hermes, the author of the *Corpus Hermeticum*. The Tablet is comprised of twelve short stanzas, two of which follow:

> 1. In truth certainly and without doubt, whatever is below is like that which is above, and whatever is above is like that which below, to accomplish the miracles of one thing.

> 7. It rises from earth to heaven and comes down again from heaven to earth, and thus acquires the power of the realities above and the realities below. In this way you will acquire the glory of the whole world, and all darkness will leave you.

"From its style, however, it is clearly of pre-Islamic origin, and as it is wholly in accord with the spirit of the Hermetic tradition—as the alchemists unanimously agree—there is no convincing reason to doubt its connection with the origins of Hermetism." Titus Burckhardt, *Alchemy*, trans. William Stoddart (Great Britain: Element Books, Ltd. , 1986), 196-197.

7. King, 10.

8. Ibid., 14.

9. A. E. Waite, *The Holy Kabbalah* (Secaucus, NJ: University Books/Citadel Press, n. d.), 548-549.

10. See Ellic Howe, *The Magicians of the Golden Dawn: A Documentary History of a Magical Order* 1887-1923, with a Foreward by Gerald Yorke (York Beach, ME: Samuel Weiser, Inc., 1984), for a full account of the history of the Golden Dawn.

11. Israel Regardie, *The Golden Dawn*, 4th ed. (St. Paul, MN: Llewellyn Publications, 1982), v.

12. Poncé, 93.

13. Poncé, 96-97.

14. Ibid., 94-101, for a fuller explanation of the Sephiroth.

15. Ibid., 101.

16. Ibid., 39.

17. Traditional Qabalistic attribution for Aries is the Hebrew letter He; Tzaddi is traditionally Aquarius. Aleister Crowley felt the attributions best represented the New Age when interchanged: Tzaddi/Aries and He/Aquarius. The numbers of the paths on the Tree remain the same. He is path 15 and Tzaddi is path 28.

18. Qabalistic attributions of the thirty-two paths can be found in: Paul Foster Case, *The Tarot: A Key to the Wisdom of the Ages*; Aleister Crowley, *777*; Dion Fortune, *The Mystical Qabalah*; David Godwin, *Godwin's Cabalistic Encyclopedia*; Gareth Knight, *A Practical Guide to Qabalistic Symbolism*; and Robert Wang, *The Qabalistic Tarot: A Textbook of Mystical Philosophy*. See bibliography for references. Any individual who would like to pursue the study of Tarot is strongly urged to contact the late Paul Foster Case's mystery school, The Builders of the Adytum, 5101-05 North Figueroa Street, Los Angeles, California, 90042.

19. Afro-American slang utilizes the verb "to be" as in "I be angry"to stress the current total state as one of Being, as opposed to the English *identification* expressed in "I Am." In Spanish, also, "ser" and "estar" denote Being as a given state

(ser) or as transitional event (estar). We have no equivalents in the English verb to be.

20. Dion Fortune, *The Mystical Qabalah*, 13th Impression (London: Ernest Benn Limited, 1957), 88-89.

21. Ibid., 13.

22. Joseph Campbell and Richard Roberts, *Tarot Revelations*, 2d ed. (San Anselmo, CA: Vernal Equinox Press, 1982), 41.

23. Fortune, 2.

24. Dane Rudhyar, *The Practice of Astrology As a Technique in Human Understanding* (Boulder: Shambhala, 1978), 50-51.

25. James Hillman, *The Dream and the Underworld* (New York: Harper & Row, 1979), 120.

26. Arthur Avalon (Sir John Woodroffe), *The Serpent Power* (New York: Dover Publications, Inc., 1974), 23.

27. Hiroshi Motoyama, *Theories of the Chakras: Bridge to Higher Consciousness*, Quest Books (Wheaton, IL: The Theosophical Publishing House, 1981), 175.

28. *The American Heritage Dictionary of the English Language.*

29. CW 5: Part 2, Chapters 2 and 3 for Jung's early work explaining the transformation of psychic energy, or libido.

30. John Whiteside Parsons, "On Magick," in *Freedom is a Two-Edged Sword: The Collected Essays of John Whiteside Parsons*, The Oriflame, No. 1. New Series (New York & Las Vegas: Ordo Templi Orientis and Falcon Press, 1989), 45-46.

31. Ibid., 47.

32. Ibid., 46.

33. Hillman, *Re-Visioning Psychology*, 12.

34. Mark P. O. Morford and Robert J. Lenardon, *Classical Mythology* (New York: David McKay Company, Inc., 1971), 25.

35. Hillman, *Re-Visioning Psychology*, 3.

36. Aleister Crowley, *Magick*, edited, annotated and introduced by John Symonds and Kenneth Grant (London: Routledge & Kegan Paul, 1973), 347.

37. CW 11, par. 6: "The *numinosum*—whatever its cause may be—is an experience of the subject independent of his will. At all events, religious teaching as well as the *consensus genitum* always and everywhere explain this experience as being due to a cause external to the individual. The *numinosum* is either a quality belonging to a visible object or the influence of an invisible presence that causes a peculiar alteration of consciousness."

Numinosity is a quality inherent in an archetypal encounter, and usually touches the person deeply. Such are the "Big Dreams" of Native Americans, or the alteration of consciousness caused by a religious experience or artistic expression.

38. Hillman, *Re-Visioning Psychology*, 57.

39. Ibid., 79.

40. Colin Wilson, *The Occult* (New York: Vintage Books, A Division of Random House, 1971).

41. Hillman, *Re-Visioning Psychology*, 134-135.

42. Ibid., 117.

43. Ibid., 140-141.

44. Ibid., 140.

45. Ibid., 141.

46. Ibid., 173.

47. Jean Shinoda Bolen, M. D. , *Goddesses in Everywoman: A New Psychology of Women*, Harper Colophon Books (New York: Harper & Row, 1984), 42.

48. "The Jungian approach amplifies dreams by using associations, analogous parallel images, symbols, legends, myths, and archetypes. We stick to the dream images and words, and look it over by a process of circumambulation." Harry A. Wilmer, *Practical Jung: Nuts and Bolts of Jungian Psychotherapy* (Wilmette, Illinois: Chiron Publications, 1987), 242.

As a process, amplification can be used any time we seek to find the archetypal and mythic meanings found in individual experiences of the image.

49. Jean Shinoda Bolen, M. D., *Gods in Everyman: A New Psychology of Men's Lives and Loves* (San Francisco: Harper & Row, 1989), x.

50. Hillman, "A Note On Story," 1.

51. James Hillman, "On Opportunism," in *Puer Papers* (Texas: Spring Publications, 1972), 162-163.

52. By wholeness I mean the full range of qualities and experiences afforded us by soul's images which contain light and dark, up and down, young and old, etc. . .

CHAPTER TWO

1. Fortune, 218.

2. Hillman, *Re-Visioning Psychology*, 13.

3. Erich Neumann, *The Origins and History of Consciousness*, *trans.* R. F. C. Hull, Bollingen Series 42 (Princeton: Princeton University Press, 1973), 315.

4. *The I Ching or Book of Changes*, The Richard Wilhelm Translation, rendered into English by Cary F. Baynes,

Bollingen Series 19 (Princeton: Princeton University Press, 1971).

A trigram is a linear figure composed of three lines, a line being either unbroken, masculine, Yang, ——— ; or broken, feminine, Yin, ———. *The Book of Changes* itself at the outset was a collection of linear signs used as oracles. There are eight trigrams, and these trigrams are conceived as images of all that happens in heaven and on earth. [xlix—l]

All unbroken lines being Yang naturally represent the archetypal masculine—the Creative:

———

———

———

The Receptive has all Yin lines:

—— ——

—— ——

—— ——

About the *Book of Changes* Richard Wilhelm writes:

Nearly all that is greatest and most significant in the three thousand years of Chinese cultural history has either taken its inspiration from this book, or has exerted an influence in the interpretation of its text. . . . Small wonder then that both of the two branches of Chinese philosophy, Confucianism and Taoism, have their common roots here. [xlvii]

5. *Book of Changes*, 3.

6. Ibid., 4.

7. See page 3.

8. *Book of Changes*, 10.

9. CW 8, par. 368.

10. Fortune, 150-151.

11. Hillman, *Re-Visioning Psychology*, 156.

12. Gregory Szanto, *Astrotherapy: Astrology and the Realization of the Self* (New York: Arkana Books, Routledge & Kegan Paul Inc., 1987), 50.

13. Kenneth Grant, *The Magical Revival* (New York: Samuel Weiser, Inc., 1973), 65. See also Neumann, *The Origins and History of Consciousness*, 282-283, for a psychological interpretation of the sequence star to Moon to Sun.

14. Mark P. O. Morford and Robert J. Lenardon, *Classical Mythology* (New York: David McKay Company, Inc., 1971), 54.

15. Richard Roess, "Messages from the Heavens," The Ascendant 12 (Fall 1988): 11.

16. The history of astrology in this chapter compiled from Francis King, *The Cosmic Influence*; Christopher McIntosh, *The Astrologers and their Creed*; Sandra Shulman, *The Encyclopedia of Astrology*; and Jim Tester, *A History of Western Astrology*. I am especially indebted to Tester's history which I have used extensively.

17. Jim Tester, *A History of Western Astrology* (New York: Ballantine Books, 1987), 13.

18. Ibid., 10.

19. Sandra Shulman, *The Encyclopedia of Astrology* (New York: The Hamlyn Publishing Group, Limited, 1976), 26.

20. Ibid., 33.

21. Tester. 58.

22. Ibid., 17.

23. Ibid., 59.

24. Ibid., 18.

25. Shulman, 33.

26. Tester, 99.

27. Ibid., 176.

28. Ibid., 240.

29. Christopher McIntosh, *The Astrologers and their Creed* (New York: Frederick A. Praeger, 1969), 85.

30. Shulman, 128.

31. Robert Anton Wilson, foreward to *The Eye in the Triangle* by Israel Regardie (Phoenix, Arizona: Falcon Press, 1982), xi-xii.

32. Nigel Calder, *Einstein's Universe* (New York: Penguin Books, 1980), 13.

33. King, *The Cosmic Influence*, chapter 2, for the discoveries listed in this paragraph.

34. Michel Gauquelin, *Cosmic Influences on Human Behavior*, trans. Joyce E. Clemow (New York: Stein and Day, Inc., 1973), chapter 2.

35. Ibid., chapter 19.

36. Ibid., 49.

37. Rudhyar, *The Practice of Astrology*, 8.

38. Ibid.

39. Liz Greene, *The Astrology of Fate* (York Beach, Maine: Samuel Weiser, Inc., 1984), 4.

40. One suspects this is may be the case in Gauquelin's *Cosmic Influences*. At the very least, Gauquelin attempted to gain the support of the scientific community which rejects anything that has the slighest odor of fate attached to it; although we are supposed to accept the inviability of physical laws. Gauquelin says of his initial work:

> The other mistake was to challenge astrologers too much. I told you yesterday about some pitfalls that the astrologers at that time were not able to avoid. And so perhaps I despised them a little bit too much, and I claimed that the evidence that I found for the Mars Effect was not astrology at all. In fact, this was some kind of awkward diplomacy on my part to flatter the scientific establishment. I hoped, with naivete, that they might be more interested in my work if I said that not only am I not an astrologer, but also that I have completely demolished astrology. But in fact that was not a good move, since the scientists never accepted my way of working or my results. And so I persisted, probably too much, in this direction. And now, as you know, after some fifteen years I have slowly changed my position—and not only for political reasons. I discovered that the scientific establishment was just putting me off (or out). . . . In "Dialogue: Michel Gauqueline and Michael Erlemine," Astro*Talk, 6, no. 1 (January1989): 2.

41. Greene, *The Astrology of Fate*, 8.

42. Active imagination is the ability to enter into psyche's imaginings while conscious, with the ego restrained. This ability slowly develops, espcially in a long term psycho-therapy setting. It is different than "idle" fantasizing, although fantasy, dreams, art works, and active imagination all come from the same place—the imaginal psyche. In active imagination one relaxes and invokes the image, many times a fragment of a dream or some other fleeting image. By containing the ego, the image is allowed to develop on its own accord without ego interference. The value of this

procedure is the ego's immediate, active, conscious involvement.

43. Stephen Arroyo, *Astrology, Karma, & Transformation: The Inner Dimensions of the Birth Chart* (Reno, Nevada: CRCS Publications, 1978), 144.

44. For the images associated with the signs of the zodiac and the planets see Greene, *The Astrology of Fate*; also, Kathleen Burt, *Archetypes of the Zodiac*, (St. Paul, Minnesota: Llewellyn Publications, 1988).

45. Jesse White-Frese, Lecture November 17, 1988 sponsored by the Astrological Society of Connecticut.

46. Bolen, *Goddesses in Everywoman*, 302.

47. Ibid., 222-223.

48. Howard Sasportas, "Subpersonalities and Psychological Conflicts" in *The Development of the Personality*, Seminars in Psychological Astrology, vol. 1 (York Beach, Maine: Samuel Weiser, Inc., 1987), 165.

49. CW 8, par. 392.

50. Table repoduced from Sasportas, "Subpersonalities and Psychological Conflicts," 208-209.

51. Bolen, *Gods in Everyman*, 312.

52. Ibid., 93.

53. Liz Greene and Howard Sasportas, *The Development of the Personality*, Seminars in Psychological Astrology, vol. 1 (York Beach, Maine: Samuel Weiser, Inc., 1987), xiv.

CHAPTER THREE

1. Hillman, "Archetypal Theory," 171.

2. Hillman, *Re-Visioning Psychology*, 173.

3. James Hillman, "On the Necessity of Abnormal Psychology: Ananke and Athene," in *Facing the Gods*, James Hillman, ed. (Dallas, Texas: Spring Publications, Inc., 1980), 17-18.

4. CW 8, par. 270, editor's note, bottom of page.

5. Ibid., par. 273.

6. Ibid., par. 280.

7. Greene, *The Astrology of Fate*, 25-26.

8. CW 8, par. 277.

9. Ibid., par 748.

10. Ibid., par. 201.

11. Ibid., par. 242.

12. Whitmont, 29.

13. CW 8, par. 402.

14. CW 14, par. 667.

15. Whitmont, 19-20.

16. Greene, *The Astrology of Fate*, 17.

17. Morford and Lenardson, 126-127.

18. Edward Tripp, *Crowell's Handbook of Classical Mythology* (New York: Thomas Y. Cromwell Company, 1970), 261.

19. Greene, *The Astrology of Fate*, 21.

20. Ibid., 25.

21. Ibid., 19.

22. See page 122.

23. Greene, *The Astrology of Fate*, 23.

24. Ibid., 25.

25. Ellenberger, 670.

26. CW 5, xxiii.

27. C. G. Jung, *Memories, Dreams, Reflections*, recorded and edited by Aniela Jaffe, trans. Richard and Clara Winsten (New York: Vintage Books, 1965), 172.

28. Ibid., 173.

29. Ibid., 173.

30. Ibid., 174.

31. Ellenberger, 671.

32. Jung, *Memories, Dreams, Reflections*, 177.

33. Ibid., 198-199.

34. Ibid., 199.

35. Ibid., 186-187.

36. Howe, *The Magicians of the Golden Dawn*, 5.

37. Herta Payson Joslin, 103-106.

38. Hillman, *The Dream and the Underworld*, 31.

CHAPTER FOUR

1. Hillman, "Archetypal Theory," 172.

2. CW 6, par. 706.

3. Marie-Louise Von Franz, "The Inferior Function," in *Lectures on Jung's Typology* (Irving, Texas: Spring Publications, Inc., 1979), 67.

4. See Kenneth Grant, *The Magical Revival*, especially the chapter on Dion Fortune, for Western magic's views on "dreaming true, " or realizing the dream.

5. R. L. Wing, *The Illustrated I-Ching* (Garden City, New York: Dolphin Books/Double Day and Company, Inc., 1982), Hexagram 14, 49. [6 Carlos Castaneda, *The Teachings of Don Juan: A Yaqui Way of Knowledge* (New York, New York: A Touchstone Book of Simon and Shuster, 1968), 182-183.]

7. James Hillman, *Archetypal Psychology: A Brief Account* (Dallas, Texas: Spring Publications, Inc., 1985), 7.

8. Barbara Kirksey, "Hestia: A Background of Psychological Focusing," in Facing the Gods, 105.

9. Hillman, *Archetypal Psychology*, 7.

10. Sheldon Cashdan, *Object Relations Therapy: Using the Relationship* (New York: W. W. Norton & Company, 1988).

11. Margery Williams, *The Velveteen Rabbit or How Toys Become Real*, illustrated by Michael Green (Philadelphia, Pennsylvania: Running Press, 1981).

12. For a variation on the hero myth where the hero does maintain a right relationship with the feminine see Hillman's "Puer Wounds and Ulysses' Scar," in *Puer Papers*.

13. Tripp, 275-295.

14. Joseph Campbell, *The Power of Myth: With Bill Moyers*, Betty Sue Flowers, ed. (New York: Doubleday, 1988), 5.

15. Ibid., 5-6.

16. Ibid., 51.

17. Ibid., 195.

18. Ibid., 51.

19. Cashdan, 23.

20. Ibid., 12.

21. For the full attributions of The High Priestess see Case, *The Tarot: A Key to the Wisdom of the Ages*, 48-55.

22. Ibid., 52.

23. Ibid., 52.

24. Hillman, *Archetypal Psychology: A Brief Account*, 6.

25. Ibid., 6-7.

26. Ibid., 7.

27. Ibid., 8.

28. Ibid., 9-10.

29. Barbara Kirksey, "Hestia: A Background of Psychological Focusing," in *Facing the Gods*, 101-113.

30. Ibid., 101.

31. Ibid., 105.

32. Ibid., 106.

33. Hillman, "On the Necessity of Abnormal Psychology: Ananke and Athene," in *Facing the Gods*, 13.

34. For full attributions of The Star see Case, 166-172.

35. Hillman, "On the Necessity of Abnormal Psychology: Ananke and Athene," 19.

36. Ibid., 13.

37. Ibid., 19.

38. Ibid., 20.

39. CW 6, pars. 821-828.

40. Hillman, "On the Necessity of Abnormal Psychology: Ananke and Athene," 19.

41. Ibid., 27-28.

42. Ibid., 21.

43. Ibid., 27.

44. Ibid., 31.

45. Hillman, *Archetypal Psychology: A Brief Account*, 49-50.

46. For the full attributions of The Lovers see Case, 84-90.

47. CW 7, par. 94, footnote 13 states, according to Jung:

> Contrary to certain views, I am not of the opinion that the "transference to the doctor" is a regular phenomenon indispensible to the success of the treatment. Transference is projection, and projection is either there or not .... The absence of projections to the doctor may in fact considerably facilitate the treatment, because the real personal values can then come more clearly to the forefront.

48. CW 7, Part 1, Chapter 7 for a full account of this process.

49. Whitmont, 58-59.

50. Murray Stein, "Hephaistos: A Pattern of Introversion, " in *Facing the Gods*, 67-86.

51. Ibid., 71.

52. Hillman, *Archetypal Psychology*: A Brief Account, 14.

CHAPTER FIVE

1. Fortune, 265.

2. Hillman, *The Dream and the Underworld*, 64-67.

3. Hillman, *Re-Visioning Psychology*, 83.

4. *The American Heritage Dictionary of the English Language.*

5. Hillman, *Re-Visioning Psychology*, 111.

6. Ibid., 101.

7. Marc Edmund Jones, *The Guide to Horoscope Interpretation* (Stanwood, Washington: Sabian Publishing Society, 1972), for detailed analysis of planetary distribution types.

8. Liz Greene, *Saturn: A New Look At An Old Devil* (York Beach, Maine: Samuel Weiser, Inc., 1976), 136.

9. James Hillman, "Senex and Puer, " in *Puer Papers*, 25-26.

10. Bolen, *Gods in Everyman*, 98-123, for a full account of the Hades God-pattern.

11. Ibid., 162-191, for a full account of the Hermes God-pattern.

12. Ibid., 192.

13. Ibid., 192-218, for a full account of the Ares God-pattern.

14. Ibid., 219-250, for a full account of the Hephaestus God-pattern.

15. Ibid., 224.

16. Ibid., 251-278, for a full account of the Dionysus God-pattern.

17. James Hillman, "Dionysos in Jung's Writings," in *Facing the Gods*, 162.

18. See pages 192-193.

19. See epigraph from Hillman, page 237 of current work.

APPENDIX

The Gods, the Tree, and the Birth Chart

A full account of the complex relationships that arise when one contemplates images, the Tree of Life, and the birth chart would require more space than this current work allows. The main focus of this book has been to introduce story and image without moving into the tyranny of a so called "final solution." My mentor in the Western magic tradition has always cautioned me against the belief that there is one way, and one way only. There is really only my way, or your way, for all prophets are true. Along this same line of reasoning, psychology must always remain descriptive—adjective rather than noun. And image is too complex a phenomenon to pigeon-hole as this or that; image is this and that and so much more for the well-spring of image appears inexhaustible.

What I present in this appendix is intended as suggestion. It occurred to me that an appendix might help the reader to tread his or her own way and come to know image thereby. I recommend this appendix as a road map only, for no psychologist, astrologer, or magician should ignore the main fantasy of science—the assumption that no discipline or individual can dispense with actual experience and carefully noted observation. What may work for me may not work for you.

The brief mythology of the God-patterns is in summary form. I recommend that anyone interested in the study of archetypes refer to the primary sources, especially, but not limited to, Carl Jung and

James Hillman. Greek mythology itself is a primary source and well worth the research. Greek mythology is so complex and the nuances within its images so subtle, that careful study is a must for the individual interested in learning the mythological basis of psyche. Jean Shinoda Bolen's two excellent books on the psychological structure of the God-patterns are also recommended reading.

The correspondences to the Tree have been taken from Aleister Crowley's 777. As a glyph of Nature, especially the natural soul, there is no symbol system equal to the Tree. Crowley attempted to condense as much information as possible within the thirty-two paths. Some of the astrological and God attributions are equivalent; as an example, Zeus/Jupiter corresponds to the sphere of Chesed, and the planet Jupiter itself is known as the mundane chakra for the sphere of Chesed by occultists. I do not agree totally with Crowley's attributions and suggest my own. Crowley did not incorporate the Gods Hestia and Hephaestus, for instance. Where a sphere is involved, as for example, Aphrodite/Venus in the sphere of Netzach, look to all the paths that radiate from that sphere for further delineation of the God-pattern.

I will stress an admonition made by Jung: we cannot readily and irresponsibly assume one-to-one correspondences between like things. The four elements, the four psychic functions, the four sons of Horus, and the four cardinal points have the archetype of four in common; but we would err in our thinking if we assumed equivalence without careful deliberation. Do we attribute the psychic function of thinking to the East and the element of air? Perhaps, but our logic must be sound; how exactly do they correspond? And ultimately, does the correspondence suggest an archetypal truth (experience)?

Some of the astrological correspondences are my own educated guesses, for we astrologers are only recently discovering the mythological ground of our craft. The astrological correspondences remain fluid and I encourage the practicing astrologer to experiment with, and broaden, the mythological knowledge base of our venerable art. It goes without saying that God-pattern emphasis in the birth chart by planet, sign, and house will manifest most strongly when the Sun, Moon, Ascendent, and Midheaven are involved in the configurations. Second consideration should be given to the natural rulerships, e.g., the planet Venus when the Sun sign is Taurus or Mars when the rising sign is Aries. The Moon and her aspects in all cases indicates the individual's capacity to receive and transmit images in a general way

Howard Sasportas's astrological types will be referred to and his table is included in Chapter Two by permission. There is no one-to-one correspondence between Sasportas's types and the God-patterns, but I believe in giving credit where credit is due. Sasportas's types can be helpful in beginning to differentiate the various themes found in a birth chart. There is one major deficit in the astrological correspondences and that is the use of the asteroids, the knowledge of which I am sincerely lacking.

Nomenclature can be a problem when the Tree, the birth chart, and the Gods are referred to simultaneously. It is perhaps best to follow the traditions of each discipline. The Greek Gods being by far the older of their Roman counterparts, when referring to the God-patterns I prefer the Greek names. When speaking astrologically, the Roman names are used. And when speaking of the Tree, the Qabalistic transliterations are important. As an example, we speak of the Ares God-pattern (Greek inheritance), the planet Mars (astrology), and the sphere of Geburah or the path of Pe (Qabalistic reference).

I would like to offer an example of how all three—image, Tree, and birth chart—can interrelate. For our example, let us take the planet Mercury in an imaginary birth chart. Mercury is the Roman name of the Greek God Hermes. In our birth chart Taurus is on the Ascendent. Mercury is in late Gemini, one of his home signs (an essential dignity), in the first house (emphasis by house placement), and makes no major or minor aspects. Virgo, Mercury's second rulership sign, is intercepted and contains no planets. A traditional astrologer might view this as a "weak" Mercury. The individual represented by our imaginary chart would probably feel out of sorts, for Mercury represents our capacity for thinking and communication.

We have an astrological problem. The Jungian perspective might guess that the Mercury archetype is not very well developed and has remained in shadow. However, psyche might overcompensate, and we may see before us an individual we would initially consider very Mercurial. The person rambles on and on, but there is no depth, no connection to something deeper—Mercury makes no aspects to the rest of the chart.

The Hermes God-pattern is present in all of us; this is the archetypal stance. And Hermes is emphasized in our imaginary chart, albeit negatively. What is lacking in a chart or in an individual psychology is just as prominent as an overemphasis. Currently, our imaginary client is experiencing a Saturn transit to his natal Mercury, a square let us say. The inner pressure increases for this person, for Saturn as a rule requires us to work and to manifest the chart energies in a concrete way. Astrologically speaking, Mercury/Hermes is being activated by the Saturn transit. How do we help this individual integrate the Mercurian functions and Hermes at its deepest level?

We allow the client to describe to us his/her experience, his/her images, about Mercury. We then suggest some reading of myth to help further activate the God-pattern. We can reference the Tree, and if the individual is so inclined, they can use the Tree's symbols to invoke Mercury; to invoke a power is to call forth that power from within psyche. Or we can suggest meditation on the Tarot Trump known as The Magician, which is a ready made pictorial representation of the archetype of Mercury. The only secret here is work and more work.

The task for our imaginary client is to create a conscious connection to Hermes/Mercury. The Saturn transit makes this so. Mercury in the first house demands it. The only caution is that we do not taint the individual's unique experience with our own perception of Mercury. We anchor ourselves within our own boundaries. The therapist, astrologer, or magician must attempt to avoid violence against the image and at all times allow the client to discover for themselves what the image means for them. We are agents and enablers.

This being a journey, we may find that Mercury begins to fashion the journey for both client and helper. Synchronistic events begin to happen. Mercury becomes the catalyst in a psychic chemical chain reaction. The God hovers above us whispering his words and immersing us in his image. We give thanks and help bring back for the client his/her newfound knowledge and experience. Mercury will always be problematical for our imaginary person, but the God, at length, is no longer a stranger, but an ally.

This example is simplistic and generalized. I will have probably offended the Jungian, the astrologer, and the magician because each can offer objections to my example from their own unique perspective. But my goal is to hopefully move each discipline a little beyond accepted disciplinary borders. Complexity and image are synonymous and psyche delights in complex relationships.

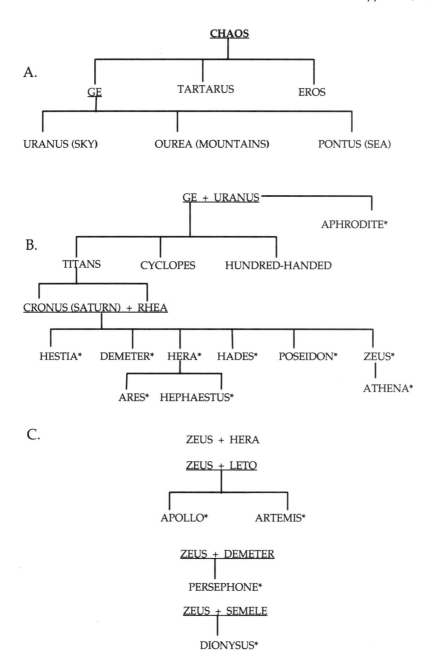

THE GREEK PANTHEON
*Denotes God-patterns in this appendix.

APHRODITE
(Venus)

Aphrodite was born from the foam of the severed genitals of Uranus that were cast into the sea by Cronus, his son. This unique birth seems to indicate that Aphrodite is a representation of the dynamic, procreative aspect of Eros. Aphrodite's most frequent epithet in Greek literature was "golden," and she was known as the Goddess of Love. She had numerous serial relationships with both mortals and Gods alike. As a Goddess she was never raped or urged into union by men or Gods—for her desirability, combined with her willingness to engage in sexual activity, precluded such aggressive advances.

Bolen refers to Aphrodite as the Alchemical Goddess. This Goddess-pattern has the ability of a focused consciousness while simultaneously being receptive to, and affected by, attention to others. She represents aspects of the lover and the creative woman. The Aphrodite archetype predisposes one to engage in serial relationships with an inability to consider the consequences of these rapturous encounters. Aphrodite is shown by one's capacity to enjoy pleasure and beauty, the ability to create, a strong procreative instinct, and the ability to nurture the creativity of others. Psychologically, Aphrodite consciousness can bridge the distance between complementary pairs of opposites such as the profane and the spiritual, the immediate and the distant, the spiritual and the sexual. Of all the Goddesses, except maybe Athena, she was the most accessible to mortal men/women. See Paul Friedrich, *The Meaning of Aphrodite*, for a full accounting of the Aphrodite Goddess-pattern.

Correspondences—Tree.
Sphere(s): Netzach, Victory
Binah, Understanding

Path	Hebrew Letter	Tarot Trump	Comments
14	Daleth	The Empress	Venus
16	Vau	Hierophant	Taurus
22	Lamed	Justice	Libra

Correspondences—Birth chart. A prominent Venus by aspect, placement, and dignity including the signs of Taurus and Libra. Venus/ Moon combinations, especially involving Capricorn. Sasportas's

Love Type describes somewhat the Aphrodite Goddess-pattern, especially Libra and the seventh house. From a non-traditional perspective, look to conflicts between Leo and Scorpio energies that include Venus for the alchemical quality of the Aphrodite Goddess-pattern.

APOLLO
(Apollo)

Apollo was the God of youth, music, prophesy, archery, and healing as well as the law giver. Apollo was the son of Zeus and Leto, and was twin to the Goddess Artemis. Apollo, along with Hermes, was a favorite son of Zeus, executing his father's will. In some areas Apollo was identified with Helios, the God of the Sun. Bolen describes Apollo's psychology as that of the extraverted future oriented thinker and intuitor. Apollo represents mental activity, emotional distance, arrogance, and his dark side is one of vindictiveness, ruthlessness, narcissism, and cruelty.

Apollo's psychology is shown by detachment and rational thought, the so-called "Apollonian" values. His roles include son and brother; there is a strong association in his mythology with his siblings, Artemis, Hermes, and Dionysus. The Apollo archetype does not incline one towards getting one's hands "dirty" emotionally, and he preferred not to become involved in the affairs of others; however, woe to the open enemy who challenged the God in any way. Apollo favors intellectual relationships. Most of his relationships ended in tragedy and the God was frequently rejected by those he courted; as an archetype he is the rejected lover. For the Greeks, the Apollo God-pattern represented the ability of a far-seeing, prophetic nature in touch with the universal laws of the cosmos itself.

Correspondences—Tree.
Sphere(s): Tiphareth, Beauty

Path	Hebrew Letter	Tarot Trump	Comments
17	Zain	The Lovers	Apollo—Diviner
18	Cheth	The Chariot	Apollo—Charioteer
25	Samekh	Temperance	Apollo—Hunter
30	Resh	The Sun	Apollo—Sun God

Correspondences—Birth chart. Sun/Jupiter combinations have a strong Apollonic component, but look to air emphasis, especially Libra, for support. Sagittarius and the ninth house by emphasis might also point towards Apollonic values.

ARES
(Mars)

Ares is traditionally known as the God of War, and Bolen also identifies him as the Dancer and the Lover. Ares was one of the least favored of Zeus's sons. One story states that Ares was born of Hera alone; as such he represents his mother's rage and her dissatisfaction with Zeus's philandering. The God delighted in the battle and in bloodshed, these being non-Olympian values. The sense of being at ease with the body is shown by Ares's various roles of lover, warrior, and dancer. Ares represents emotional reactivity, and the movement between assertion and aggression. Ares indicates the abilities of intense activity, emotional expressiveness, and protection of others. Negatively, the Ares God-pattern can manifest in bullying others, alcohol addiction, paranoia, jealousy, and low self-esteem.

Correspondences—Tree.
Sphere(s): Geburah, Severity

Path	Hebrew Letter	Tarot Trump	Comments
24	Nun	Death	Scorpio
27	Pe	The Tower	Attributed to Mars
28	Tzaddi	The Emperor	Aries

Correspondences—Birth chart. Sasportas's Will type describes some of the Ares temperament. Emphasis on Mars by aspects (especially to Sun), placement, and essential dignity can describe an Ares man. Do not forget Mar's rulerships of Aries and Scorpio. Look especially for Water/Fire conflicts that involve Mars.

ARTEMIS
(Diana)

Artemis was the Goddess of childbirth, youth, and wild animals. She was also identified with the Moon. Artemis was very protective of her honors, and actively punished those who forgot her in their worship. She chose to remain virgin and ruthlessly protected her chastity. She was favored by Zeus, along with Athena. Artemis's favorite haunts were the wilds of the forest where she spent her time with other young virgin women and wood nymphs. She was a huntress and roamed the woodlands with her entourage and hunting dogs. As Diana, she represented one aspect of Triple-Faced Hecate having rulership over the nighttime skies. According to Bolen, as one of the virgin Goddesses she represents one aspect of feminine focused consciousness. Like her brother Apollo, she represents emotional distance, ruthlessness, and unbridled rage. Activity is the cornerstone for an Artemis woman. The Artemis archetype is present when the abilities of concentration, setting and achieving goals, independence, autonomy, and strong friendships with women are apparent. The Artemis energy is also in touch with Nature. Artemis inclines towards brotherly relationships with men; however, Artemis can be said to be woman-identified and the champion of women's causes.

Correspondences—Tree.
Sphere(s): Binah, Understanding
Yesod, The Foundation

Path	Hebrew Letter	Tarot Trump	Comments
13	Gimel	High Priestess	The Moon
29	Qoph	The Moon	Instincts/Body

Correspondences—Birth chart. The Goddesses are the most difficult to pinpoint in the chart since there are only two feminine planets, the Moon and Venus. Feminine energies can also be ascribed to Neptune and Pluto. The Artemis woman is many times embodied by the Aries woman in conjunction with Aquarian energy. Look to Sasportas's Will Type for clues, but count on Moon/Uranus (Aquarius) combinations. The planets do not have to be in actual contact. A strong Lunar emphasis with concurrent Uranian energy might require the activation of the Artemis pattern for integration of both energies. A back-up in the chart of both fire and earth energies can also be helpful in finding the Artemis Goddess-pattern.

ATHENA
(Minerva)
Athena was the Goddess of wisdom, arts and crafts, and war.

Athena is said to have been born an adult in full battle armor from the head of Zeus. This birth seems to indicate that Athena is a strongly male- identified Goddess. She is one of Bolen's virgin Goddess with the ability of a focused feminine consciousness. Athena was known as a Goddess of Men, giving counsel and nurturing heroes who were usually fathered by Zeus; her relationships with women were distant and competitive. The Athena archetype can exhibit emotional distance, guile, and a lack of empathy. Athena's shadow side is represented by what Bolen describes as the Medusa effect—the ability to take away the spontaneity, vitality, and creativity of persons unlike her. Athena's strengths include the ability to set and achieve goals, creating effective strategy, practicality, and producing tangible results—she presided over women's crafts.

Correspondences—Tree.
Sphere(s): Chokmah, Wisdom

Path	Hebrew Letter	Tarot Trump	Comments
15	He	The Star	Aquarius
17	Zain	The Lovers	Gemini
22	Lamed	Justice	Libra

Correspondences—Birth chart. See Artemis. Like Artemis, look to Moon/Uranus combinations, but determine if the Moon/Uranus energies are backed up by seventh house and Air emphasis, Libra especially. Athena is the more cerebral of the two Goddesses so that air energy is to be suspected. In my own work, I have found the Athena pattern co-existing side by side with the Artemis pattern, especially if the woman is strongly feminist.

DEMETER
(Ceres)

Demeter was the Goddess of the Grain and fertility and represents one aspect of the Universal Mother. Demeter is one of Bolen's vulnerable Goddesses, the others being Hera and Persephone. The vulnerable Goddesses, unlike the virgin Goddesses, are receptive to and welcoming of significant others in their lives and in their self-perceptions. Demeter represents the mother and nurturer. The Demeter archetype is intimately connected with the mother-daughter relationship. When her daughter Persephone was abducted by

Hades, Demeter caused the crops to fail and wandered aimlessly about the Earth until her daughter was returned to her. The Demeter Goddess-pattern brings with it one form of the descent, or the emotion of depression. When Persephone was abducted she roamed aimlessly, as her functional abilities relied upon the presence of another. She would have starved mankind had not the Gods, Zeus in particular, intervened. From this we can appreciate the ability in this Goddess-pattern to withhold affection and nurturance when her needs are not met. This Goddess-pattern is heavily identified with the fulfillment of child-bearing, the involvement with an active male partner being secondary.

Correspondences—Tree.
Sphere(s): Binah, Understanding
Malkuth, The Kingdom

Path	Hebrew Letter	Tarot Trump	Comments
19	Teth	Strength	Leo—Procreatrix
32	Tau	The World	Saturn—Preserver

Correspondences—Birth chart. Sasportas's Maintenance Type comes to mind. Moon/Venus/Earth, especially Capricorn, Moon/Water/Earth combinations, especially Taurus, Cancer, and Virgo. Saturn/Moon combinations in Earth and Water signs.

DIONYSUS
(Bacchus)

Dionysus was the Greek God of wine and vegetation. Dionysus, although pursued by Hera, was nonetheless nurtured and protected by his father Zeus. A key to understanding Dionysian consciousness is to remember that along with Hephaestus, Dionysus remained close to the feminine ground of being. Dionysus was a God of women. He also represents an aspect of the puer, or eternal adolescent. As the God of the Vine, he is the "Loosener." The Dionysus experience can bring with it psychosis and psychic dismemberment. Along with Ares, this God-pattern predisposes one towards an experience of the body, or more precisely, the middle ground where body and psyche interface. He is the God of extreme opposites, and of ecstasy. Dionysus's shadow manifests in distortions of self-perception, substance abuse, and poor self-esteem. Passionate intensity is Dionysus's cornerstone. Bolen suggests that personal committed love and the journey to the Underworld are the inherent challenges for the Dionysus man. One singular aspect of the Dionysus archetype is suggested by Walter Otto in Dionysus: Myth and Cult. This is the fact that Dionysus himself was mad, madness being an archetypal situation of the God's imaginal landscape. At his presence, women would leave their looms and homes to sport in the mountains and woodlands, dancing and honoring the God with wild abandon. These maenads would alternately succor and dismember the animals of the forest. Dionysus would also make mad those who would oppose his worship, death being the end result for these individuals. Pentheus is an example. A Theban king, he was torn apart by his mother and aunts as he tried to spy upon the mysteries of the God.

Correspondences—Tree.
Sphere(s): Kether, The Crown
Tiphareth, Beauty

Path	Hebrew Letter	Tarot Trump	Comments
26	Ayin	The Devil	Capricorn
31	Shin	Last Judgement	Fire

Correspondences—Birth chart. See Sasportas's Mystic Type. Neptune/Pluto combinations aspecting Sun, followed by Pisces and the twelfth house. Some Saturn in the configuration can accentuate the Neptune/Pluto/Sun energies. Neptune/Uranus/Sun conflicts are also suspect, especially if Pluto is also strong in the chart.

HADES
(Pluto, Dis)

Hades was the God of the Underworld. Psychologically, the Underworld is also the realm of souls and of the unconscious. Hades is one of the Kings of the Olympian pantheon. He rarely left his domain. He is a loner and a recluse. His wife, whom he'd abducted, was Persephone, daughter of Demeter. That which is below consciousness, that which is dark, that which the ego rejects, that which is not beautiful all find their way to Hades's realm. Violence, power and control issues, and suppressed rage can also accompany

Hades's presence. The Hades individual is sensitive to the shadow side of others. Depression, social invisibility, distortion of reality, and low self-esteem can be present in the Hades God-pattern. Hades confers the ability to access the images of the unconscious and the ability to be detached from life experiences. The archetypal situation of the descent is to be found in Hades's mythology.

Correspondences—Tree.
Sphere(s): The imaginary sphere of Daath said to be found between Chokmah and Binah and child of their union. Daath is the twin son to Tiphareth representing the Sun's antithesis in shadow.

Path	Hebrew Letter	Tarot Trump	Comments
24	Nun	Death	Scorpio
27	Pe	The Tower	Mars/Fire
31	Shin	Last Judgement	Fire

Correspondences—Birth chart. Pluto/Sun contacts, Pluto, Scorpio, and the eighth house generally. Saturn/Pluto combinations also. Look to Earth element as back-up, especially Taurus and Capricorn.

HEPHAESTUS
(Vulcan)

Hephaestus was the God of fire and metalworking. One aspect of Hephaestus that immediately stands out is that of all the Gods, he was the only one that worked. This God-pattern contains the archetypal situation of the outsider. According to Bolen, he manifests in one's psychology as the ability to toil, labor, and create with unremitting persistence. Hephaestus's creativity is founded upon the feminine ground of experience. Passion in all its intensity focused in laboring is strictly Hephaestian. Zeus rejected Hephaestus outright for his homeliness, casting the child headfirst from Olympus in a fit of rage. He is one of the rejected sons, for Hera also rejected him. He is also the rejected lover; even though he was married to Aphrodite, she preferred the company of Ares, her lover. Hephaestus's mythology indicates the attributes of social inappropriateness, buffoonery, and low self-esteem; he was the peacemaker when visiting Olympus, using humor to quell the easily aroused passions of the Gods. This God-pattern can also represent the Wounded-Healer; creatively working on soul-making can be a Hephaestian specialty.

Correspondences—Tree.
Sphere(s): Geburah, Severity

Path	Hebrew Letter	Tarot Trump	Comments
17	Zain	The Lovers	Gemini
31	Shin	Last Judgement	Fire

Correspondences—Birth chart. Moon/Pluto/Saturn combinations with Fire/Earth elements as back-up. Sun/Pluto/Fire configurations are also suspect. Sasportas's Pragmatist Type, marginally.

HERA
(Juno)

Hera was the Goddess of marriage and childbirth, and the Queen of Heaven. She represents the archetype of wife and commitment maker. Hera is one of Bolen's vulnerable Goddesses in that self-perception and self- definition includes significant others. She was the wife of the King of the Gods, Zeus. Hera's career was pursuing and tormenting Zeus's many paramours and illegitimate offspring. The Hera archetype is often described in the phrase, "Behind every successful man there lies a woman." One of the positive attributes of Hera is the ability to re-enact the Hieros Gamos or Sacred Marriage where the opposites find fulfillment uniting with each other. Renewal is found in Hera's mythology, for it was said that every year Hera would bathe in a sacred spring and become virgin again. An important task for the Hera identified individual is learning to turn rage into creative self-expression, for Hephaestus was said to have been born parthenogenically from Hera alone.

Correspondences—Tree.
Sphere(s): Binah, Understanding
Malkuth, The Kingdom

Correspondences—Birth chart. See Aphrodite and Demeter. Sasportas's Love Type combined with his Maintenance Type. Moon/Venus/Earth and seventh house combinations supported by Fire/Water conflicts.

HERMES
(Mercury)

Hermes was the Messenger of the Gods. Bolen reminds us that he was also the Guide of Souls, the great Communicator, the Trickster, and Traveler. Hermes was one of the favored sons of Zeus. He is usually depicted as bearing the caduceus, the winged wand which represented his sovereignty over communications and his role as Zeus's right hand man. Cleverness is found in the Hermes pattern. It is said in myth that on his first day of birth he stole some of Apollo's cattle, and when brought before Zeus by his brother lied unabashedly. To appease Apollo's anger, he presented his brother with the lyre which he invented from a tortoise shell and strings. Hermes represents one aspect of the eternal adolescent. He was a friendly God, and the Hermes man can develop easy and fluid relationships with men. Bolen describes Hermes as the gregarious loner. Sociopathy can also accompany the Hermes God-pattern, as the God is clever, will lie through his teeth, and will justify any action. The Trickster aspect is especially important to remember when dealing with the Hermes archetype. Hermes was also the psychopomp, the guide of souls on their way to the Underworld and he was found throughout the mythologies of the other Gods and of heroes during times of initiation and transitions. He was the deliverer of the word of Zeus; in this respect he represents Logos manifest.

Correspondences—Tree.
Sphere(s): Hod, Splendor

Path	*Hebrew Letter*	*Tarot Trump*	*Comments*
12	Beth	The Magician	Mercury
17	Zain	The Lovers	Gemini
20	Yod	The Hermit	Virgo

Correspondences—Birth chart. Mercury emphasis by aspect, placement, and essential dignities. Mercury/Jupiter/Sun combinations. Look to Gemini and Virgo for further support of the Hermes pattern. Mercury/Saturn and Mercury/Pluto can also indicate a strong Hermes presence.

HESTIA
(Vesta)

Hestia was identified with the hearth and as the Goddess of the Hearth. She requested to remain virgin and this request was honored by the Gods. Hestia is described by Bolen as one the virgin Goddesses with an ability for focused feminine consciousness. In the Greek tradition images of Hestia were no where to be found for the Goddess was imaged through structure and form, especially the domed inner sanctuary of the Temple. Of all the God-patterns, Hestia consciousness is the most inward focused from a meditative stance. Another image for Hestia is the point/center of the Temple where the fire burned continuously. Hestian psychology is decidedly introverted. When we acknowledge Hestia's presence, we begin to appreciate that even within the most mundane of tasks, spiritual meaning can be found; Hestia's psychology is one of centeredness and reflection.

Correspondences—Tree
Sphere(s): Kether, The Crown
Malkuth, The Kingdom

Path	Hebrew Letter	Tarot Trump	Comments
13	Gimel	High Priestess	The Moon

Correspondences—Birth chart. Moon/Pluto/Neptune/Earth combinations. Hestia is the most elusive of the God patterns to find within the chart. Surprisingly, I have often found the Hestia personality in Scorpio women, even when they are committed to the roles of spouse and mother.

PERSEPHONE
(Proserpina)

Persephone was known as Kore—the Maiden. She is the Queen of the Underworld. Bolen assigns the roles of Receptive Woman and Mother's Daughter to this Goddess-pattern. Persephone is one of Bolen's vulnerable Goddesses; she was abducted by her uncle Hades to be his wife and rule with him in the Underworld. Introversion, also seen in Hestia, is an aspect of this Goddess-pattern. Persephone's presence can also manifest in depression, manipulation, and withdrawal into unreality. Upon her arrival to the Underworld after her abduction, she refused to eat and was inconsolable no matter how often Hades attempted to make her feel welcomed. The Persephone woman can be aware of the unconscious and its images, and can indicate a confrontation with psychosis. The Persephone woman can be all women to the same man, in that being overly receptive, she reflects back to others what they wish to see. A major challenge for the Persephone identified woman is to develop a personality in her own right that has ego strength, for only such a woman can truly be a Queen, especially Queen of the Underworld. Before this can happen, however, the Persephone woman must confront her own darkness, her own despair, and depression. Then she can become a guide to others in their own descent to Hades.

Correspondences—Tree.
Sphere(s): Binah, Understanding
Malkuth, The Kingdom

Path	*Hebrew Letter*	*Tarot Trump*	*Comments*
32	Tau	The World	Earth

Correspondences—Birth chart. Moon/Pluto/Saturn/Earth combinations with seventh house emphasis; maybe Venus/Pluto. Scorpio and the eighth house generally, especially when the Moon is involved. Saturn/Moon influence can indicate the depression and vulnerable aspect of the Persephone pattern.

POSEIDON
(Neptune)

Poseidon was the God of the Sea. Bolen further states that the Sea can be symbolic of the world of emotion and instinct. Poseidon was a father-king of his domain. He was also known as Poseidon Earth-shaker for it was believed by the Greeks that he caused earthquakes when angry. The Poseidon man has access to feelings, a capacity not overly valued in today's Western culture. He can hold a grudge for years, but unlike Hephaestus who turns his rage into creative self-expression, Poseidon will turn his anger against the perceived object of his grievances. Instinctual self-expression is also a manifestation of the Poseidon archetype. Negatively, the Poseidon God-pattern can manifest in a loss of boundaries with others, consuming all he touches with diffuse and overwhelming emotion.

Correspondences—Tree.
Sphere(s): Kether, The Crown

Path	Hebrew Letter	Tarot Trump	Comments
23	Mem	Hanged Man	Water
29	Qoph	The Moon	Instincts/Body

Correspondences—Birth chart. Neptune emphasis by aspects, placement, and essential dignity. Look to Fire/Earth emphasis, also the water houses, and Pisces.

ZEUS
(Jupiter)

Zeus was King of the Gods and reigned without challenge on Mt. Olympus. Greek mythology is populated with his numerous offspring and constant philandering. Generativity is the cornerstone of the Zeus archetype; one need only follow the mythologies of his offspring, both mortal and divine. He represents the sacral kingship archetype in its Western form. Zeus is the source, the beginning and end of the Olympian pantheon, and we come to know his many aspects as we study Greek mythology in general. The Zeus archetype is the favored role in our culture for men. He is the God of the Western patriarchy in all its positive and negative aspects.

Correspondences—Tree.
Sphere(s): Chesed, Mercy

Path	Hebrew Letter	Tarot Trump	Comments
21	Kaph	Wheel of Fortune	Jupiter
25	Samekh	Temperance	Sagittarius
29	Qoph	The Moon	Pisces

Correspondences—Birth chart. Sun/Jupiter emphasis by aspects, placement, and essential dignities. Sagittarius and the ninth house. Sasportas's Change Type to a certain degree.

Annotated Bibliography

Bolen, Jean Shinoda. *Goddesses in Everywoman: A New Psychology of Woman*. Harper Colophon Books, New York: Harper & Row, Inc., 1985.

Working from Jung's theory of the archetype, Bolen develops the seven goddess patterns, archetypes of behavior for women (and men) based upon the seven Greek goddesses: Artemis, Athena, Hestia, Hera, Demeter, Persephone, and Aphrodite. She divides them into three groups: Artemis, Athena, and Hestia represent focused consciousness. These goddesses do not include the needs of others in their behaviors, at least not from a dependent nurturant perspective. Hera, Demeter, and Persephone represent diffuse consciousness and as the Wife, the Mother, and the Daughter, respectively, these goddesses include patterns of behavior that focus heavily on relationships. Aphrodite, alone, represents a combination of the first two groups, needing relationships, yet always true to her own goals. Aphrodite is the alchemical goddess.

This is a helpful book when one contemplates the roles that women fulfill. Bolen thoroughly explores each goddess pattern, including the developmental aspect: what do these patterns of behavior look like in childhood, adulthood, old age? And rare for most works, she includes what these patterns might look like for Lesbians. On the whole the book is straight–forward, a quality I personally appreciate in any written work. Clarity and simplicity rate high on my list, and this book certainly meets these requirements.

_____. *Gods in Everyman: A New Psychology of Men's Lives and Loves*. San Francisco: Harper & Row, 1989.

Bolen divides the God patterns for men into the Father Gods—Zeus, Neptune, and Hades; and the generation of Sons—Apollo, Hermes, Ares, Hephaestus, and Dionysus. This volume follows the foremat of her previous work, *Goddesses* ... I find that both volumes are very helpful in beginning work on myth with clients.

Burckhardt, Titus. *Alchemy: Science of Cosmos, Science of Soul*. Translated from the German by William Stoddart. Great Britain: Element Books Ltd., 1986.

The subtitle "Science of the Cosmos, Science of the Soul" tells us from what perspective Burckhardt approaches the subject of alchemy. He states clearly that we cannot understand the alchemists by simply reducing their symbols to be reflective of psychological processes. Alchemy is a philosophy of man, god, and cosmos, and their inter–relationships taken from the Emerald Tablet of Hermes usually paraphrased "As above, so below." Alchemy attempts to create a vessel, the soul, that can contain the divine essence. Burckhardt gives the essential concepts in alchemical work. He does not go into the details, but gives his understanding of what the alchemists were saying in their extensive writings. It is a good introductory volume giving the major alchemical ideas.

Burt, Kathleen. *Archetypes of the Zodiac*. St. Paul, Minnesota: Llewellyn Publications, 1988.

Kathleen Burt writes about what she considers to be the archetypes of each of the astrological signs using traditional sign rulerships and esoteric planet rulerships. She elaborates each sign using myths from different cultures.

There has been much work done in the past decade on myths and astrological signs. The strong points of the book include the gathering of many myths and Kathleen Burt's insights gained from many years of astrology practice. Not everyone agrees on what myths and gods and goddesses pertain to which signs. Also, it is dangerous to assume that knowing the myth is knowing the archetype, or that an archetype manifests the same way for each person.

Ellenberger, Henri F. *The Discovery of the Unconscious*. New York: Basic Books, Inc., 1970.

This amazing volume covers nine hundred pages. The research involved is enormous. Ellenberger traces the history and evolution of dynamic psychiatry, beginning with folk medicine and shamanism, moving to exorcism, magnetism, hypnosis, and finally, modern dynamic psychiatry. He utilizes the known historical, social, and cultural environment, the personality of a theory's originator, and their own life story and experiences to explain a given theory. The chapters on Janet, Freud, Adler, and Jung are thorough as Ellenberger gives and analyzes the main theses in each man's system of psychology.

I strongly recommend this volume for anyone that is serious about the study of psychology, especially its history and evolution. However, as Ellenberger repeatedly states, the chapters can at best be an overview of any particular system. He succeeds in placing the theories and the men behind the theories in an historical and conceptual framework. His writing is clear and logical and more than makes up for the eight hundred pages of text.

Greene, Liz and Sasportas, Howard. *The Development of the Personality*. Seminars in Astrological Astrology, Vol. 1. York Beach, Maine: Samuel Weiser, Inc., 1987.

Liz Greene's perspective is that of a Jungian analyst and Howard Sasportas's perspective comes from his humanistic psychology and psychosynthesis training. Together, they offer new insights into the use of the natal chart as a basis for psychological understanding of the person for whom one is doing the chart. I believe their work to be on the forefront of modern research into the dynamics of the psyche as correlated with astrology's rich and powerful symbols. Their psychological knowledge is sound and the way they weave together the two disciplines offers a model for future work. They prove to the reader the viability of merging astrology and psychology, and for this reason is good reading for the psychologist and the astrologer alike.

There are four chapters in this initial volume: "The Stages of Childhood" and "Subpersonalities and Psychological Conflicts" by Howard Sasportas, and "The Parental Marriage in the Horoscope" and "Puer and Senex" by Liz Greene. Sasportas reviews several human developmental models and incorporates the astrological planets and signs most prominent during different stages of childhood from birth through puberty in the chapter on "Stages of Childhood." His second chapter on subpersonalities incorporates psychosynthesis theory pertaining to personalities outside of the individual ego, subpersonalities that can be inferred from astrological symbolism; and alternately, that one can work with a specific astrological configuration by personifying.

Greene's two chapters, are, as always in her writings, well researched and to the point. She writes about the sun and moon as being indicative of the parents in the chart, sun as symbolic of father and moon of mother. The chapter on the puer is also well researched and keeps to Jungian archetypal theory. This first volume is hopefully indicative of their future work together.

_____. Dynamics of the Unconscious. Seminars in Psychological Astrology, Vol. 2. York Beach, Maine: Samuel Weiser, Inc., 1988.

Liz Greene writes "Depression" and "Alchemical Symbolism in the Horoscope." The chapter on depression is well written. Greene explores Melanie Klein's depressive stance and describes the process of depression, its suffering, but also its potential for a liberative resolution and creativity. The chapter on alchemical symbolism explores the four elements as described in alchemical literature and Greene relates each of the four processes of calcinatio, solutio, coagulatio, and sublimatio and their corresponding psychological and astrological processes. Howard Sasportas does the subject of aggression justice, identifying when aggression is healthy and important and when it degenerates to violence. The planetary significator for aggression is Mars, and he explores the archetype well. The chapter on the sublime offers insights into the planet Neptune, the sign Pisces and the quest and/or aversion to the experience of merging with something or someone other than ourselves.

Hillman, James. *Archetypal Psychology: A Brief Account.* Dallas: Spring Publications, Inc., 1985.

The total number of pages of text number less than sixty. Hillman presents all his concepts in very concise and condensed form, defining for the reader the parameters of his archetypal psychology. Each definition is loaded, taut, like the elastic thread that comprises a golf ball and like a golf ball; each definition soars towards its goal. Included in this work is a bibliography of authors who have expanded upon Hillman's work and a complete listing of Hillman's own prodigious writings.

I was struck by Hillman's emphasis on the image. I agree with his opinion that the culling and nurturing of the image extends beyond the psychopathological into all areas of who and what we are as human beings. He turns the image inside-out, preferring to believe that the image creates us, not we the image, a highly radical but necessary shift in emphasis. The bibliography and complete list of his works are a treasure and orients the reader towards further exploration of Hillman's writings.

_____. *The Dream and the Underworld*. New York: Harper/Colophon Books, Harper & Row, 1979.

This book includes six chapters. Hillman begins with Freud's theory of dreams, elaborates his thought that we must look to the myths of the Underworld, especially Hades, Night and her children, and approach dreams and the images in dreams as attempts at soul–making to be accepted as a reality of their own. Dreams are a process of soul. They belong to the Underworld which has its own topography, its own rules, its own existence apart from the ego. Hillman is adamant that to take dreams as tools for the ego robs the image and soul of its vitality. Ego and life tend not to understand psyche as soul. Death beckons from the Underworld, and Hillman explains that images of death and disease are the images we need to pay attention to in our dreams, places where life is transformed into psyche. Hillman forces us to re-examine our use of dreams, but mostly challenges us to put aside ego defenses and truly enter into the house of Hades. Pluto means "riches" and alludes to another aspect of Hades, once we meet him on his own ground.

_____. *Re-Visioning Psychology*. New York: Harper/Colophon Books, Harper & Row, 1975.

This is a very powerful book that challenges the assumptions and practices of modern psychology while suggesting an alternative which Hillman has come to call archetypal psychology, or a logos of soul. He compares the modern era to the Renaissance, a time of decay that offers us the opportunity to "re–vision" psychology. Hillman is thorough in his research and his ideas are supported, first, by the clarity of his writing, second, by the passion of his offensive, and third, by the depth of his thinking. The book has four chapters that correspond to the process of what he calls soul-making: personifying, pathologizing, psychologizing, and dehumanizing.

This book was like coming home. After reading many books on analytical psychology, I was beginning to feel trapped into a "system" of psychology. Jung's work is monumental, but I have found it confining. Hillman not only explores his theses well, but in turn gives one the permission to imagine, which is to say, to give primacy to the image.

Hillman, James, et al. *Facing the Gods*. James Hillman, ed. Dallas, Texas: Spring Publications, 1980.

This volume is comprised of nine essays by Hillman and some of his associates including Murray Stein and Barbara Kirksey, on the Gods: Amazons, Dionysos, Hestia, Hermes, Athene, Rhea, Artemis, Ariadne, Hephaistos. The scholarship moves us to depth, and the God–images, psycholologically explored, are nothing less than powerful. A must reading for anyone researching the psychological impact of God-images.

Hillman, James, et al. *Puer Papers*. James Hillman, ed. Dallas, Texas: Spring Publications, 1979.

The puer aeternus, or eternal youth, was an archetype that Jung explored in his own work and which Hillman and others explore in these nine essays. To quote the back cover: "... the radiant youth, aloof, sensitive, and eternal: an archetype in myth and poetry, a symptom in psychotherapy, a figure in dreams, a leitmotif in biography." All these images of the puer are found in these essays, and Hillman's own writings are excellent expositions on the puer conflicts.

Jacobi, Jolande. *Complex/Archetype/Symbol in the Psychology of C.G. Jung*. Translated from the German by Ralph Manheim. Bollingen Series 57. Princeton: Princeton University Press, 1959.

This volume contains two essays:
"Complex/Archetype/Symbol" and "Archetype and Dream." I read only the former. Mrs. Jacobi explains what Jung meant by complex, archetype, and symbol and how they interrelate. She

uses quotes from Jung and fills in the gaps where necessary.

Jung, C.G. *Analytical Psychology, Its Theory and Practice*: *The Tavistock Lectures*. Pantheon Books. New York: Random House, 1968.

    Carl Jung was invited to give a series of five lectures at the Institute of Medical Psychology (Tavistock Clinic) in London, England. These lectures took place on September 30 to October 4, 1935 and a stenographic record of each lecture was taken. The lectures are contained in this volume. They include most of Jung's therapeutic psychology in one form or another. Each presentation was followed by a discussion period. This affords us some insight into Jung's personality; the fact that these were lectures also forced Jung to define his concepts in only sentences instead of paragraphs. This volume has a relaxed, easy style making for enjoyable reading. Jung's lecture on the association test is the most understandable of all his works that I have read which describe this test.

_____. *Collected Works of C.G. Jung*. *Bollingen Series XX*. Translated by R.F.C. Hull and edited by H. Read, M. Fordham, G. Adler, and Wm. McGuire (Princeton, N.J. : Princeton University Press, and London: Routledge & Kegan Paul, Inc., 1953-1973).

    The series of twenty volumes constitutes most of what is available and accessible in English of Jung's vast work. More recently, also in the Bollingen Series, we have the letters of Jung in English and book format. If one is to work with images and archetypes at all, primary reading of Jung is indispensable. My first reading of the *Collected Works* began eleven years ago, one summer, and they have influenced my life immensely, most importantly my journey through young adulthood. Carl Gustav Jung has been one of two persons who have most influenced my development and has been a constant companion in fantasy.

    Approaching the *Collected Works* as a master's degree candidate is a bit like coming home after college, there is a familiarity and a distance simultaneously. Volumes such as *Symbols of Transformation* or *The Archetypes and the Collective Unconscious*, which focus primarily on the definition and evolution of the archetype, I have read previously in my own personal quest. For this study I have focused on those volumes that pertain particularly to the art and practice of psychotherapy.

_____Volume 7. Two Essays on Analytical Psychology. 2d. ed. Bollingen Series XX. Princeton: Princeton University Press, 1953.

   In the first of the two essays in this volume, "On the Psychology of the Unconscious," Jung explores Freud's eros theory followed by an exploration of Adler's inferiority theory. These two points of view are to Jung the representatives of the two attitude–types: the introvert and the extravert. Jung further explains that the ideal would be to utilize the synthetic method where there is room for both introversion and extraversion. He then explains how each attitude-type responds to the demands of the unconscious and from there explains the nature of archetypes and the therapeutic approach one takes when confronting unconscious material. The second essay is titled "The Relations Between the Ego and the Unconscious" and explains Jung's therapeutic approach to the unconscious. He defines ego, persona, shadow, anima, animus, the mana-personality, and self as each pertains to the individuation process.

   This volume is different from many others of the *Collected Works* in that it written in a sequential, if artificial, manner. Jung's definition of the individuation process is shown step by step with few footnotes and the definitions themselves are clear and accessible to the reader.

_____Volume 8. The Structure and Dynamics of the Psyche. 2d. ed. Bollingen Series XX. Princeton: Princeton University Press, 1959.

   This volume contains eighteen essays divided into seven sections. As I read them, I made three divisions: The majority of essays, as the title implies, do indeed define the structure and dynamics of the psyche. In this division I also include those essays describing analytical psychology. Into the second division I place the essays on Spirit and stages of life. The third division consists of one essay, "Synchronicity: An Acausal Connecting Principle." These divisions seem logical to me on the basis of the contents of the essays.

   The structure and dynamics of the psyche are manyfold. Jung describes modalities; energy dynamics based upon the science of physics while defining his concept of libido as different from Freud's. He defines conscious, personal unconscious, and collective unconscious repeatedly. The essay detailing the theory of the complex and the two essays on dreams provide invaluable information, while the section on the relationship between instincts and archetypes in "Instinct and the Unconscious" challenges one to understand more fully Jung's theory of the archetypes. Since the essays were originally published at various points in Jung's career, one can appreciate the difficulties he had in creating appropriate definitions of his concepts, and it becomes clear as one reads that Jung was very careful and meticulous when articulating his theories.

I found myself carefully pondering most of these essays while taking many notes. I know this to be a volume I will return to repeatedly in my work since there are many definitions. Particularly important for my future work is his use of the word "image" in various essays, which seems to point to the fact that the image has many levels of meaning.

_____Volume 16. The Practice of Psychotherapy. 2d. ed. Bollingen Series XX. Princeton: Princeton University Press, 1954.

Part I of this volume contains nine essays delivered at various times, places, and to different audiences. They outline many important considerations for the modern psychotherapist. One primary consideration that appears in many of the essays is the need for the therapist to take an active role in the healing process, using for navigation the client's own individuality. Jung calls for the admittance into therapy of a philosophy of life, a demand that the therapist confront self before attempting to heal others. He explores the necessity of having an awareness of the relationship between individual and society, and repeatedly places the science of psychology into its historical niche as the natural evolution of civilized humankind.

Part II consists of three essays. "The Therapeutic Value of Abreaction" is Jung's views on the process of abreaction, that is, the retelling of events as done from client to therapist. This process is more than simple confession. It calls upon the therapist's strength of personality if the confession is to become actual healing work. It is the therapist's responsibility to utilize the retelling of events towards the greater goal of healing. "The Practical Use of Dream–Analysis" is truly a gem of an essay. Jung's usual writing style is one of synthesis. He uses many images and references when he writes and it taxes patience and ability to follow the thread which he is expounding. Not so with this essay. He writes about the proper attitude in dream work, which is one of total openness, where the therapist knows that pre–judgements can be noxious to the interpretation of dreams. Other practical considerations are the need for the therapist to have a broad knowledge background, especially myths; the importance of placing a dream in the person's unique life context, including his or her philosophy of life; and the importance of not making dream interpretations fit any one particular therapeutic doctrine. The third essay, "The Psychology of the Transference" is difficult to read and understand. Jung uses a series of alchemical prints and text to illustrate the psychology of the transference. At times it becomes more an alchemical narrative, although perseverance allowed me to glean the practical aspects to be found intermittently throughout the text.

_____. *The Undiscovered Self.* Translated from the German by R.F.C. Hull. An Atlantic Monthly Press Book. Boston: Little, Brown, and Company, 1958.

This small essay by Jung in his later years addresses the plight of modern day individuals as they struggle to reconcile their inner promptings towards individuation and their responsibility both to themselves and the group. Jung points out that both modern day society and religion are creating a vacuum since neither institution nurtures individuation and the quest for meaning in life. More than any other essay, this one asserts what Jung maintained: if there is something wrong with society, then there is something wrong with me, and if there is something wrong with me, then it is my responsibility to address it. It can only be through the individual that society as a whole can be healed.

King, Francis. *The Cosmic Influence.* London: Aldus Books, 1976.

An easy and enjoyable book, as are most of King's histories, that nonetheless contains much information, in summarized format, on the history of astrology, and includes many photographs and illustrations. This book follows the "coffee-table" book format that can be misleading; although it may appear glossy, King presents us with much serious thought.

Mattoon, Mary Ann. *Jungian Psychology in Perspective*. New York: The Free Press, A Div. of Macmillan Publishing Co., Inc., 1981.

One more of the numerous volumes that have been written on the psycholoy of Jung. This book is good because Mattoon branches out into current research and critical approaches to Jung that produces some exciting conclusions and challenges to some of Jung's ideas.

Neumann, Erich. *The Origins and History of Consciousness*. Forward by C.G. Jung. Translated from the German by R. F. C. Hull. Bollingen Series, no.42. Princeton: Princeton University Press, 1973.

In his forward, Jung states that Neumann has created a unified whole in his analysis and description of the evolution of consciousness. Neumann accomplishes this task by incorporating the mythological as well as the psychological components of ego development. He uses the image of the uroboros, the serpent holding its tail in its mouth, as the symbol of the original unity of conscious and unconscious. Contained in this original unity is the embryonic ego. Neumann then traces the development of the ego and its eventual birth from the unconscious, its growth, its return to the unconscious as Mother, usually symbolized by the incest motif, and finally the resolution of ego as the center of consciousness. In the first half of the book Neumann utilizes myths and symbols as the representatives of this process, while in the second half of the book he presents a psychological interpretation of individual growth within and away from the group.

Most notable for me is his exposition of the myths detailing the hero's journey. In Part I hero and ego are synonymous. He asserts, as did Jung before him, that the incest taboo originates not from an Oedipal father who will punish the hero, but simply because the new–formed ego as Hero is in danger of being reabsorbed by the unconscious as Mother, a danger further complicated by the ego's desire to return to its place of origin. The author also reminds us that the ego is in danger of being absorbed by the archetypal Father as well as the archetypal Mother, a concept I have yet to read elsewhere. Part II is a psychological analysis of the separation of various systems out of the group which give rise to the individual/group antinomy. Neumann describes the experience of the archetypes of shadow and anima/animus as necessary in the development of personality if the individual is to survive and contribute to the group from which they evolved.

Neumann is thorough in his presentation. He has had the benefit of Jung's pioneer work and this has enabled him to bring all the pieces together. There is much in this book that has clarified for me the evolution of consciousness from an archetypal perspective.

Payson Joslin, Herta. "The Transformative Image: A Feminine Approach to Therapy." Submitted in partial fulfillment of the requirements for the degree of Master of Arts, Goddard Graduate Program, Vermont College/Norwich University, November 1981.

The author in this makes the case for a therapy that is based on the image as essentially a feminine approach. This is illustrated by the inclusion of personal and client material. There are two levels to this work, one is the written text, while the second is the sharing of images that requires a different way of appreciation.

Poncé, Charles. *Kabbalah: An Introduction and Illumination for the World Today.* 2d., Quest Books, Wheaton, IL: The Theosophical Publishing House, 1980.

There do not exist many books on the Kabbalah that the average person can read and understand without having knowledge of esoteric doctrine. This book by Poncé is one of those texts that must be included in the reading list of anyone seriously wishing to contemplate the Kabbalah. Poncé gives the traditional Jewish mysticism's history and major beliefs, then adds modern correspondences to the system. His insights and astuteness on the subject are helpful, but the major strength of the book is its simplicity and clarity coupled with Ponce's enthusiasm and deep respect for the topic under consideration.

Shulman, Sandra. *The Encyclopedia of Astrology.* New York: The Hamlyn Publishing Group, Limited, 1976.

A "coffee–table" book with hundreds of photos and illustrations and good historical coverage of astrology.

Singer, June. *Boundaries of the Soul.* New York: Doubleday & Company, 1972.

June Singer tells us, in her introduction, that from the start of her own training to become a Jungian analyst she recognized the need for Jung's psychology to become accessible to laypeople. *Boundaries of the Soul* is her attempt to consolidate all of Jung's concepts into a format easier to assimilate by the person who has not had training in Jung's psychology. She covers all the major areas of Jungian analysis: the relationship between client and therapist; the theory of complexes; the archetypes, including the shadow, anima/animus, self; psychological types; understanding dreams, including active imagination; death and dying. She makes extensive use of dreams and drawings, and succeeds in her original intent of clarifying for us the healing process as developed by Jung.

This is written strictly from the teachings of Jung. There are no excursions into new territory. I recommend this book as the most accessible summation of Jungian analysis as handed down from the Zurich school. The eloquent chapters for me were "Analyst and Analysand," "Complexes by Day and Demons by Night," "Understanding our Dreams," and "We Were Born Dying." It is clear throughout that the author is committed to her work and has learned the essence of Jungian psychology. The author shares a very personal account of her work with others and this indirect thread teaches us just as much as the written text.

Storr, Anthony, comp. *The Essential Jung*. Princeton: Princeton University Press, 1983.

Anthony Storr has selected and arranged Jung's writings from the Collected Works and other sources in a way he felt best presented Jung. He devised ten chapters beginning with "Jung's Early Work" and ending with "Man and His Future." Mr. Storr as compiler qualifies the selection of text as his own, yet his selections do justice to Jung's ideas. His selection and presentation of Jung's main ideas gives the reader an opportunity to sample Jung's numerous works and decide if further in–depth reading is desirable.

Szanto, Gregory. *Astrotherapy: Astrology and the Realization of the Self*. London: Arkana Books by Routledge & Kegan Paul Ltd., 1987.

The author of this work feels that astrology and psychotherapy compliment each other. Gregory Szanto writes that the individual horoscope is unique and that the goal of therapy is to help the individual become whole. The first half of the book is devoted to reviewing psychotherapy models, which Mr. Szanto does well. He then incorporates the Cabalah which he posits as a symbol for the archetypal human psyche. The last third of the book he devotes to giving examples of what he means by astrotherapy. This last part seemed to me rather weak, but overall the book is a valiant attempt at synthesizing two divergent but mutually helpful disciplines.

Tester, Jim. *A History of Western Astrology*. New York: Ballentine Books, 1987.

One cannot work with Jungian concepts and not meet with synchronous experiences. This book was published in 1987 after the death of the author. I had read many books on the history of astrology many years ago, and had planned to do so again for this work, not overly excited, I must add. I discovered this book on the shelves in early 1988 and thought, "What a coincidence." It was published just in time for my own work. Tester's history is about the best I have read. It is scholarly, well written and well researched. Tester's writing style is easy but elegant and his sense of humor fills the pages. He was a man in love with history and with classical studies, as this work is more historical and classical than astrological. This is why the book works, for Tester does not have an agenda for or against astrology. This book is enjoyable (though not always easy reading) because Tester delights in the subject at hand. And with his knowledge of history, Tester places astrology within the context of its development. This is not a book on the thought and theory of astrology, but on its development within the historical world views of each time period from 300 B.C. to the 1700s A.D.

Whitmont, Edward C. *The Symbolic Quest: Basic Concepts of Analytical Psychology*. Princeton: Princeton University Press, 1969.

Whitmont approaches the explanation of Jung and analytical psychology by beginning with the symbolic way of perceiving and the symbolic approach and moving into the realm of the archetype which is the objective psyche. He defines the complex, psychological types, persona, shadow, anima/animus and self, and the process of individuation. He ends with the definition of ego and how the ego functions in relationship to the archetypes and the symbolic quest. He moves from objective to subjective, a sequence rather different from the traditional presentation, including Jung's.

I found the early chapters like "The Symbolic Approach" and "The Approach to the Unconscious" and the ending chapters on the ego and "Therapy" to be the most instructive since in these chapters Whitmont's understanding of Jung's concepts are blended with his own unique thought.

Wilmer, Harry A. *Practical Jung*. Wilmette, IL: Chiron Publications, 1987.

The author states in his introduction that the current book evolved from his forty years plus of work with others. Dr. Wilmer has had a traditional Freudian training and prefers to call himself an "eclectic Jungian." This is apparent, for he uses many different modes of expression: his own drawings, cartoons, reproductions of photographs that illustrate his point, case histories, dream material, quotes from Jung, and quotes from other authors. He alternates between what he calls "rules of thumb" and explanations of Jungian concepts. The rules are poignant statements of his own experience. They are presented directly with justification based on case material. Jung's psychology is taken one idea at a time, using Jung's own words and enriched by Wilmer's eclectic style.

Jung has written that the psychotherapist cannot divest himself of a philosophy of life, nor can effective therapy happen without taking into account the client's own philosophy of life. This leads at times to a feeling that Jungian therapy is too much in the clouds and not enough on terra firma. Wilmer brings practical and theoretical together. He addresses issues such as money, gifts, hugs, self–inventory, limitations, hubris, life in the bureaucracy, life transitions, and more, and simultaneously presents such Jungian concepts as the transcendent function, the nature of dreams, etc . . .

I recommend this book highly for its humaneness. I found the "practical" rules to be invaluable at the beginning stages of my own Masters work. Wilmer's presentation of case material alternately touched me or had me laughing out loud, but always a chord was struck and the message delivered. Wilmer's sense of humor projects warmth and compassion without ever lapsing into cynicism.

Selected Bibliography

Books

Avalon, Arthur (Sir James Woodroffe). *The Serpent Power*. New York: Dover Publications, Inc., 1974.

Arroyo, Stephen. *Astrology, Karma, & Transformation: The Inner Dimensions of the Birth Chart*. Reno, Nevada: CRCS Publications, 1978.

Bolen, Jean Shinoda. *Goddesses in Everywoman: A New Psychology of Woman*. Harper Colophon Books, New York: Harper & Row, Inc., 1985.

_____. *Gods in Everyman: A New Psychology of Men's Lives and Loves*. San Francisco: Harper & Row, 1989.

Burckhardt, Titus. *Alchemy*. Translated from the German by William Stoddart. Great Britain: Element Books Ltd., 1986.

Burt, Kathleen. *Archetypes of the Zodiac*. St. Paul, Minnesota: Llewellyn Publications, 1988.

Calder, Nigel. *Einstein's Universe*. New York: Penguin Books, 1980.

Campbell, Joseph. *The Power of Myth*. New York: Doubleday, 198.

Campbell, Joseph and Roberts, Richard. *Tarot Revelations*, 2d. ed. San Anselmo, CA: Vernal Equinox Press, 1982.

Case, Paul Foster. *The Tarot: A Key to the Wisdom of the Ages*. Richmond, Virginia: Macoy Publishing Company, 1975.

Cashden, Sheldon. *Object Relations Therapy: Using the Relationship*. New York: W.W. Norton & Company, 1988.

Castaneda, Carlos. *The Teachings of Don Juan: A Yaqui Way of Knowledge*. New York: A Touchstone Book of Simon and Shuster, 1968.

Crowley, Aleister. *777 And Other Qabalistic Writings of Aleister*

Crowley. York Beach, Maine: Samuel Weiser, Inc., 1973.

_____. *Magick*, edited, annotated, and introduced by John Symonds and Kenneth Grant. London: Routledge & Kegan Paul, 1973.

Ellenberger, Henri F. *The Discovery of the Unconscious*. New York: Basic Books, Inc., 1970.

Fortune, Dion. *The Mystical Qabalah*, 13th Impression. London: Ernest Benn Limited, 1957.

Frazier, Sir James George. *The Golden Bough: A Study in Magic and Religion*, abridged ed. New York: Macmillan Publishing Company, Inc., 1950.

Gauquelin, Michel. *Cosmic Influences on Human Behavior*. Trans. by Joyce E. Clemow. New YorK: Stein and Day, Inc., 1973.

Godwin, David. *Godwin's Cabalistic Encyclopedia: A Complete Guide to Cabalistic Magick*. n.p.: Llewellyn, 1979.

Grant, Kenneth. *The Magical Revival*. New York: Samuel Weiser, Inc., 1973.

Graves, Robert. *The White Goddess*. New York: Farrar, Straus and Giroux, 1987.

Greene, Liz. *The Astrology of Fate*. York Beach, Maine: Samuel Weiser, Inc., 1984.

_____. *Saturn: A New Look At An Old Devil*. York Beach, Maine: Samuel Weiser, Inc., 1976.

Greene, Liz and Sasportas, Howard. *The Development of the Personality*. Seminars in Psychological Astrology, Vol. 1. York Beach, Maine: Samuel Weiser, Inc., 1987.

_____. *Dynamics of the Unconscious*. Seminars in Psychological Astrology, Vol. 2. York Beach, Maine: Samuel Weiser, Inc., 1988.

Hillman, James. *Archetypal Psychology: A Brief Account*. Dallas: Spring Publications, Inc., 1985.

_____. *The Dream and the Underworld*. New York: Harper/Colophon Books, Harper & Row, 1979.

_____. *Loose Ends: Primary Papers in Archetypal Psychology*. Dallas, Texas: Spring Publications, 1975.

_____. *Re-Visioning Psychology*. New York: Harper/Colophon Books, Harper & Row, 1975.

Hillman, James, et al. *Facing the Gods*. James Hillman, ed. Dallas, Texas: Spring Publications, 1980.

_____. *Puer Papers*. James Hillman, ed. Dallas, Texas: Spring Publications, 1979.

Howe, Ellic. *The Magicians of the Golden Dawn: A Documentary His-*

tory of a Magical Order. York Beach, Maine: Samuel Weiser, Inc., 1984.

Jacobi, Jolande. *Complex/Archetype/Symbol in the Psychology of C.G. Jung*. Translated from the German by Ralph Manheim. Bollingen Series 57. Princeton: Princeton University Press, 1959.

Jones, Marc Edmund. *The Guide to Horoscope Interpretation*. Stanwood, Washington: Sabian Publishing Society, 1972.

Jung, C.G. *Analytical Psychology, Its Theory and Practice: The Tavistock Lectures*. Pantheon Books. New York: Random House, 1968.

_____. *Collected Works of C.G. Jung*. Bollingen Series XX. Translated by R.F.C. Hull and edited by H. Read, M. Fordham, G. Adler, and Wm. McGuire (Princeton, N.J.: Princeton University Press, and London: Routledge & Kegan Paul, Inc., 1953- 1973), especially the following:

Vol. 5. *Symbols of Transformation*. 1956.

Vol. 6. *Psychological Types*. 1971.

Vol. 7. *Two Essays on Analytical Psychology*. 1953.

Vol. 8. *The Structure and Dynamics of the Psyche*. 1959.

Vol. 9. Part 1. *The Archetypes and the Collective Unconscious*. 1959.

Vol. 11. *Psychology and Religion*: West and East. 1958.

Vol. 14. *Mysterium Coniunctionis*. 1965.

Vol. 16. *The Practice of Psychotherapy*. 1954.

_____. *Memories, Dreams, Reflections*. Recorded and edited by Aniela Jaffe. Trans. by Richard and Clara Winsten. New York: Vintage Books, 1965.

_____. *The Undiscovered Self*. Translated from the German by R.F.C. Hull. An Atlantic Monthly Press Book. Boston: Little, Brown, and Company, 1958.

King, Francis. *The Cosmic Influence*. London: Aldus Books, 1976.

_____. *Magic: The Western Tradition*. New York: Avon Books, 1975.

Knight, Gareth. *A Practical Guide to Qabalistic Symbolism*. York Beach, Maine: Samuel Weiser, Inc., 1965.

Mattoon, Mary Ann. *Jungian Psychology in Perspective*. New York: The Free Press, A Div. of Macmillan Publishing Co., Inc., 1981.

McIntosh, Christopher. *The Astrologers and their Creed*. New York: Frederick A. Praeger, 1969.

Motoyama, Hiroshi. *Theories of the Chakras: Bridge to Higher Consciousness*. Wheaton, IL: The Theosophical Publishing House, 1981.

Neumann, Erich. *The Origins and History of Consciousness*. Forward by C.G. Jung. Translated from the German by R. F. C. Hull. Bollingen Series, no.42. Princeton: Princeton University Press, 1973.

Parsons, John Whiteside. *Freedom is a Two-Edged Sword: The Collected Essays of John Whiteside Parsons*. The Oriflame, No.1, New Series. New York & Las Vegas: Ordo Templi Orientis and Falcon Press, 1989.

Ponce, Charles. *Kabbalah: An Introduction and Illumination for the World Today*. 2d., Quest Books, Wheaton, IL: The Theosophical Publishing House, 1980.

Regardie, Israel. *The Golden Dawn*, 4th ed. St. Paul, MN: Llewwellyn Publications, 1982.

_____. *The Eye in the Triangle*. Phoenix, Arizona: Falcon Press, 1982.

Rudhyar, Dane. *The Practice of Astrology As a Technique in Human Understanding*. Boulder: Shambhala, 1978.

Shulman, Sandra. *The Encyclopedia of Astrology*. New York: The Hamlyn Publishing Group, Limited, 1976.

Singer, June. *Boundaries of the Soul*. New York: Doubleday & Company, 1972.

Storr, Anthony, comp. *The Essential Jung*. Princeton: Princeton University Press, 1983.

Szanto, Gregory. *Astrotherapy: Astrology and the Realization of the Self*. London: Arkana Books by Routledge & Kegan Paul Ltd., 1987.

Tester, Jim. *A History of Western Astrology*. New York: Ballentine Books, 1987.

Von Franz, Marie-Louise and Hillman, James. *Lectures on Jung's Typology*. Irving, Texas: Spring Publications, Inc., 1979.

Waite, A.E. *The Holy Kabbalah*. Secaucus, N.J.: University Books/Citadel Press, n.d.

Wang, Robert. *The Qabalistic Tarot: A Textbook of Mystical Philosophy*. York Beach, Maine: Samuel Weiser, Inc., 1983.

Whitmont, Edward C. *The Symbolic Quest: Basic Concepts of Analytical Psychology*. Princeton: Princeton University Press, 1969.

Wilhelm, Richard, translater. *I Ching or Book of Changes*, rendered into English by Cary F. Baynes. Bollingen Series XIX. Princton, N.J.: Princeton University Press, 1971.

Williams, Margery. *The Velveteen Rabbit or How Toys Become Real*. Illustrated by Michael Green. Philadelphia, Pennsylvania: Running Press, 1981.

Wilmer, Harry A. *Practical Jung*. Wilmette, IL: Chiron Publications, 1987.

Wilson, Colin. *The Occult*. New York: Vintage Books, A Division of Random House, 1971.

Wing, R.L. *The Illustrated I-Ching*. New York: Dolphin Books/Double Day and Company, Inc., 1982.

Reference Books

Eliade, Marcia, editor in chief. *The Encyclopedia of Religion*. New York: Macmillan Publishing Comapny, 1987.

Morford, Mark and Lenardson, Robert. *Classical Mythology*. New York: David McKay Company, Inc., 1971.

Morris, William, editor. *The American Heritage Dictionary of the English Language*. Boston: Houghton Mifflin Company, 1976.

Tripp, Edward. *Crowell's Handbook of Classical Mythology*. New York: Thomas Y. Cromwell Company, 1970.

Turabian, Kate L. *A Manual for Writers of Term Papers, Theses, and Dissertations*. Fifth ed. Chicago: The University of Chicago Press, 1982.

Warkins, Floyd C.; Dillingham, William B.; and Martin, Edwin T. *Practical English Handbook*. 4th ed. Boston: Houghton Mifflin Company, 1974.

Periodicals

Roess, Richard. "Messages from the Heavens." The ASCendant 12 (Fall 1988).

Gauquelin, Michel and Erlewine, Michael. "Dialogue: Michel Gauquelin and Michael Erlewine." Astro*Talk 6, no.1 (January 1989).

Manuscripts

Payson, Herta Joslin. "The Transformative Image: A Feminine Approach to Therapy." Submitted in Partial Fulfillment, Degree of Master of Arts, Goddard Graduate Program, Vermont College/ Norwich University, November 1981.

INDEX

STAY IN TOUCH

On the following pages you will find listed, with their current prices, some of the books and tapes now available on related subjects. Your book dealer stocks most of these, and will stock new titles in the Llewellyn series as they become available. We urge your patronage.

However, to obtain our full catalog, to keep informed of new titles as they are released and to benefit from informative articles and helpful news, you are invited to write for our bi-monthly news magazine/catalog. A sample copy is free, and it will continue coming to you at no cost as long as you are an active mail customer. Or you may keep it coming for a full year with a donation of just $5.00 in U.S.A. ($20.00 overseas, first class mail). Many bookstores also have *The Llewellyn New Times* available to their customers. Ask for it.

Stay in touch! In *The Llewellyn New Times'* pages you will find news and reviews of new books, tapes and services, announcements of meetiongs and seminars, articles helpful to our readers, news of authors, advertising of products and services, special money-making opportunities, and much more.

The Llewellyn New Times
P.O. Box 64383-Dept. 006, St. Paul, MN 55164-0383, U.S.A.
• • •
TO ORDER BOOKS AND TAPES

If your book dealer does not have the books and tapes described on the following pages readily available, you may order them direct from the publisher by sending full price in U.S. funds, plus $1.50 for postage and handling for orders *under* $10.00; $3.00 for orders *over* $10.00. There are no postage and handling charges for orders over $50. UPS Delivery: We ship UPS whenever possible. Delivery guaranteed. Provide your street address as UPS does not deliver to P.O. Boxes. UPS to Canada requires a $50 minimum order. Allow 4–6 weeks for delivery. Orders outside the U.S.A. and Canada: Airmail—add retail price of book; add $5 for each non-book item (tapes, etc.); add $1 per item for surface mail.

FOR GROUP STUDY AND PURCHASE

Because there is a great deal of interest in group discussion and study of the subject matter of this book, we feel that we should encourage the adoption and use of this particular book by such groups by offering a special "quantity" price to group leaders or "agents."

Our Special Quantity Price for a minimum order of five copies of *PSYCHOLOGY, ASTROLOGY & WESTERN MAGIC* is $38.85 cash-with-order. This price includes postage and handling within the United States. Minnesota residents must add 6-1/2% sales tax. For additional quantities, please order in multiples of five. For Canadian and foreign orders, add postage and handling charges as above. Credit card (VISA, Master Card, American Express) orders are accepted. Charge card orders only may be phoned free ($15.00 minimum order) within the U.S.A. or Canada by dialing 1-800-THE-MOON. Customer service calls dial 1-612-291-1970. Mail Orders to:

LLEWELLYN PUBLICATIONS
P.O. Box 64383-Dept. 006/St. Paul, MN 55164-0383, U.S.A.

HORARY ASTROLOGY: The History and Practice of Astro-Divination
by Anthony Louis

Horary Astrology is a how-to-guide for the intermediate astrologer on the art of astrological divination. Horary is the best method for getting answers to questions of pressing personal concern: Where are my lost keys? Will the house burn down? Will I ever have children?

The premise is that a question, like a person, comes into the world at a particular significant moment. A horoscope cast for the birth of an inquiry is called a horary chart. An analysis of that chart reveals the circumstances surrounding the question and its eventual outcome. When used wisely, horary acts like a trusted advisor to whom you can turn in times of trouble. Hard to believe? Numerous examples offer proof!

0-897542-394-9, 592 pgs., 6 x 9, illus., softcover $18.95

MAGIC AND THE WESTERN MIND: Ancient Knowledge and the Transformation of Consciousness
by Gareth Knight

Magic and the Western Mind explains why intelligent and responsible people are turning to magic and the occult as a radical and important way to find meaning in modern life, as well as a means of survival for themselves and the planet.

First published in 1978 as *A History of White Magic*, this book illustrates, in a wide historical survey, how the higher imagination has been used to aid the evolution of consciousness—from the ancient mystery religions, though alchemy, Renaissance magic, the Rosicrucian Manifestoes, Freemasonry, 19th century magic fraternities, up to psychoanalysis and the current occult revival. Plus it offers some surprising insights into the little-known interests of famous people.

The Western mind developed magic originally as one of the noblest of arts and sciences. Now, with the help of this book, anyone can defend a belief in magic in convincing terms.

0-87542-374-4, 240 pgs., 5–1/4 x 8, illus., softcover $12.95

20TH CENTURY MAGIC AND THE OLD RELIGION: DION FORTUNE, CHRISTINE HARTLEY, CHARLES SEYMOUR
by Alan Richardson

This magical record details the work of two senior magicians—Charles Seymour and Christine Hartley—within Dion Fortune's Society of the Inner Light during the years 1937 to 1939.

Using juxtaposed excerpts from Seymour and Hartley's magical diaries together with biographical prefaces containing unique insights into the background and nature of the Society, Alan Richardson paints a fascinating picture of Dion Fortune and her fellow adepts at the peak of their magical careers.

Originally published as *Dancers to the Gods,* now with a new introduction and the addition of Seymour's long essay, "The Old Religion," a manual of self-initiation, this new edition retains Dion Fortune's "lost" novels, the past-life identities of her Secret Chiefs, and much more.

The simple act of reading these juxtaposed diaries of a true priest and priestess can cause a resonance with the soul which will ultimately transform those who so desire it
0–87542–673–5, 288 pgs., photographs, 6 x 9   **$12.95**

THE WHEEL OF DESTINY:
The Tarot Reveals Your Master Plan
by Patricia McLaine

Here is an irresistible new tool for self knowledge found nowhere else. *The Wheel of Destiny* delves into the "Master Plan Reading" of the Tarot's Major Arcana and provides detailed information about the individual, much like a reading of an astrological birth chart.

The book explains how to lay out the 22 cards and delineates the meaning of each card in whatever position it falls. The reading provides deep and specific information on divine purpose; strengths and weaknesses; talents; past lives; karmic patterns; relationships; physical, emotional, and spiritual development; and much more. All the reader needs is this book and a Tarot deck. No previous knowledge of the Tarot is required, yet serious students of the Tarot will find many new truths and profound perspectives.
0-87542-490-2, 480 pgs., 7 x 10, illus., softcover   **$17.95**

GODWIN'S CABALISTIC ENCYCLOPEDIA
by David Godwin
This is the most complete correlation of Hebrew and English ideas ever offered. It is a dictionary of Cabalism arranged, with definitions, alphabetically, alphabetically in Hebrew, and numerically. With this book the practicing Cabalist or student no longer needs access to a large number of books on mysticism, magic and the occult in order to trace down the basic meanings, Hebrew spellings, and enumerations of the hundreds of terms, words, and names that are included in this book.

This book includes: all of the two–letter root words found in Biblical Hebrew, the many names of God, the Planets, the Astrological Signs, Numerous Angels, the Shem Hamphorash,the Spirits of the Goetia, the Correspondences of the 32 Paths, a comparison of the Tarot and the Cabala, a guide to Hebrew Pronunciation, and a complete edition of Aleister Crowley1s valuable book Sepher Sephiroth.

He re is a book that is a must for the shelf of all Magicians, Cabalists, Astrologers, Tarot students, Thelemites, and those with any interest at all in the spiritual aspects of our universe.

0–87542–292–6, 500 pgs., 6 x 9, softcover $15.00

A GARDEN OF POMEGRANATES
by Israel Regardie
The Tree of Life is the ground plan of the Qabalistic system–a set of symbols used since ancient times to study the Universe. It is a geometrical arrangement of ten sephiroth, or spheres, each of which is associated with a different archetypal idea, and 22 paths which connect the spheres.

This system of primal correspondences has been found the most efficient plan ever devised to classify and organize the characteristics of the self. Israel Regardie has written one of the best and most lucid introductions to the Qabalah.

A Garden of Potnegranates combines Regardie's own studies with his notes on the works of Aleister Crowley, A.E. Waite, Eliphas Levi and D.H. Lawrence. No longer is the wisdom of the Qabalah to be held secret! The needs of today place the burden of growth upon each and every person–each has to undertake the Path as his or her own responsibility, but every help is given in the most ancient and yet most modern teaching here known to humankind.

0-87542-690-5, 176 pg., softcover $7.95